Private Military and Security Companies (PMSCs) and the Quest for Accountability

Private Military and Security Companies (PMSCs) have constituted a perennial feature of the security landscape. Yet, it is their involvement in, and conduct during, the ongoing wars in Iraq and Afghanistan that have transformed the outsourcing of security services into such a pressing public policy and world-order issue. The PMSCs' ubiquitous presence in armed conflict situations, as well as in post-conflict reconstruction, their diverse list of clients (governments in the developed and developing world, non-state armed groups, intergovernmental and non-governmental organizations, and international corporations) and, in the context of armed conflict situations, involvement in instances of gross misconduct, have raised serious accountability issues. The prominence of PMSCs in conflict zones has generated critical questions concerning the very concept of security and the role of private force, a rethinking of "essential governmental functions," a rearticulation of the distinction between public/private and global/local in the context of the creation of new forms of "security governance," and a consideration of the relevance, as well as limitations, of existing regulatory frameworks that include domestic and international law (in particular international human rights law and international humanitarian law).

This book critically examines the growing role of PMSCs in conflict and post-conflict situations, as part of a broader trend towards the outsourcing of security functions. Particular emphasis is placed on key moral, legal, and political considerations involved in the privatization of such functions, on the impact of outsourcing on security governance, and on the main challenges confronting efforts to hold PMSCs accountable through a combination of formal and informal, domestic as well as international, regulatory mechanisms and processes. It will be of interest to scholars, policymakers, practitioners and advocates for a more transparent and humane security order.

This book was published as a special issue of *Criminal Justice Ethics*.

George Andreopoulos' research focuses on the intersections of international relations and international law with special emphasis on international organizations and on international human rights and humanitarianism.

John Kleinig works and publishes in moral, social, and political philosophy, with a special interest in criminal justice ethics.

Private Military and Security Companies (PMSCs) and the Quest for Accountability

Edited by
George Andreopoulos and
John Kleinig

Routledge
Taylor & Francis Group

LONDON AND NEW YORK

First published 2015 by Routledge

2 Park Square, Milton Park, Abingdon, Oxon OX14 4RN
711 Third Avenue, New York, NY 10017, USA

Routledge is an imprint of the Taylor & Francis Group, an informa business

First issued in paperback 2017

British Library Cataloguing in Publication Data
A catalogue record for this book is available from the British Library

ISBN 13: 978-1-138-85474-1 (hbk)
ISBN 13: 978-1-138-05752-4 (pbk)

Typeset in Palatino
by RefineCatch Limited, Bungay, Suffolk

Publisher's Note
The publisher accepts responsibility for any inconsistencies that may have arisen during the conversion of this book from journal articles to book chapters, namely the possible inclusion of journal terminology.

Disclaimer
Every effort has been made to contact copyright holders for their permission to reprint material in this book. The publishers would be grateful to hear from any copyright holder who is not here acknowledged and will undertake to rectify any errors or omissions in future editions of this book.

Contents

Citation Information

The chapters in this book were originally published in *Criminal Justice Ethics*, volume 31, issue 3 (December 2012). When citing this material, please use the original page numbering for each article, as follows:

Chapter 7
A U.N. Convention to Regulate PMSCs?
José L. Gómez del Prado
Criminal Justice Ethics, volume 31, issue 3 (December 2012) pp. 262–286

Chapter 8
Transparency as a Core Public Value and Mechanism of Compliance
Allison Stanger
Criminal Justice Ethics, volume 31, issue 3 (December 2012) pp. 287–301

Chapter 9
The Stability Operations Industry: The Shared Responsibility of Compliance and Ethics
Doug Brooks and Hanna Streng
Criminal Justice Ethics, volume 31, issue 3 (December 2012) pp. 302–318

Please direct any queries you may have about the citations to
clsuk.permissions@cengage.com

Acknowledgements

The special issue was based on papers presented at a research workshop jointly organized by the Center for International Human Rights (CIHR) and the Institute of Criminal Justice Ethics (ICJE) held at the John Jay College of Criminal Justice, CUNY, October 7–8, 2011. The editors would like to thank the following: Shawna Brandle, Aferdita Hakaj, Shelby Prue, Ksenia Armstrong, Margaret Smith, Elizabeth Yukins and Jonathan Jacobs. In addition, they would like to acknowledge the generous support of the Centre for Applied Philosophy and Public Ethics (CAPPE), an Australian Research Council Special Research Centre. Last, but not least, they would like to thank all the participants who contributed to the deliberations of the two-day workshop.

Revisiting the Role of Private Military and Security Companies

GEORGE ANDREOPOULOS* AND SHAWNA BRANDLE

This essay addresses the role of private military and security companies (PMSCs) in security governance. In this context, it offers a historical overview of some of the main developments in the evolution of private warfare and critically discusses some of the key challenges confronting the quest for holding PMSCs accountable in accordance with international human rights and humanitarian norms.

Introduction: Definition and Key Issues

This special issue of *Criminal Justice Ethics* examines the growing role of private military and security companies (PMSCs) in conflict and post-conflict situations, as part of a broader trend towards the outsour-

George J. Andreopoulos is Professor of Political Science at John Jay College of Criminal Justice and at the Graduate Center, CUNY, and founding director of the Center for International Human Rights at John Jay College of Criminal Justice. Corresponding author. Shawna Brandle is a PhD candidate at the Graduate Center of the City University of New York, studying human rights, international law, and media.

cing of security functions. Particular emphasis is placed on key moral, legal, and political considerations involved in the privatization of such functions, on the impact of outsourcing on security governance, and on the efforts to hold PMSCs accountable through a combination of formal and informal regulatory mechanisms and processes.

There is little doubt that PMSCs have been with us for a long time and have been important actors in recent conflicts in places such as Angola, Sierra Leone, and Liberia in Africa, Colombia in Latin America, and Papua New Guinea, among others.[1] However, it is primarily as a result of the ongoing wars in Iraq and Afghanistan that the outsourcing of national security services (for example, logistical support, weapons procurement, war zone security needs, prisons, psychological warfare, and covert operations) has become such a pressing public policy and world order issue. The PMSCs' ubiquitous presence in armed conflict situations, as well as post-conflict reconstruction, their diverse list of clients (governments in the developed and developing world, non-state armed groups, intergovernmental and non-governmental organizations, and international corporations) and, in the context of armed conflict situations, instances of gross misconduct have raised serious accountability issues. The prominence of PMSCs in conflict zones has generated critical questions concerning the very concept of security and the role of private force, as well as the rearticulation of the distinction between public/private and global/local in the context of the creation of new forms of "security governance."[2] Questions have also been raised about the relevance, as well as limitations, of existing regulatory frameworks that include domestic and international law (in particular international human rights law, international humanitarian law, and international criminal law).

At the start, a few remarks on the term used to designate these entities, and on the "mercenary" label that has often been attached to them, are in order. Private military companies (PMCs) appeared in the 1990s, while private security companies (PSCs) have been around, in various forms, since the 1970s.[3] The precise term used for the designation of the various private security sector entities has been a subject of debate. Some analysts draw a distinction between PMCs and PSCs on the basis of their active involvement in conflict and the extent of legitimate control: PMCs are those private business entities that are directly engaged in combat and combat-related activities, while PSCs are those private business entities that avoid combat operations. Instead, PSCs are primarily engaged in military advice and training, operational/tactical support, logistical support, and security/policing activities. In addition, PSCs, in contrast to PMCs, operate under a greater degree of (usually home state) control.[4] Other analysts, though, draw no such distinctions; instead they use terms such as privatized/private military firms (PMFs),[5] security companies,[6] or the more expansive private military and security companies (PMSCs),[7] while others use the inaccurate (and value-judgment-laden) term "mercenaries." For our project, we will use the broader term PMSCs to designate all private sector security-related businesses "that provide governments with professional services intricately linked to warfare."[8] We use this term bearing in mind that the line between active combat and some of the activities that entities, designated as PSCs, routinely undertake (operational/tactical support activities) is often rather thin indeed. For example, during the 2003 Operation Enduring Freedom in Iraq, security contractors operated missile guidance systems on U.S. ships, and computer systems for unmanned aerial vehicles (UAVs).[9] It can be argued that such activities transform PSC personnel into civilians directly participating in hostilities, thus resulting in the loss of their civilian status, and trigger the corresponding provisions of international humanitarian law. In addition, there is a continuous flow of personnel from PMCs to PSCs, a trend that has intensified as a result of the decline of PMCs and the exponential growth of PSCs. The realization that there is a substantial overlap between PMCs and PSCs is also reflected in the Montreux Document, probably the most important soft-law document on the existing legal obligations of states in their relations with PMSCs. The Montreux Document does not draw any distinction between PMCs and PSCs; it uses the term PMSCs.[10] Having said that, we also acknowledge that there are areas of activity that fall within the PSC domain. A good example of the latter would be the provision of security-related services to the NGO sector.[11] Thus, while strict compartmentalization between PMC and PSC functions is unsustainable, it is also true that not all PSC activities are combat-related.[12]

A common criticism against PMSCs is that they constitute a modern form of mercenarism. While this characterization is not accurate,[13] there is, according to one analyst, "a clear line of continuity" between mercenaries and these private security entities;[14] continuities that, according to another analyst, indicate that these entities "represent . . . the corporate evolution of the age-old profession of mercenaries."[15] At the most basic level, the increasing privatization of security services (broadly defined) paves the way for new forms of security governance with adverse implications for the relationship between the state and the citizen. In particular, implications for legitimacy expectations that state action must meet in such a vital issue area, if such action is to elicit and sustain public support. It is no accident, therefore, that the rising profile of PMSCs has raised serious accountability issues and calls for strengthening regulatory controls to ensure effective oversight.

The quest for regulatory control has become a pressing moral, legal, and, ultimately, governance issue. Both supporters and critics of PMSCs seem to agree on one point: the demand for private sector security services has increased and PMSCs carry out actions that, for a variety of reasons, governments are unable or unwilling to undertake. Such reasons cover a broad spectrum ranging from a government's basic inability to deal with a security threat and restore public order to a government's desire to lower the political costs of a particular policy. A good example of the former would be the case of the government of Sierra Leone in the mid-1990s. In 1995, the government hired Executive Outcomes (EO), a South African PMSC, to help it defeat the forces of the Revolutionary United Front (RUF), a rebel group that had been waging, since 1991, a campaign of terror against the civilian population.[16] In this task, EO proved to be successful; its offensives against the RUF were a key contributing factor to the RUF's eventual decision to participate in peace talks with the government, which led to the signing of the Abidjan Accord in 1996.[17] A good example of the latter would be the U.S. government's military involvement in the Colombian civil war and in Iraq. By outsourcing parts of the U.S. mission in these two countries, the Bush administration managed to shield the size, scope, and costs of its involvement from public scrutiny and effective congressional oversight.[18]

Since the privatization of security functions is here to stay (and this clearly seems to be the case), then the key tasks at hand include: (1) to understand its origins, causes, and multiple manifestations; and (2) to devise an effective regulatory framework that would be consistent with the exigencies of democratic control and would adhere to fundamental international rules and standards, in particular those drawn from international human rights, international humanitarian law, and international criminal law.

In order to set the stage for the contributions that follow, we will offer a historical note on private warfare, and we will briefly discuss and assess some of the challenges confronting the quest for accountability and the efforts at ensuring PMSC compliance with international human rights and humanitarian law norms and standards.

A Historical Note on Private Warfare: From Antiquity to the Emergence of PMSCs

States have authorized the use of force by a variety of non-state actors that have included mercenaries, privateers, and mercantile companies.[19] The use of non-state entities in conflict situations dates back to antiquity, with the first account recorded in the West being the unsuccessful use of mercenaries by Cyrus, a contender for the Persian throne, in 401 BC,[20] and the first recorded account from the East occurring even earlier—during the reign of King Shulgri of Ur between 2094 and 2047 BCE.[21] Mercenaries were an essential part of the Chinese army for over 500 years, from the late T'ang Dynasty until the fall of the Sung Dynasty.[22] Sarah Percy traces the advancement and retrenchment of the history of the use of private forces, starting in the twelfth century. Mercenaries were individuals or groups banded together to sell their skills at war-making to powers who would pay. "Independent, roving bands of mercenaries of common birth, like the *routiers* and *cotereaux* of the twelfth and thirteenth centuries, fought for themselves rather than a lord or king," while Swiss mercenaries, who would continue to fight for the French through 1793, first appeared in the thirteenth century.[23] The history of restraining the use of private forces dates back almost as far, though the Lateran Council of 1179 only condemned those forces who were fighting for themselves, and tended to attack the Church; this left those with just title unaffected.[24] The Magna Carta required the expulsion of all foreign mercenaries in 1215,[25] and Florence developed a code of conduct regarding mercenary use in 1337.[26]

Despite these attempts at reducing or regulating the use of private force, mercenaries and free companies continued to be in high demand throughout the thirteenth and fourteenth centuries, until a break in the Hundred Years' War from 1360 to 1369 left demobilized mercenaries roving the French countryside "with entrepreneurial zeal."[27] In Italy, during the Renaissance period, northern city-states began hiring freelance commanders (condottieri), whose task was to supply troops for specified military services.[28] Condottierri were more interested in capturing their opponents in the battlefield than in killing them, since their main aim was to raise ransom money.[29]

A series of attempts to reduce the use of private forces followed from several levels of authority—in 1364, bulls from Pope Urban "excommunicated mercenaries, granted indulgences to those who fought against them, forbade assisting mercenaries, and tried to restrict the payment of protection money to get the mercenaries to leave various areas,"[30] while a French *routier* captain was executed for not having proper authorization for his wartime actions in 1391,[31] and, in 1422, Zurich tried to prevent its citizens from fighting for other powers.[32] Other methods of controlling the use of private military forces included the prototype of a standing army as devised by Charles II of France in the mid-fifteenth century,[33] and Machiavelli's advice that mercenaries are less effective than one's own troops.[34] Contrary to these moves towards contraction, the Perpetual Peace Treaty of 1516 spelled out increased French use and control of Swiss mercenary troops, including rules for recruitment and pay.[35] Over time, though, increased state control is what really began to reduce the overall use of private forces; as of 1648, "the mercenaries remaining were no longer independent and were generally hired out from one state to another in situations of tight control and even as part of an alliance."[36]

In addition to land-based mercenaries, another category of state-sponsoredprivate force was privateering. Privateering was a wartime practice in which individuals and groups were authorized by states to attack the enemy's commercial shipping and to keep part of what was seized as remuneration for their actions.[37] The basis for this authorization was the granting of letters of marque that entitled private actors to act under the authority of the state issuing such letters.[38] The granting of these letters was what separated privateers from pirates; the former engaged in these prac-

tices under the authority of the state, while the latter did so on their own authority and exclusively for their own benefit. Needless to say, this wartime practice, which amounted to state-sponsored piracy, enabled states to advance their military and strategic objectives, while reducing the risk of attack on their own naval assets.[39]

England set the stage with its use of privateers in the thirteenth century; English monarchs issued the first privateer commissions in 1243, and the first letter of marque, directed against Portugal, was issued in 1295.[40] Generally, two periods are considered as particularly important for the role of privateering in English naval warfare: the first from 1544 to 1618, and the second from 1708 until about the middle of the nineteenth century.[41] For France, on the other hand, the "golden age" of privateering was between the latter part of the seventeenth century and the first half of the nineteenth century. In particular, the wars between 1689 and 1713, by disrupting the trade in the Mediterranean and Atlantic seas, were instrumental in generating demand for privateering services among French merchants.[42]

The practice of privateering was significantly reduced by the Armed Neutrality Declaration, which began with several major powers signing in 1780. The declaration finally gained the approval of Great Britain in an 1801 side agreement conceding "the immunity of convoyed vessels from search by privateers."[43] This was coupled with the U.S. beginning to actively deter French privateering in 1793,[44] and wide accession to the Declaration of Paris in 1856, that declared privateering abolished and recognized that a neutral country's flag protected enemy goods (except contraband).[45] With these developments and decrees privateering was effectively eliminated by the end of the nineteenth century.

Last, but not least, there was another set of private actors that engaged in the use of force: mercantile companies. These companies "were state-created institutions that used violence in the pursuit of economic gain and political power for both the state and non-state actors."[46] The most notable cases included the Dutch East India Company, chartered in 1602, and the English East India Company; the latter, initially chartered in 1600, assumed its final form in 1702, as a result of a merger.[47] Both companies were granted, by their respective governments, such extensive powers that they eventually became, in many areas of activity, indistinguishable from sovereign entities.

On the economic front, these mercantile companies secured privileges that included a monopoly on trade in a particular commodity, or with a specific region. On the political/military front, they had the authority, among other things, to govern their own nationals, raise an army or a navy, build forts, make war, and issue their own money.[48] When their monopoly privileges were threatened, the companies were more than eager to resort to force, usually with a combination of local and European mercenaries. For example, the Dutch East India Company employed 20,000 local mercenaries and 5,000 Europeans between 1715 and 1719 in order to recapture its fort in Calcutta;[49] the English East India Company, as a result of its victory at the Battle of Plassey (1757) against the forces of the

Nawab of Bengal, firmly established its threatened control over Bengal. This victory, coupled with its success at the Battle of Bhaksar in 1764, led the Mughal Emperor to formally acknowledge British dominance in the region.[50]

States' use of private armed forces continued throughout the nineteenth century, in the War of Greek Independence, the dynastic struggles in Portugal and Spain, the 1830 war between Brazil and Argentina, and the Crimean War.[51] At the same time, however, more and more states began to adopt legislation preventing their own citizens from serving other states that were at war with states friendly to their own—the U.S., Britain, and France all enacted such legislation.[52] As national standing armies became the more popular form of state force, mercenary forces were increasingly used only in the colonies.[53]

In the first half of the twentieth century, state use of private force included "35,000 foreigners—mostly Europeans—[who] volunteered to serve in the Spanish Civil War" in 1936–39[54] and Ghurka forces being hired to fight for both India and Great Britain.[55] The United States used civilian contractors in limited non-combat roles in both world wars.[56] The 1960s through 1980s brought about the "dogs of war" period of mercenarism, including "French, South African, Rhodesian, Spanish, Italian, British, and Belgian mercenaries [who] served in the Congo, on both sides of the conflict."[57] Mercenaries fought on both sides of the Nigerian Civil War in 1967–70,[58] and one of the most infamous "dogs of war," the Frenchman Bob Denard, was notoriously hired to depose the president of the

Comoro Islands, which he did, and then hired by different parties three years later to replace the president he had helped put into office.[59] Mid-to-late twentieth-century use of military contractors is not restricted to developing countries, of course. "At the height of hostilities in Vietnam, an estimated nine thousand civilian contractors accompanied U.S. servicemen" while "in the 1991 Gulf War, the U.S. government; utilized approximately five thousand private contractors to support the war effort."[60] Estimates for the number of contractors range from one for every uniformed U.S. service person in Iraq to contractors outnumbering the uniformed U.S. service people in country.[61]

As illustrated, although the private use of force has existed in one form or another since antiquity, the concept of the PMSC is relatively new. In terms of self-identification, all of the private military and security firms seek to convey the image of themselves as respectable companies; as official, formal organizations, and as "corporations similar to other corporations."[62] The professional background of PMSC members is routinely used as an argument to bolster such an image: PMSCs are often staffed by ex-military members, led by a core of the elite forces of the major military powers throughout the world, including but not limited to former American Navy SEALs and special forces, British SAS, and South African and former Soviet commandoes. In fact, the growth of the PMSC industry is widely attributed to the massive downsizing that happened in most militaries when the Cold War ended.

The secretive tendencies of PMSCs desperate to maintain "proprietary information" for a competitive edge makes it difficult to know for sure the exact number of PMSCs and their employees.[63] In the appendix to *Corporate Warriors*, Peter Singer lists 70 PMFs and their websites;[64] the membership of the International Stability Operations Association, a U.S. trade association of PMSCs, boasts 52 members.[65] These numbers, though large, would tend towards an underestimation of the industry, since only the largest and most reputable PMSCs would have widely publicized websites or pay dues to be involved with an American-based trade association. As Singer notes, "the global number is estimated to be in the mid-hundreds."[66] Looking at some additional information, a better picture of the actual size of the industry begins to emerge. Take DynCorp, a PMSC with major contracts with the U.S. Department of Defense, Justice, and Treasury, as well as the Drug Enforcement Agency and other U.S. agencies. DynCorp has more than 17,500 employees, over 550 operating facilities throughout the world, and annual revenues of more than $1.3 billion.[67] Military Professional Resources, Inc. (MPRI), a Virginia-based PMSC, also specializes in contracts for the U.S. government, to the tune of $12 million in annual revenue.[68] According to Jackson Nyamuya Maogoto, PMSCs "presently make up roughly 20% of the U.S. military personnel assisting the Columbian security forces in the ongoing military campaign against drug cartels and Marxist guerilla rebels, at a cost running into hundreds of millions of dollars."[69]

Unlike the individual mercenaries or bands of free companies from days gone by, PMSCs are legal entities organized as corporations. PMSCs range in size from small consulting firms to large corporations employing hundreds at a time.[70] Although they are formal, legal organizations, most PMSCs do not maintain large full-time employment; instead, they tend to consist of a few full-time staff who maintain databases of eligible personnel, allowing for flexibility and quick build-ups to meet contract requirements.[71] This was the model of such PMSCs as Executive Outcomes and Sandline.[72] Beside the skeleton-staff model of PMSCs, there exists also the large-scale multi-service PMSCs that employ hundreds, if not thousands, of full-time workers in a variety of military and defense-related fields; examples include MPRI, BoozAllen, Betac, and Vinnell.[73] PMSCs have been involved in all aspects of armed conflict, including from MPRI's training of African military staffs as part of the U.S. State Department's African Crisis Response Initiative,[74] to Executive Outcome's planning, leading, and participating in offensive operations to remove the threats posed by rebel groups to the regimes of Angola and Sierra Leone.[75] In addition, there are thousands of contracts underway in Iraq for such myriad services as security for diplomats, guarding the U.S. embassy, snipers, and interrogators.[76]

The Quest for Accountability and the Relevance of Human Rights and Humanitarian Law Norms

The growing profile of PMSCs in security governance has raised critical questions concerning the prospects for holding them accountable. Before we address some of the issues and challenges that such a quest faces, a few preliminary observations on accountability are in order.

Accountability is by definition a relational concept. At the most basic level, an entity is responsible for some act or failure to act in ways that are consistent with certain accepted standards of behavior, as well as to someone or some institutional entity. Accountability, as Ruth Grant and Robert Keohane have noted, is premised on the idea that some entities/actors have a right to hold others to such standards, to judge them in accordance to these standards, and to sanction them in cases of failure to uphold them.[77] The existence of sustainable processes for judging and sanctioning are indispensable components of any credible accountability mechanism. As Marcus Hedahl notes in his contribution, "accountability is a response to right and wrong actions."[78] Accountability presupposes a shared understanding of the legitimacy of the operative standards for exercising accountability, as well as of the authority of the parties involved in this relationship (one entity expected/assigned to exercise certain powers, while the other expected to hold them to account for such exercise).[79]

What are the legitimate operative standards for exercising accountability in the case of PMSCs? Clearly one important source derives from international human rights and humanitarian norms. Although many of these norms are legalized, and thus can be adjudicated and enforced before the appropriate fora, others are advanced through an increasingly dense network of transnational processes, which expose non-adherence with the concomitant reputational costs for violators.[80] For example, contracting and host states should ensure that PMSC personnel respect the right of individuals to be free from torture and cruel, inhuman, or degrading treatment or punishment (a fundamental right in international human rights, as well as in international humanitarian law), and the principle of distinction between combatants and non-combatants in conflict situations (a fundamental principle of international humanitarian law). Beyond such established norms, other types of conduct that are addressed in soft-law instruments of varying strength[81] can be promoted in different ways that often include peer pressure and public exposure. In such a context, violations can have adverse material (loss of contract) and moral consequences (isolation). Last, but not least, standards of legitimacy would include the relevant provisions of domestic laws, in the civilian as well as the military realm, which in some instances have an extra-territorial jurisdictional reach.[82]

As far as the parties involved in the landscape of accountability are concerned, two sets of relationships emerge: one set of relationships involves PMSCs and external (to the industry) entities and processes, and the other set involves PMSCs and internal industry monitoring mechanisms and processes. The former would include legislation and administrative directives developed/issued by states, whether these are Contracting, Territorial, or Home States,[83] while the latter would involve industry codes of conduct and self-generated monitoring mechanisms in an effort to advance socially responsible corporate conduct. An example of the latter would be the Code of Conduct of the International Stability Operations Association (ISOA) and its provision for a Standards Committee.[84]

What are the main mechanisms for accountability which have the potential for contributing to improved practices? We would argue that three mechanisms are of particular relevance to our discussion: legal accountability, peer accountability, and public reputational accountability.[85] Legal accountability would refer to the requirement that the relevant actors/entities abide by formal rules and that these rules constitute the frame of reference for their actions before courts and related judicial entities. Peer accountability would refer to mutual evaluation of actors/entities by their counterparts. Public reputational accountability is the form of accountability that combines aspects of the previous ones. Reputation provides a certain form of accountability both on its own terms, when other mechanisms are absent, as well as in conjunction with them. For example, legal – as well as peer – stigmatization invariably incurs reputational costs for the offender, even if the impact of such costs often leaves a lot to be desired. Until the recent criminalization of the gravest abuses of human rights, public reputational accountability constituted the main form of accountability for such abuses.

While legal accountability provides by far the strongest form of accountability, it faces, in the context of PMSCs, several challenges. First, early attempts to designate PMSC personnel as mercenaries and apply to them the corresponding provisions of international law have not advanced the cause of accountability. For several reasons, PMSC personnel must be considered as separate and distinct from mercenaries. The international legal framework that covers mercenarism is drawn from Article 47 of the 1977 Additional Protocol I to the Geneva Conventions, which denies POW status to mercenaries, and defines them as any person who

(a) Is specially recruited locally or abroad in order to fight in an armed conflict;

(b) Does, in fact, take a direct part in the hostilities;

(c) Is motivated to take part in the hostilities essentially by the desire for private gain and, in fact, is promised, by or on behalf of a Party to the conflict, material compensation substantially in excess of that promised or paid to combatants of similar ranks and functions in the armed forces of that Party;

(d) Is neither a national of a Party to the conflict nor a resident of territory controlled by a Party to the conflict;

(e) Is not a member of the armed forces of a Party to the conflict; and

(f) Has not been sent by a State which is not a Party to the conflict on official duty as a member of its armed forces.[86]

Further codification on the issue of mercenarism continued at the regional level, culminating in the Organization of African Unity's Convention for the Elimination of Mercenarism in Africa, which specified the definition of mercenaries further referring directly to the purpose of their employment, "specifically if they were hired for the overthrow of governments or OAU-recognized liberation movements."[87] This definition purposely left open the possibility of states lawfully hiring mercenaries for other purposes,

an opportunity of which several states availed themselves.[88]

In addition, the U.N. General Assembly adopted in 1989 the International Convention Against the Recruitment, Use, Financing, and Training of Mercenaries. It expanded on the 1977 definition by including an additional set of characteristics mercenaries must meet cumulatively.[89] Such a development has ensured that almost no one is guilty according to the latest definition; Geoffrey Best famously quipped that anyone found guilty under the definition "deserves to be shot – and his attorney with him!"[90] In fact, one of the arguments used by proponents of the U.N. Draft Convention is precisely the inapplicability of the mercenary label to PMSC employees.[91]

Moreover, each of these frameworks refers to individual mercenaries, not to corporate entities, so by stressing their formal, corporate nature, PMSCs can easily avoid being painted as mercenaries: "It is the *corporatization* of military service provision that sets them apart."[92] For the most part, PMSC employees must be considered civilians, although some actions, such as the use of arms in circumstances other than self-defense, may subject them to consideration as combatants.[93] In the context of the Geneva Conventions, such use of arms would constitute direct participation in hostilities, a term that has generated considerable debate. This debate has been rekindled as a result of a recently issued interpretive guidance by the International Committee of the Red Cross (ICRC).[94]

The second problem, related to the first, refers to gaps in the existing international legal framework.

This issue is extensively addressed in the contributions by Kristine Huskey, Benjamin Perrin, Nigel White, and José Gómez del Prado, so there is no need to repeat the main arguments here. Suffice to say that several of the gaps result from the state-centric nature of international law and its concomitant inability to effectively address the changes in the structure and functions of states and international organizations. More specifically, concerning states, such state centrism is anchored in a Westphalian conception of sovereignty that reinforces an outdated understanding of state responsibility and a corresponding failure to effectively address states' due diligence obligations. Moreover, while individuals are coming under increasing international – as well as domestic – legal scrutiny, corporate entities (such as PMSCs), given their status in international law, would at best undertake non-binding initiatives in corporate social responsibility.[95]

Last, but not least, it is important to bear in mind that legal accountability is almost invariably a reactive tool, rather than a proactive one. This is true even in situations where legal instruments expressly refer to prevention.[96] Therefore, and in the context of our subject matter, the fulfillment of due diligence obligations on the part of states and international organizations would necessitate complementarity between legal and peer accountability mechanisms. The latter, if properly designed and implemented, have the potential of filling an important gap. The prospects for an effective regulatory framework would be enhanced by focusing on the potential intersections between the proposed U.N. Convention and the Montreux Process.

Peer accountability faces the challenges that confront all self-regulatory initiatives. First, as soft-law initiatives, they are not backed by state sanctions.[97] Second, as voluntary instruments, they have a selectivity problem: these instruments would only apply to those entities willing to participate, not all. In addition, and related to the previous point, voluntary instruments tend to attract, whether for instrumental or normative reasons (or a mixture of both), those entities more eager to abide by the standards outlined in the document; "good" entities will most likely join, while the bad ones will stay away. Last, but not least, such initiatives often lack well-developed monitoring mechanisms and assessment tools, and/or provide little information on how these would work. For example, the ICoC, adopted in 2010, is noticeably weak on regulation, and it has still to finalize the Charter of the Oversight Mechanism.[98] Turning to another example, it is not clear how the ISOA Code of Conduct works to ensure compliance among "misbehaving" companies. To be sure, most peer accountability proponents, including Brooks and Streng in this issue, make it clear that such mechanisms and procedures are not and cannot be substitutes for legal accountability. In fact, the challenge here would be to explore ways in which legal and peer accountability could interact in mutually reinforcing ways.[99]

As the previous discussion has indicated, information is a crucial variable in the design and operation of accountability mechanisms. In fact, transparency, understood here as the "widespread availability of information,"[100] underscores all initiatives in this critical issue area. If, for example, one looks at the different oversight procedures and mechanisms provided for by the United Nations Draft Convention (Committee on the Regulation Oversight and Monitoring of PMSCs, and the proposed subsequent establishment of an International Register of PMSCs as well as the Periodic Reports Mechanism, and the Inquiry Procedure),[101] there is little doubt that one of the key aims is to generate more reliable information that, if appropriately channeled and used, will strengthen accountability.

In her essay, Allison Stanger argues that increased transparency of PMSCs, including more information collection and sharing, and more public and elite scrutiny of their activities, as part of their contracts and/or contract-approval processes would go a long way towards improving PMSCs' adherence and accountability to international humanitarian law. Such transparency would make them more present and accountable to the government and the public.[102] Once more information has been gathered and analyzed by individual states contemplating the hiring of PMSCs, states can make better decisions about how much PMSC involvement will help them achieve their objectives in a way consistent with international humanitarian and domestic law. Movements towards such transparency for the sake of accountability are emerging. Unfortunately, calls for increased transparency and domestic regulation tend to come in response to crises, such as particularly gruesome deaths of PMSC employees or massive, publicized PMSC atrocities. Calls for increased transparency and accountability in PMSCs are even beginning to come from congressional representatives

about the use of contractors in Iraq. One Representative "has introduced legislation to force the government to release detailed records on the use of contractors in Iraq and the names and job descriptions of all those killed and injured, information that is virtually impossible to get right now."[103] Furthermore, in the wake of Blackwater Security's unprovoked attack on unarmed civilians in Iraq, both houses of Congress are considering bills to limit and regulate PMSCs.

Increased transparency of these firms and their activities through better information sharing, oversight, and domestic regulation could also help ensure restraint on the part of PMSCs and their employees. PMSCs shroud themselves and their activities in secrecy, shielded by propriety information protections. Because of this secrecy, it is difficult to know what PMSCs are doing, where and how they are doing it, who is being affected, and how much it all really costs. One example is the mystery surrounding contractors in Iraq. Firms are not required to release information about their employees, and the Pentagon does not keep track of contractor casualties;[104] it is, in fact, difficult to get an accurate account of how many contractors are actually in Iraq. Furthermore, while the main argument in favor of privatization is cost-effectiveness, there is little empirical evidence to show that privatizing military functions has been effective in saving money. The lack of transparency allows PMSCs to "overcharge and underdeliver."[105] If the need for contractor and equipment escort and protection is factored in – since, to remain civilians, they cannot take up arms to protect their own equipment or anything but themselves – it is questionable whether privatization is a cost-savings at all.[106] Marcus Hedahl's piece in this volume examines the lack of accountability for large sums of money spent on contracting by the U.S., and argues that if PMSC contracting were revised to provide sufficient accountability and transparency, the amount of contracting would shrink dramatically.

Compounding the transparency concerns noted above, the use of PMSCs also has additional hidden costs or negative externalities, like the drain on resources and staff of national militaries; when states pay for PMSCs, they cannot afford to spend as much on their militaries, while at the same time the PMSC industry they are supporting has the tendency to woo away their best and brightest military men and women with higher salaries and better benefits.[107] If states are to avoid the negative spiral of a "self-perpetuating market for force" that "is likely to diminish both the quality and the extension of the security coverage, as well as the legitimacy of those providing it,"[108] they must make more thorough cost-benefit analyses and ensure that the information produced by these analyses is disseminated widely, so as to inform public debate. It seems counterintuitive that states would contract PMSCs, whose entire costs often include higher wages and profits. At least when considering the major militaries, such as the U.S., perhaps instead of hiring contractors it might make more sense to beef up the home state's military. The state could use the money that would have gone to the PMSC to achieve the multiplier effect of building a strong, effective, in-house military that is responsive to the military and politi-cal chain of command. Such a military would be clearly responsible under international human rights and international humanitarian law. In his essay, Marcus Hedahl proposes a hybrid approach using federally funded research and development centers as a model.

The preceding remarks by no means exhaust all the pertinent focal issues and questions. In an effort to set the stage for the essays that follow, we have sought to offer a broader historical context in the evolution of private warfare and touch upon some of the most pressing issues that confront the quest for accountability. The essays in this volume address certain key moral, legal, and political considerations involved in the privatization of security functions, the impact of outsourcing on security governance, and the efforts to hold PMSCs accountable through a combination of formal and informal regulatory mechanisms and processes. In the preparation of their essays, we asked our contributors to take into consideration at least some of the following focal issues and questions:

- What are the ethical, legal, political, and military implications of outsourcing to PMSCs?

- What are the responsibilities of these entities and of the other relevant actors in zones of conflict?

- What are the gaps in the international and domestic legal frameworks and how can they be addressed?

- What are the international/regional/national mechanisms and processes that can contribute to greater transparency and to efforts at inducing compliance?

Andrew Alexandra considers the ethical implications of outsourcing to PMSCs, arguing that outsourcing complicates keeping the state accountable to the people for its use of the military, and makes it more difficult for the people to act as a restraining force on the way in which the military is used. He begins his examination of this issue by offering an overview of the liberal view of violence and its implications for organizations dedicated to its use. He then proceeds with an analysis of the salient characteristics of the three historically dominant forms of armies and concludes with a critical assessment of the current situation, characterized by the uneasy coexistence of these three forms of armies.

Marcus Hedahl tackles the concept of accountability, and argues that the current accountability system for PMSCs is woefully inadequate. According to him, mere enhancements in oversight cannot hope to remedy that failing. He emphasizes that once we recognize the kind of accountability required of PSMCs, we will realize that radical changes in the foundational relationship between PSMCs and the state are required. More specifically, in order to be appropriately accountable, members of PMSCs must become a part of or, at the very least, directly responsible to the legitimate authoritative military or police structures. Futhermore, there must be a clear and precise delineation of responsibility among public officials for holding individual members of PMSCs criminally liable.

Kristine Huskey considers different ways of analyzing the existing legal regimes for holding PMSCs accountable. The rapidly growing presence of PMSCs in armed conflict and post-conflict situations in the last decade has engendered scrutiny of available mechanisms for criminal and civil accountability of the individuals whose misconduct causes harm, as well as drawn attention to the responsibility of states and international organizations for harm that occurs. Huskey's essay proposes a practical construct of three phases based on PMSC operations—Contracting, In-the-Field, and Post-Conduct—for analyzing the existing international legal regime. In offering this paradigm, she critically discusses whether and to what extent the legal regime provides "accountability for" PMSCs and their personnel.

Continuing the discussion about the international legal framework, Benjamin Perrin examines the common claim that there are gaps in international law that undermine accountability of private military and security companies. He uses a multiactor analysis in relation to the commission of international crimes, violations of fundamental human rights, and ordinary crimes. Perrin identifies six significant gaps in the existing framework that should be of greatest priority to address. According to him, without this critical first step of identifying these deficiencies, the debate about how to enhance accountability within this sector is likely to be misguided at best.

Nigel D. White argues that the increasing inapplicability of the Westphalian concept of sovereignty constitutes a major impediment in the way of international regulation of PMSCs. He critically discusses current and proposed regulatory regimes, placing particular emphasis on the Montreaux Process, and on the U.N. Draft Convention on PMSCs. White argues that the optimal accountability outcome would be for them to emerge as complementary – as opposed to rival – regimes. According to him, the debate on "inherently governmental functions" should not stand in the way of promoting effective regulation. The most effective approach would be to recognize that certain functions are acts of states, irrespective of who performs them. In this context, such functions give rise to state responsibility that, in contradistinction to state functions, can never be outsourced.

Turning his attention to one of the key proposed regulatory instruments, the U.N. Draft Convention on PMSCs, José Gómez del Prado traces its evolution and assesses the challenges that it confronts in the face of opposition from the U.S., the U.K., and other Western governments—as well as from PMSCs, which prefer self-regulation. Del Prado critically discusses the record of PMSCs in the field and argues that the adoption of the Draft Convention is necessary to fill an important protection gap.

The quest for accountability must address the issue of transparency. In her essay, Allison Stanger argues that American foreign policy has been privatized across the three Ds of defense, diplomacy, and development. She examines the reasons for and unintended negative consequences of this outsourcing of American power. She argues that the federal government must pursue contracting in ways that do not undermine the public interest. It can do this by identifying the things that should never be outsourced and ensuring that the letter and spirit of the Federal Funding Transparency and Accountability Act is upheld. Greater transparency in contractor–government relations will foster private security contractor compliance with ethical norms while bolstering our capacity for self-government.

As representatives of the Stability Operations industry (ISOA), Doug Brooks and Hanna Streng bring to this discussion on accountability and compliance the much-needed industry perspective. Their essay argues that companies in the stability operations industry have been subjected to painstaking scrutiny, while critics have ignored the value that they bring to contingency operations and government clients. Moreover, the scope of the industry is often overlooked by critics who paint a picture of uncontrollable companies making enormous profits. They challenge some of the common criticisms that are levied against the industry by the media and academics. According to them, the far larger problem of waste due to poor client planning and oversight is invariably glossed over. Their essay discusses industry self-policing efforts that have emerged to support the use of professional and compliant businesses in stability operations. While not a substitute for legal mechanisms, Brooks and Streng argue that such efforts demonstrate the willingness of ethical companies to improve standards in the industry.

The debate on the privatization of security functions is by no means settled. While the issue of what governments should and should not outsource goes on, it is important to bear in mind that outsourcing should not be equated with abdication of state responsibility for the actions of the private entities that assume security-related functions. Human rights and humanitarian norms constitute widely accepted standards of legitimacy that should guide state and international institutional action in this critical issue area. In this context, the most promising way to address existing gaps in the regulatory framework would be to focus on the growing intersections between hard and soft-law accountability mechanisms to ensure that they operate in mutually reinforcing ways.

Notes

"Private Security Forces and African Stability: The Case of Executive Outcomes," *Journal of Modern African Studies* 36, no. 2 (1998): 307–31; Sarah Percy, *Mercenaries: The History of a Norm in International Relations* (Oxford, UK: Oxford University Press, 2007), 208–18; and Major Michael E. Guillory, "Civilianizing the Force: Is the United States Crossing the Rubicon?" *Air Force Law Review* 51 (2001): 111–42.

2 A critical causal factor in the discussion on the nature and function of the state and its relation to the citizen is the rise of neo-liberal ideology; this issue is addressed in Andrew Alexandra's contribution in this issue.

3 Percy, *Mercenaries*, 206.

4 Ibid., 62–63.

5 Singer, *Corporate Warriors*, 8; and P. W. Singer, "Outsourcing War," *Foreign Affairs* 84, no. 2 (March/April 2005): 119.

6 Juan Carlos Zarate, "The Emergence of a New Dog of War: Private International Security Companies, International Law, and the New World Disorder," *Stanford Journal of International Law* 34, no. 1 (Winter 1998): 76.

1 We use the generic term PMSCs to designate all private sector security entities involved in conflict zones, although we are mindful of the distinction that some analysts have drawn between private military companies (PMCs) and private security companies (PSCs) (see below). For a discussion of the involvement of PMSCs in these conflicts, see P. W. Singer, *Corporate Warriors: The Rise and Fall of the Privatized Military Industry* (Ithaca: Cornell University Press, 2008), esp. chap. 7; H. M. Howe,

7. See, for example, Antenor Hallo de Wolf, "Modern *Condottieri* in Iraq: Privatizing War from the Perspective of International and Human Rights Law," *Indiana Journal of Global Legal Studies* 13, no. 2 (Summer 2006): 315–356.

8 Singer, "Outsourcing War," 120.

9 Percy, *Mercenaries*, 225–26.

10 The Montreux Document on Pertinent International Legal Obligations and Good

Practices for States Related to Operations of Private Military and Security Companies during Armed Conflict, Montreux, Switzerland September 17, 2008, http://www.icrc.org/eng/assets/files/other/icrc_002_0996.pdf. The International Code of Conduct (ICoC) which built on the Montreux Document, as well as on the "Respect, Protect, Remedy" framework developed by the former Special Representative of the U.N. Secretary General on Business and Human Rights, uses the term "Private Security Service Providers;" http://www.icoc-psp.org/Home_Page.html. On the Montreux Document, see Nigel White's and Kristine Huskey's contributions in this issue.

11 Deborah Avant, "Think Again: Mercenaries," *Foreign Policy*, July 1, 2004, http://www.foreignpolicy.com/articles/2004/07/01/think_again_mercenaries?print=yes&hidecomments=yes&page=full

12 Among the participants in our workshop, there was near consensus on the broader PMSC term as the appropriate term to designate the entities under study. See, however, the contribution by Brooks and Streng in this issue, which challenges this designation as "inherently faulty and deceptive."

13 Avant, "Think Again: Mercenaries," and Jose Gomez del Prado's contribution in this issue. See also our brief discussion of the legal framework in this essay.

14 Percy, *Mercenaries*, 236.

15 Singer, "Outsourcing War," 120.

16 This is discussed in Zarate, "Emergence of a New Dog of War," 95–97.

17 Ibid., 96–97.

18 Singer, "Outsourcing War," 125–26.

19 Daphne Richemond-Barak, "Rethinking Private Warfare," *Law & Ethics of Human Rights* 5, no. 1 (2011): 167.

20 Zarate, "Emergence of a New Dog of War," 82.

21 Daniel P. Ridlon, "Contractors or Illegal Combatants? The Status of Armed Contractors in Iraq," *Air Force Law Review* 62 (June 2008): 209.

22 Ibid., 210.

23 Percy, *Mercenaries*, 73.

24 Ibid., 80.

25 Ibid., 71.

26 Ibid., 86.

27 Ibid., 81.

28 Zarate, "Emergence of a New Dog of War," 84.

29 Ibid.

30 Percy, *Mercenaries*, 82.

31 Ibid., 72.

32 Ibid., 84.

33 Ibid., 83.

34 Ibid., 83.

35 Ibid., 83–84.

36 Ibid., 91.

37 Janice E. Thomson, *Mercenaries, Pirates and Sovereigns: State-Building and Extraterritorial Violence in Early Modern Europe* (Princeton: Princeton University Press, 1994), 22.

38 Kendall Stiles, "Banning Piracy: The State Monopoly on Military Force," in Wayne Sandholtz and Kendall Stiles, *International Norms and Cycles of Change* (New York: Oxford University Press, 2009), 35; Thomson, *Mercenaries, Pirates and Sovereigns*, 22–23; and Richemond-Barak, "Rethinking Private Warfare," 163.

39 Stiles, "Banning Piracy," 35; and Richemond-Barak, "Rethinking Private Warfare," 163.

40 Thomson, *Mercenaries, Pirates and Sovereigns*, 22.

41 Christopher Kinsey, *Corporate Soldiers and International Security: The Rise of Private Military Companies* (New york: Routledge, 2006), 37. By the 1750s, privateering had become such an integral part of English naval strategy that political lobbies were formed to advance the interests of privateers; ibid.

42 Ibid According to Kinsey, one of the key differences between English and French privateering was that, in the former case, privateers were auxiliary to the Royal

Navy, while, in the latter case, privateers constituted, in all respects, the French navy.

43 Thomson, *Mercenaries, Pirates, and Sovereigns*, 70.

44 Ibid., 78.

45 Ibid., 71.

46 Ibid., 41.

47 Ibid., 169, note 118.

48 Ibid., 35.

49 Ibid., 39.

50 H. V. Bowen, *The Business of Empire: The East India Company and Imperial Britain, 1756–1833* (Cambridge, UK: Cambridge University Press, 2006), 3. For an insightful commentary on the East India Company's inhumane administrative practices in India on the occasion of the 250th anniversary of the Battle of Plassey, see Amartya Sen, "Imperial Illusions: Britain and India, and the Wrong Lessons," *New Republic*, December 31, 2007; http://www.tnr.com/article/books/imperial-illusions

51 Thomson, *Mercenaries, Pirates, and Sovereigns*, 88–89.

52 Ibid., 81, 88.

53 Ridlon, "Contractors or Illegal Combatants?," 211.

54 Thomson, *Mercenaries, Pirates, and Sovereigns*, 93.

55 Ibid., 91.

56 David. L. Snyder, "Civilian Military Contractors on Trial: The Case for Upholding the Amended Exceptional Jurisdiction Clause of the Uniform Code of Military Justice," *Texas International Law Journal* 44, no. 1/2 (Winter 2008), 69.

57 Thomson, *Mercenaries, Pirates, and Sovereigns*, 93.

58 Ibid.

59 Ibid.

60 Snyder, *Civilian Military Contractors on Trial*, supra note 53 at 69 and 70.

61 Rian Kelty, "Citizen Soldiers and Civilian Contractors: Soldiers' Unit Cohesion and Retention Attitudes in the 'Total Force'," *Journal of Political & Military Sociology* 37, no. 2 (Winter 2009): 133–59.

62 Anna Leander, "The Market for Force and Public Security: The Destabilizing Consequences of Private Military Companies," *Journal of Peace Research* 42, no. 5 (2005): 608.

63 Singer, *Corporate Warriors*, 152–55, 192–95; John M. Broder and James Risen, "Contractor Deaths in Iraq Soar to Record," *New York Times Online*, May 19, 2007.

64 Singer, *Corporate Warriors*, 261–62.

65 http://stability-operations.org/index.php (accessed March 18, 2012).

66 Singer, *Corporate Warriors*, 79.

67 Daniel Burton-Rose and Wayne Madsen, "Corporate Soldiers: The U.S. Government Privatizes the Use of Force," *Multinational Monitor* 20, no. 3 (March 1999): 18.

68 As of 1998! It is expected that this number is significantly higher today; Zarate, "The Emergence of a New Dog of War," 104.

69 Jackson Nyamuya Maogoto, "Subcontracting Sovereignty: Commodification of Military Force and Fragmentation of State Authority," *Brown Journal of World Affairs* 13, no. 1 (Fall/Winter 2006): 153.

70. P. W. Singer, "War, Profits, and the Vacuum of Law: Privatized Military Firms and International Law," *Columbia Journal of Transnational Law* 42, no. 2 (Spring 2004): 522.

71 Singer, *Corporate Warriors*, 7.

72 Steven Brayton, "Outsourcing War: Mercenaries and the Privatization of Peacekeeping," *Journal of International Affairs* 55, no. 2 (Spring 2002): 306–07.

73 Singer, *Corporate Warriors*, 73.

74 Burton-Rose and Madsen, "Corporate Soldiers," 17.

75 Brayton, "Outsourcing War," 311–13; see also notes 16, 17.

76 Broder and Risen, "Contractor Deaths in Iraq Soar to Record."

77 Ruth W. Grant and Robert O. Keohane, "Accountability and Abuses of Power in

World Politics," *American Political Science Review* 99, no. 1 (2005): 29–30.

78 Marcus Hedahl, "Unaccountable: The Current State of Private Military and Security Companies," this issue. See section on The Accountability Problem.

79 Grant and Keohane, "Accountability and Abuses of Power in World Politics," 29.

80 By legalization, we refer to a form of institutionalization that is characterized by *obligation* (actors are legally bound by a rule), *precision* (rules "unambiguously define the conduct they require"), and *delegation* (third parties have, among other things, the authority "to implement, interpret and apply the rules'); see Kenneth W. Abbott et al., "The Concept of Legalization," in *Legalization and World Politics*, ed. Judith L. Goldstein, Miles Kahler, Robert O. Keohane, and Anne-Marie Slaughter (Cambridge, MA: MIT Press, 2001), 17. On the legalization front, one of the most important developments in the last 20 years has been the international criminalization of human rights violations.

81 Two of the most commonly cited soft-law instruments in the case of PMSCs are the Montreux Document and the International Code of Conduct for Private Security Service Providers (ICoC). The Montreux Document is applicable to states, and the International Code of Conduct to PMSCs. While no document creates new legal obligations for the entities concerned, the Montreux Document reflects existing due diligence obligations on states under international law; the Code, on the other hand, is much weaker on this front, since there are no such obligations for corporate entities in international law. Some of the key principles that the personnel of PMSCs, which are signatories to the ICoC, should adhere to include fundamental human rights norms, such as prohibition of the use of torture and of slavery and forced labor. These two documents constitute the Montreux Process. See also Nigel White's contribution, in this issue.

82 In the case of the U.S., relevant domestic laws would include the Alien Tort Claims Act, the Federal Tort Claims Act, the Military Extraterritorial Jurisdiction Act (MEJA), as well as the amended Uniform Code of Military Justice (UCMJ),

which extends jurisdiction "over persons serving with or accompanying U.S. armed forces in the field in times of declared war or a contingency operation," Memorandum for Secretaries of the Military Departments, http://www.justice.gov/criminal/hrsp/docs/03-10-08dod-ucmj.pdf. For a list of key US laws applicable to PMSCs, see Kevin Lanigan, "Legal Regulation of PMSCs in the United States: The Gap between Law and Practice," http://www.privatesecurityregulation.net/files/Microsoft%20Word%20-%20PMSC%20Article,%20US,%20Kevin%20Lanigan,%20Final.pdf

83 Here we use the terminology of the Montreux Document.

84 The ISOA Code of Conduct can be found at http://www.privatesecurityregulation.net/files/Microsoft%20Word%20-%20PMSC%20Article,%20US,%20Kevin%20Lanigan,%20Final.pdf. For a discussion of the ISOA Code of Conduct, see the contribution by Doug Brooks and Hannah Streng, in this issue.

85 This typology is drawn from Grant and Keohane, "Accountability and Abuses of Power in World Politics," 36–37. In our view, these are the main mechanisms, but not the only ones.

86 Adam Roberts and Richard Guelff, eds., *Documents on the Laws of War*, 3rd ed. (Oxford: Oxford University Press, 2000), 447.

87 Singer, "War, Profits, and the Vacuum of Law," 528.

88 Ibid., 529.

89 See http://treaties.un.org/doc/publication/UNTS/Volume%202163/v2163.pdf for the full definition.

90 Kevin H. Govern and Eric C. Bales, "Taking Shots at Private Military Firms: International Law Misses its Mark (Again)," *Fordham International Law Journal* 32, no. 1 (2008): 57, note 17.

91 See Jose Gomez del Prado's contribution in this issue. For the text of the United Nations Draft Convention on Private Military and Security Companies, see Human Rights Council. Promotion and Protection of all Human Rights, Civil, Political, Economic, Social and Cultural Rights, Including the Right to Development. *Report of*

the Working Group on the use of mercenaries as a means of violating human rights and impeding the exercise of the right of peoples to self-determination. A/HRC/15/25, 2 July 2010; http://www2.ohchr.org/english/issues/mercenaries/docs/A.HRC.15.25.pdf

92 Singer, *Corporate Warriors*, 45 (original emphasis).

93 Colonel Steven J. Zamparelli, "Privatization: Contractors on the Battlefield – What Have We Signed Up For?" *Air Force Journal of Logistics* 23, no. 3 (Fall 1999): 17.

94 Nils Melzer, *Interpretive Guidance on the Notion of Direct Participation in Hostilities under International Humanitarian Law*, International Committee of the Red Cross, 2009; http://www.icrc.org/eng/assets/files/other/icrc-002-0990.pdf. For a critique of the "continuous combat function" category in the Interpretive Guidance, see United Nations General Assembly, Human Rights Council, Report of the Special Rapporteur on Extrajudicial, Summary or Arbitrary Executions, Addendum: Study on Targeted Killings, A/HRC/14/24/Add.6, May 28, 2010; http://reliefweb.int/sites/reliefweb.int/files/resources/A38037358F1EF91B492577370006546B-Full_Report.pdf

95 We are referring here to the fact that corporations are not subjects of international law; see also Nigel White's contribution on this point.

96 The best example here is the Convention on the Prevention and Punishment of the Crime of Genocide which is both an international human rights and an international humanitarian law instrument. The title gives a misleading impression; the Convention addresses the issue of punishment, but not that of prevention.

97 On this issue, see also Human Rights Council, *Why We Need an International*

Convention on Private Military and Security Companies (PMSCs). Submission by the Working Group on the use of mercenaries as a means of impeding the exercise of the right of peoples to self-determination, A/HRC/WG.10/CRP.1, 17 May, 2011.

98 Draft Charter of the Oversight Mechanism for the International Code of Conduct-for Private Security Service Providers; http://www.icoc-psp.org/uploads/Draft_Charter.pdf. The Draft Charter was issued in January 2012. As of October 1, 2012, 511 companies from 63 countries have signed the ICoC.

99 In the case of the ISOA, it would be interesting to examine the extent to which the existence and operation of the Code may have strengthened those voices in the industry which supported the adoption of the Civilian Extraterritorial Jurisdiction Act (CEJA), as well as the expansion of the Military Extraterritorial Jurisdiction Act (MEJA).

100 See Grant and Keohane, "Accountability and Abuses of Power in World Politics," 39

101 See note 91.

102 Brayton, "Outsourcing War," 318.

103 Broder and Risen, "Contractor Deaths in Iraq Soar to Record"

104 Ibid

105 Maogoto, "Subcontracting Sovereignty," 152.

106 Zamparelli, "Privatization: Contractors on the Battlefield," 17–18.

107 Leander, "The Market for Force and Public Security," 617.

108 Ibid., 618.

Private Military and Security Companies and the Liberal Conception of Violence

ANDREW ALEXANDRA*

The institution of war is the broad framework of rules, norms, and organizations dedicated to the prevention, prosecution, and resolution of violent conflict between political entities. Important parts of that institution consist of the accountability arrangements that hold between armed forces, the political leaders who oversee and direct the use of those forces, and the people in whose name the leaders act and from whose ranks the members of the armed forces are drawn. Like other parts of the institution, these arrangements are responsive to changes in military technology and needs, to geopolitical facts, and to moral and political norms. In particular, they are sensitive to the forms that military organization takes. Since the emergence of modern states in Europe some 500 years ago, there have been three main such forms: private providers—in the form of mercenaries, in early modern Europe—then professional standing armies, which in turn developed into citizen armies. Although elements of the three organizations have coexisted in many armies, the citizen army model has dominated until recently. That model brought with it a particular conception of the accountability relations between the army, the state, and the people. The state had authority over and directed the army, which was accountable to it. In turn the state was accountable for its use of the army to the people, on whose behalf it acted.

The dominance of state authority over the military is now under strain, with the professional and private elements—in the form of private military and security companies

Andrew Alexandra is Director of the Australian Research Council Special Research Centre for Applied Philosophy and Public Philosophy (CAPPE), University of Melbourne Division. He has a number of publications on topics in war and peace, including the co-edited collection Private Military Companies: Ethics, Theory and Practice *(Routledge, 2008).*

(PMSCs)—having increasing importance. As those elements increase in power and presence, so it becomes more difficult to make the state accountable to the people for its use of the military, and more difficult for the people to act as a restraining force on the way in which the military used.

In this essay, I outline and assess these developments—with particular emphasis on the emergence of PMSCs—in the light of a liberal view of (political) violence. The essay focuses on the situation in the United States, which possesses by far the most important military force in the world today, and in which the use of PMSCs is most developed. The paper has three main sections and a brief conclusion: the first section sketches the liberal view of violence and its implications for organizations dedicated to its use; the second outlines the salient characteristics of the three historically dominant forms of armies; and the third looks at the current situation in which the three forms coexist uneasily.

1. Introduction

Wars involve a clash between the military forces of organized political groups. Those clashes occur within a broader framework of rules, norms, and organizations—what, following John Rawls, we can call the institution of war. For Rawls, an institution is

a public system of rules which defines offices and their positions with their rights and duties, powers and immunities, and the like. These rules specify certain forms of action as permissible, others as forbidden; and they provide for certain penalties and defenses, and so on, when violations occur.

Rawls goes on to give examples of what he calls "institutions ... games and rituals, trials and parliaments, markets and systems of property."[1] Modern war has gradually become institutionalized in this Rawlsian sense. In the first instance, following the emergence of recognizably modern states in Italy in the late fifteenth century, the institutionalization of war was internal to the state, with the subordination of the providers of military force to political control, and their dedication to the realization of political goals.[2] Subsequently, a set of international rules has evolved governing international relations, including wars, and covering such things as the reasons for which war can be entered into, how wars can be fought, and what follows from their termination.[3]

Some of those rules are long-standing, such as the Westphalian division of the world into a number of sovereign states, each of which claims sovereignty over a discrete territory, and the delineation therein of the rights entailed by sovereignty. Others are more recent. Of particular relevance to this essay is the emergence of a broadly liberal conception of justified political violence during the twentieth century and especially after World War II. According to the liberal conception of violence in general, an individual's basic rights—such as the rights to bodily integrity and autonomy—entail that others are not justified in using violence either as an end in itself or as a means to the achievement of some pre-existing end, where doing so would violate the rights of the subject of violence. Notwithstanding, violence, or the threat of violence, can become justified (and in some cases obligatory) where it is a necessary means to deter or prevent the violation of basic rights or to rectify such violations if they nevertheless occur. Importantly, according to this conception violence has no intrinsic value, although it can have instrumental value deriving from its effectiveness in limiting rights violations that would otherwise occur.

The liberal conception of violence has a number of implications for the institution of war. First, it implies that peace is the (desired) state of normality and war the (unwanted) exception. Second, it implies that the purpose of war—and of the organizations dedicated to its pursuit—is the restoration of peace. It thus imposes limits both on the grounds on which states can justifiably go to war—in response to an unjustified attack on their own, or some other, state, and to defend groups against egregious violations of their basic rights—and the goals which they can thereby aim to achieve—the restoration of the status quo ante in the case of defensive war, and the cessation of human rights violations in the case of humanitarian interventions. This stands in contrast to the view of war as a legitimate tool for the extension of political power. Third, the liberal conception of violence has important implications for the role and structure of the state organizations dedicated to the prevention of,

preparation for, and fighting of wars. According to the liberal conception, the ideal world is one in which there is no violation of rights and hence no need for violence, and a fortiori no place for organizations of violence. The best possible world is one in which as much as possible of what would happen in the ideal world still happens. Organizations of state violence are guardians, dedicated to the realization of this world. There are thus two overriding pragmatic desiderata for such organizations and the regulatory framework within which they operate: effectiveness in preventing and limiting violence and other rights violations; and what might be called neutrality. This notion of neutrality connotes that the operations of these organizations should impinge as little as possible on the legitimate activities of the public they protect. It also suggests that they should allow the resumption of normal life as fully and quickly as possible after conflict. Of course, in practice they will always have some impact, if only because they are costly, so a system of taxation or the like will have to be put in place to fund them. Though these two desiderata—effectiveness and neutrality—are not logically incompatible, there is a kind of de facto tension between them. Many of the most obvious ways of increasing the effectiveness of institutions of violence, such as giving them greater powers to monitor and restrict suspect actions or people, clearly reduce neutrality. In any case, because these organizations have no independent intrinsic value, the desideratum of neutrality tells us that they should be as small and non-intrusive as is compatible with their effectiveness.

2. Armed Forces: Three Models

The organizations at the heart of the institution of war, of course, are the armed forces. In the approximately 500 years that the modern state system has been evolving, there have been three main forms of military organization. Until well into the seventeenth century, mercenaries were the primary source of military force for European powers.[4] Mercenary forces were spectacularly poor in terms of both the desiderata outlined above (effectiveness and neutrality) and with states ravaged by the very forces that were supposedly protecting them Europe in this period was devastated by bloody and protracted wars. The need to generate steady revenue streams to pay for mercenary forces stimulated the development of centralized state finance bodies, enabling European states to employ soldiers on a permanent basis and form standing professional armies. These armies were organs of the state and, at least in their officer class, largely composed of nationals. However, in their modes of fighting, culture, and isolation from civilian life, and their role as agents of the rulers of the state—as useful for protection against domestic subversion as foreign usurpation—they resembled their mercenary forebears.[5]

The second major transformation was the move from professional standing armies to citizen armies. The French Revolutionary Army was the model for this transformation. Faced with defeat in its war against its continental neighbors, the French revolutionary government decreed a levee en masse, according to the following terms:

Henceforth, until the enemies have been driven from the territory of the Republic, the French people are in permanent requisition for army service. The young men shall fight; the married men shall forge arms and transport provisions; the women shall make tents and clothes and shall serve in the hospitals; the children shall turn old lint into linen; the old men shall betake themselves to the public squares in order to arouse the courage of the warriors and preach hatred of kings and the unity of the Republic.[6]

This decree of 23 August 1793 presupposes a radical understanding of the relationship between members of a nation and the state that is its political expression (the state being understood here as the corporate entity that exercises political authority within a region). The state is charged with preparing for and, if necessary, prosecuting war, and it is entitled to draw on all the human and material resources of the nation to do so. The people are sovereign, and with popular sovereignty comes not simply universal rights of political participation and control, but universal duties to support and defend the nation. At the very least, citizens are obligated to contribute to the war effort, and, more specifically, the young men need provide military service. According to this conception, the role of the soldier becomes a political office: civic status and military service are two sides of the one coin—there are no longer citizens, or soldiers, but rather "citizen-soldiers." Relatedly, the armed forces are seen as continuous with and at the service of the nation, rather than the preserve of a separate military caste beholden to a ruling elite, as it had been in the Ancien Régime. Conscription becomes a means both to generate the manpower required by mass armies, especially in times of war, and to distribute the burdens of service equitably.

There is no necessary incompatibility between mercenary, professional, and citizen forces; indeed, many armies have been composed of some mix of such forces. The U.S. military through the first three-quarters of the twentieth century, for instance, is described by Elliot Cohen as an example of an "expansible/selective service military" which "consists of a relatively small, professional, peacetime army, conceived as a kind of framework around which a potentially much larger wartime army can be built."[7] That wartime army, of course, was mainly constituted by citizen-soldiers for whom military service was an interruption in the arc of their lives. Military service remained embedded in the broader society. Hence, although it contained an essential professional core, in its war-fighting incarnation the U.S. military was a citizen army.[8]

On the other hand, while Western states continued to draw on mercenaries—especially in foreign wars and colonial missions—well into the nineteenth century, there is clearly a tension, if not outright conflict, between the patriotic values and attachments that ideally motivate the citizen-soldier and the commercial ones characteristic of the mercenary. It is not surprising that the rise of the citizen-army saw mercenaries increasingly pushed into the margins of conventional military activity, while national, regional, and international laws and conventions progressively criminalized mercenarism and activities associated with it, such as recruitment.

Over the past couple of centuries, citizen armies have undoubtedly been more effective than either purely mercenary or purely professional armies could have been. As the success of Napoleon's Grande Armée demonstrated, mass mobilization was necessary for military success in the kind of interstate wars that remained a possibility for most advanced states from the early nineteenth century until late into the twentieth century. For pragmatic reasons other European powers were obliged to follow the French model, even when placing military power into the hands of the masses had the potential to subvert the status quo.[9]

Popular sovereignty brought with it a particular conception of the accountability relations among the army, the state, and the people. The state had authority over and directed the army, which was accountable to it.[10] In turn, the state was accountable for its use of the army to the people, on whose behalf it acted.[11] The nature of citizen armies meant that it was difficult for the state to avoid such accountability. Because citizen armies are composed of soldiers whose lives remain intertwined with that of the civilian population, and because the burden of military service is broadly spread through the population, citizens have a powerful incentive to concern themselves with the military decisions of the state. Conversely, since the state can effectively prosecute a war using a citizen army only with the ongoing support of the populace, it is obliged to act in ways that will generate and maintain that support. Members of democratic societies, in particular, have shown a willingness to make the sacrifices necessary to prevail in armed conflicts that threaten the survival of their states or those of their allies, and a disinclination to do so for conflicts that do not.[12] As Cheyney Ryan puts it, "The way to prevent irresponsible war-making was to ensure that its sacrifice would be borne by everyone."[13] Citizen armies thus can be seen as providing at least some degree of insulation against both internal oppression and external aggression.

3. An Unstable Amalgam

Although all nations retain standing armies, the nature of those armies, at least in Western states, is undergoing what is arguably the most significant change since the French Revolution. There are two interconnected reasons for this, both reflecting the radically altered geopolitical environment following the fall of the U.S.S.R. and the end of the Cold War. In the first place, those changes have arguably done away with the need for mass citizen armies. The end of the Cold War saw the disappearance of the realistic possibility of large-scale interstate war, which had been the primary raison d'être of those armies. In post-World War II Europe, for example, peace was kept through the Cold War by massed, conscript-based line-defenses backed by a nuclear deterrent. As the Cold War neared its end in 1988, and with it the possibility of interstate conflict in Europe, European NATO forces consisted of 3.1 million active troops and 5.5 million reservists, most of whom were conscripts; three years later these figures had been reduced by over 40%.[14] As the Cold War wound down, other threats emerged, including the growth of international terrorism, the proliferation of weapons of mass destruction, uncontrolled mass movement of peoples, and the growth of intra-state conflicts. At the same time, advanced states were increasingly called to use their military power for "humanitarian interventions" to prevent or end serious violations of human rights and to keep or make peace (often in multinational operations).

Although they have remained dependent on financial support from the state, contemporary armies no longer need ongoing injections of large numbers of new recruits to maintain the mass of militarily trained citizens who could be rapidly mobilized in case of war. This development is reflected in the phasing out of conscription in many states. The new calls on the military are also likely to place troops in harm's way, generating the political risks attendant on conscript casualties, even if it is possible to deploy them. Furthermore, technologies such as networked information systems have become increasingly important as "force multipliers." Conscripts are less likely to possess the skills needed to handle such systems than specialist professionals, and the costs associated with extensive conscript intakes eat into the budget available for high-tech equipment and training.

The second reason for the changing nature of armies is the rethinking of the relationship between state and citizen consequent on the ascendancy of neo-liberal ideology among policy elites. That ideology has altered the understanding of the role of the state in delivery of services to its citizens—from "government" to "governance." Although the state still takes responsibility for the availability of a range of services, it oversees the provision of such services rather than delivering them directly through its own agencies. As part of this change many state agencies have been privatized. There appear to be two main motivations for such privatization. First, it is held that private agencies, subject to the discipline of the market, will provide the needed services more efficiently than public sector organizations. But, second, it is often thought that there is a fund of available resources, skills, and so on, locked up in public sector organizations that can generate greater economic returns, first, for the state itself, and then for the community more generally, if their economic potential is exploited in the market.

Neo-liberal ideology thus renders the provision of military services by private, rather than public, providers at least prima facie desirable. At the same time, neo-liberalism has also contributed to the need for private provision by changing the relationship among citizens, mediated through state institutions. Fraternity has long been one of the animating values of Western states, expressed, for example, in welfare programs such as age pensions and health care systems. Norms of loyalty, mutuality, exclusivity, and preparedness to sacrifice individual interests for the greater good—all of which can be

seen as specifications of the value of fraternity—have also been embodied in institutional arrangements for national defense as well as in attitudes to those arrangements (furthermore, as implied above, hostility to mercenaries and mercenary forces reflect their incompatibility with the value of fraternity). With the ascendancy of neo-liberalism, fraternal social values have been eroded. In effect, risk has been re-privatized. But, of course, norms of sacrifice and the like, on which the citizen army has been founded, inevitably are undermined in such circumstances.

These changes in the mission of modern armies, and in the relationship between state and citizen, have produced consequential alterations in the structure and nature of those armies, and their relation to the nation they serve. In the U.S., for example, despite involvement in major conflicts in Iraq and Afghanistan over the past decade, a smaller percentage of the population belong to the armed forces than at any time since before World War II (currently around 0.5% of the population is in the military, compared to 9% in World War II and about 2% in the Vietnam War). As well as remaining in the services for longer periods than previous generations, members of the military are also less typical of the U.S. population as a whole—service members are disproportionately drawn from the rural South, far more likely than the rest of the population to have a parent who served in the military, and less likely to come from either very poor or very well-off backgrounds.[15] They are increasingly likely to identify themselves as politically partisan (in the main, supporters of the Republican Party) and, for the first time in over 100 years, military veterans are now under- rather than over-represented in Congress.[16] In the light of these facts, it is not surprising that in a recent survey of military veterans and civilians, both groups overwhelmingly agreed with the proposition that "the public understands the problems that those in the military face either 'not too well' or 'not well at all'" (84% of recent veterans and 71% of civilians).[17]

As the U.S. military has become increasingly detached from the broader society, so members of that society have decreasingly come to see involvement in the nation's war effort as part and parcel of being a citizen. The military had difficulty in finding sufficient recruits to fight the wars in Iraq and Afghanistan, even when there was overwhelming public support for them. Initiatives to generate the required numbers included significantly increasing financial incentives such as enlistment bonuses, scholarships, and mortgage assistance; targeting minorities, including non-citizens (by 2006, 30,000 non-citizens were serving in the U.S. military); and lowering standards— by 2007, almost 30% of recruits had to be granted a waiver for behavior (including criminal felonies) or conditions (such as medical problems or low aptitude scores) that would have previously disqualified them.[18] Notably, recruitment campaigns emphasized the personal benefits of enlistment rather than service to the community, in part at least to forestall the resistance of parents to their children's enlistment[19] (though patriotic concerns do remain important in motivating recruits[20]).

In short, although the U.S. army is (largely) composed of citizens, it is moving away from the ideal of a citizen force and in the direction of a professional army. At the same time, in the U.S., as in a number of other countries, private military and security companies are increasingly doing work that was previously undertaken by members of national armed forces.

The emergence and rapid growth of PMSCs is clearly one of the most significant developments in military affairs over the past two decades since the end of the Cold War. PMSCs are descendants of the mercenary organizations of earlier times—they provide military services, including the provision of coercive force, for a fee. But they differ in important, perhaps fundamental ways from those organizations. As Peter W. Singer puts it, the "critical factor is their modern corporate business form."[21] Although PMSCs came to public attention with the military involvement of groups such as Sandline International and Executive Outcomes in conflicts in Sierra Leone and Angola in the 1990s, the major PMSCs are domiciled in First-World countries, which are also their principal clients. The services that PMSCs provide to national forces include logistical support, training, guarding personnel and installations, operation of weapons systems, and gathering of intelligence. With estimated annual revenues in the tens of billions, PMSCs—including such substantial corporations as DynCorp, Northrop Grumman, Xe Services LLC (formerly Blackwater), and KBR (formerly Kellogg, Brown & Root)—have come to play a significant role in the military activities of states, especially the United States. PMSCs have become central to U.S.—and hence to global—military activity. For example, in the first Gulf War in 1991 the ratio of members of U.S. state forces to contractors is estimated to have been in the order of 50:1; in the second Gulf War and in the U.S.-led war in Afghanistan, the ratio is close to 1:1.[22] Moreover, those contractors are overwhelmingly non-American: in Afghanistan in 2011, only 1% of the almost 19,000 Department of Defense contractors were U.S. citizens, with 95% being Afghanis.[23]

If contractors are counted as part of the armed forces, then it would seem that the U.S. army, at least, has become a hybrid private/national force, and one whose members are increasingly drawn from foreign countries. This conclusion tends to be resisted by appealing to the supposedly non-combatant role of PMSC members in conflict zones. The laws of war[24] draw a categorical distinction between combatants and civilians in countries involved in war. These categories are both exhaustive—there is no other applicable category—and exclusive: a person in one category is excluded from the other. The combatant/civilian distinction and associated norms are of central importance to the liberal view of war outlined above, aiming to draw a bright line between those who fight a war and those who carry on the peaceful life that is the purpose of war to protect. Very different rights, duties, and immunities attach to members of these two categories. Combatants have the right to participate in hostilities, whereas civilians do not; combatants have the right to intentionally target hostile combatants, but no right to intentionally target civilians unless such civilians directly participate in hostilities; combatants have the right to be accorded prisoner-of-war status if apprehended by the enemy, whereas civilians do not,[25] even if in fact they have taken part in hostilities; and

combatants are immune from prosecution for their role in hostilities provided they have fought according to the laws of war, whereas civilians are liable to criminal prosecution for such actions. While civilians are legally forbidden from "direct participation" in hostilities, by, for example, taking up arms, obviously they might in fact participate. If they do, they are classified as "unlawful/unprivileged combatants" and forfeit their immunity from attack, but only "unless and for such time as they take a direct part in hostilities."[26] The term "unlawful combatant" is potentially misleading, implying as it does a third legal category, somewhere between that of (lawful) combatant and civilian. "Unlawful combatants" are, rather, civilians whose illegal actions have caused them to forfeit temporarily their immunity and to incur criminal liability.[27]

Hence, even though, as indicated above, members of PMSCs employed by the U.S. government in Iraq and Afghanistan have taken on many of the tasks traditionally assumed by members of the armed forces, they do not thereby come to have the status of combatants. In determining what their status actually is, it is helpful to look at the structure and function of PMSCs. Singer has influentially suggested a "tip of the spear" typology of PMSCs, with military provider firms (MPFs) offering front-line command and combat operations at the offensive tip of the spear, followed by military consultancy firms (MCFs) providing training and advisory programs, and then military support firms (MSFs) offering logistical support services.[28] The larger PMSCs typically will be able to offer services of all three kinds, although military consultancy and military support are the most important of their functions. In terms of this typology, members of MPFs in conflict zones will clearly count as (lawful or unlawful) combatants. Military provider firms are, however, a relatively minor part of the PMSC industry and the operations of PMSCs in the conflicts in Iraq and Afghanistan do not involve MPFs.

Contractors undertaking military consultancy and military support roles may become lawful combatants in one of two ways. First, states can make it a condition of granting contracts to PMSCs that members who undertake certain functions enlist as reservist members of the armed forces, becoming part of the military chain of command when on active service. The United Kingdom has done this in its "Sponsored Reserve" scheme.[29] Second, Protocol I Additional to the Geneva Conventions allows that a "paramilitary or armed law enforcement agency" (which could include PMSCs) may be incorporated in the armed forces of a party to a conflict, provided that the party doing so notifies the opposing side.[30]

The United States, at least, chooses not to take either of these routes to bestowing combatant status on its contractors in conflict zones. Such contractors are neither enlisted in the armed forces, nor in the military chain of command; they remain employees under the direction of companies that have a contractual relationship with the state. Hence, given the dichotomous nature of the combatant/civilian distinction, and the current criteria for drawing that distinction, it is at least prima facie plausible that, as U.S. policy documents state, "[c]ontractors accompanying the armed forces . . . are civilians accompanying the U.S. Armed Forces."[31]

Because members of PMSCs working for the United States are not lawful combatants, they are civilians. That status is, of course, compatible with them being unlawful combatants. Are they? Here it is useful to consider the similarities between the organizational articulation of PMSCs—as described, for example, in Singer's "tip of the spear" typology of PMSCs—and that of modern armies. It will be recalled that in Singer's typology, military provider firms offering front-line command and combat operations are placed at the offensive tip of the spear, followed by military consultancy firms offering training and advisory programs, and then by military support firms offering logistical support services. Singer's delineations reflect similar distinctions between the main functional divisions of the armed forces—known respectively as the combat arm, the combat support arm, and the combat support service.[32] The combat arms are (in army terms) infantry and armor—those elements of the army that aim to engage with and fight the enemy. Combat support covers those elements that directly help the combat arms close with and kill the enemy: engineers, artillery, air, and intelligence fall within this category. Finally, combat service support encompasses those areas (logistics, signals, medical services, and so on) that support the overall military effort. The metaphor describing the relationship between the combat arm and the other arms is that of "tooth to tail."

Although fighting is primarily the mission of members of the combat arms, all members of the armed forces bear arms,[33] have had at least basic combat training, are expected to engage in combat, if required, and are counted as combatants. The status of members of armed forces as combatants is, it seems to me, overdetermined. An armed force engaged in ongoing conflict is a kind of corporate entity, all the members of which share a common animating end. It is composed of a number of interacting subunits (such as the artillery and the intelligence units), which are defined by the different specialized means they use to help realize their common goal. The interdependence of the various subunits means it is a tactical matter as to where resistance to achievement of their common goal is best focused and the form it takes. That is, resistance at any time may or may not take the form of the exercise of violent force (it might, for example, take the form of a denial of material support) and, if violence is used, it might be most effectively directed at units other than those that belong to the combat arms. It might be wiser to attack "the tail" than "the tooth." At the same time, the functional divisions within the armed forces are not rigid; if necessary, any member can be called on to engage in combat (or other tasks). Potentially, at least, all members are both liable to and capable of attack.

Although U.S. government contractors in conflict zones have not been integrated into the command structure of the armed forces, they nevertheless fit into the corporate structure described in the previous paragraph. They share a common goal with the armed forces and interacted with elements of it to achieve that goal. According to official U.S. doctrine, "contractor employees cannot lawfully perform military functions and should not be working in

scenarios where they might be conceived as combatants."[34] While it is true that, as civilians, contractors may not legally take "direct part" in hostilities, when they are as integral a part of the military mission as they have been in Iraq and Afghanistan, it is fanciful to think that they will not be conceived of and treated as combatants, not simply by opposition forces, but by the state for which they work.

Consider two well-documented chains of events in Iraq in 2004. The first was sparked by the notorious killing of four Blackwater employees in the city of Falluja, which had become one of the principal centers of resistance to the U.S. occupation and the scene of fierce and ongoing fighting, with significant civilian casualties. The local population greeted the killing of the Blackwater employees with jubilation. According to The New York Times, "[m]any people in Falluja said they believed that they had won an important victory on Wednesday."[35] The U.S. government and armed forces worried that the killings could undermine U.S. resolve in Iraq and embolden the resistance—as the downing of Black Hawk helicopters had in Somalia in 1993—unless there was a large and successful display of U.S. force in response. The second chain of events began with a firefight in the holy city of Najaf, with followers of the cleric Muqtada Al-Sadr on one side and U.S. soldiers and Blackwater employees guarding the Coalition Provisional Authority (CPA) headquarters on the other. It is uncertain who was responsible for initiating the firefight,[36] but it is clear that not only did the Blackwater employees play a leading role, including directing the actions of the soldiers, but three Blackwater helicopters were given permission by CPA staff to deliver ammunition and evacuate a wounded marine during the course of the fight.[37] In both cases, U.S. forces soon engaged in full-blown, bloody assaults on the towns—assaults that were clearly precipitated by, and responding to, the events involving Blackwater staff.

In situations in which contractors are becoming involved in large-scale firefights alongside uniformed troops, are directing and providing material assistance for such troops, and where targeting contractors is an effective tool in influencing enemy tactics, it is hard to maintain that they are not combatants—albeit unlawful ones. Moreover, the contractors appear to pose a particular danger to the civilian population. Figures for civilian casualties in Iraq and Afghanistan are speculative and highly contested,[38] and there seems no reliable way of working out the relative contributions of contractors and uniformed troops to those casualties. There have been, however, a number of well-publicized cases of contractors injuring and killing civilians without just cause, such as the "Nisoor Square Massacre" in which Blackwater employees escorting a convoy of U.S. State Department vehicles shot dead 17 Iraqi civilians in Baghdad.[39] According to the American journalist Scott Horton, "[d]ozens of incidents . . . comparable to the Nisoor Square case have been referred to [the] Justice [Department]."[40]

There is a variety of plausible explanations for the tendency of contractors to use unjustified deadly force against civilians, including inadequate screening of recruits, poor training, lack of local knowledge, and so on. To some extent at least, however, it stems from the incentive

structures within which PMSCs currently operate. Consider the situation confronting Blackwater in providing personal security services to Paul Bremer in his role as Head of the Coalition Provisional Authority in Iraq in 2003–04. This was a period of extreme disorder in Iraq (arguably exacerbated by some of Bremer's own decisions, such as dissolving the Iraqi army) and Bremer was a highly visible and attractive target for forces hostile to the U.S. occupation. Osama Bin Laden offered "10,000 grams of gold to whoever kills the occupier Bremer"[41] and Bremer himself recounted that a U.S. Secret Service survey had reckoned him to be "the most threatened American official anywhere in the world."[42] At a time when the market opportunities for PMSCs in Iraq were rapidly expanding, preventing a successful attack on Bremer became a commercial imperative for Blackwater. As the man charged with reconstructing the Iraqi armed forces, Colonel Thomas Hammes, put it:

> You may lose an ambassador in an insurgency—that's a fact; the British did in Malaya—but you have other ambassadors . . . But if Blackwater loses a principal, they're out of business, aren't they? Can you imagine being Blackwater, trying to sell your next contract, saying, "Well, we did pretty well in Iraq for about four months, and then he got killed." And you're the CEO who's going to hire and protect your guys. You'll say, "I think I'll find somebody else." . . . For the military, if the primary gets killed, that's a very bad thing. There will be after-action reviews, etc., but nobody's going out of business.[43]

Unsurprisingly, Blackwater staff were prepared to be extremely aggressive in protecting their charge, trying to ensure that his progress from place to place would be unimpeded, for example, by forcing other vehicles off the road or even shooting at them. Blackwater fulfilled their brief in protecting Bremer, but did so in a way that alienated locals and arguably set back the overall U.S. mission. According to Hammes:

Their interests are fundamentally different than ours....Blackwater's an extraordinarily professional organization and they were doing exactly what they were tasked to do: protect the principal. The problem is in protecting the principal they had to be very aggressive, and each time they went out they had to offend locals... making enemies each time they went out. So they were actually getting our contract exactly as we asked them to and at the same time hurting our counterinsurgency effort.[44]

More generally, under current policies, with PMSCs operating outside the military chain of command, there is likely to be, at best, only an accidental coincidence between the broad politico/strategic goals of the state that employs a PMSC and the much narrower ones the PMSC is tasked to achieve.

As currently structured, the relationship between PMSCs and U.S. national forces in conflict zones is undesirable in terms of both of the desiderata for armed forces that were outlined above. The legal status of contractors as civilians and their actual status as combatants is blurring the important line between combatant and civilian, making it harder to draw a line around a sphere that should be, as far as possible, protected from conflict. And the behavior of contractors toward the civilian population breaches that line. Moreover, that behavior also undermines the effectiveness of the state forces by alienating the local population and generating conflict.

4. Conclusion

Clearly, the way in which the U.S. in particular is using PMSCs in conflict situations is undesirable in terms of both of the aforementioned desiderata for armed forces (effectiveness and neutrality). In terms of effectiveness, although PMSCs may be successful in pursuit of their narrowly defined goals, that success can come at the cost of undermining the effectiveness of the broader effort of which they are part. They can, for example, alienate the local population and generate conflict. In terms of neutrality, the legal status of contractors as civilian and their actual status as combatants blurs the important line between combatant and civilian, making it harder to draw a line around a sphere that should, as far as possible, be protected from conflict. In addition, the behavior of contractors toward the civilian population often breaches that line.

One way of dealing with these problems would be to restrict the kinds of services that PMSCs can offer, or perhaps ban them outright. As a matter of fact, the likelihood of this occurring seems slight. Moreover, without denying the obvious need to better integrate members of PMSCs with those of state militaries when they are operating together, PMSCs would seem to have a legitimate role in providing needed capabilities in areas such as logistics. They can assist in many of the tasks that modern armies are called on to undertake, for example, by intervening to protect civilian populations in times of crisis. The events occasioning such interventions are generally unpredictable in timing or location or both. Not even the most powerful state can maintain armed forces possessing the full range of resources and capabilities needed across the possible range of situations that they might face. Calling on the services of PMSCs increases states' capacities to provide swift, effective responses to situations requiring humanitarian intervention.

There are obviously good reasons for the U.S. and other states which make extensive use of PMSCs to follow the British example and make PMSC employees in conflict zones members of the armed forces, falling under the military chain of command. They therefore become unequivocally lawful combatants, whose actions may be directed to conform to the overall strategic goals of the armed forces. There have been, in fact, some significant, albeit insufficient, developments in the direction of integrating PMSC employees into the U.S. armed forces—for example,

the 2006 amendment of the Military Extraterritorial Jurisdiction Act to permit the court-martialling of contractors[45] and the inclusion of contractors in the official account of U.S. forces.[46] There have also been moves at both the international and industry levels to develop codes of conduct for the private security industry, codes that aim inter alia to provide accountability mechanisms.[47]

Given the continuing use of PMSCs, these are positive developments. But however accountable PMSCs become to the state that employs them, and however well integrated they are into the armies whose mission they share, fundamental concerns remain. PMSCs, by their nature, remain disconnected from the people in whose name that state is acting. Moreover, they are growing in influence at a time when the militaries that they supplement are themselves moving away from the citizen-army form. This form could ensure at least a good deal of accountability—and hence some kind of assurance against military adventurism—by the states to the people in whose name they supposedly act.

Notes

1 John Rawls, *A Theory of Justice* (Cambridge, MA: Belknap/Harvard University Press, 1973), 55.

2 See F. H. Hinsley, *Nationalism and the International System* (London: Hodder & Stoughton, 1973), esp. chap. 6, "The Modern Pattern of Peace and War"; Michael Howard, *War in European History* (Oxford: Oxford University Press, 1984).

3 Hinsley sees the modern international system emerging in post-1815 Europe "as a body of assumptions and restraints that

was accepted by governments, and not merely advocated by theorists." Hinsley, *Nationalism and the International System*, 85. For an account of the historical development of the regulation of war, see James Turner Johnson, *Ideology, Reason, and the Limitation of War* (Princeton: Princeton University Press, 1974).

4 This is not to suggest that mercenaries were the only such source. Local militias, for example, also played a role. Moreover, often there was no sharp break between a primary reliance on mercenary forces and

the institution of a standing army, with mercenaries increasingly incorporated into state structures over time, a process that occurred earlier in Italy than in northern Europe. For more detailed discussion, see Andrew Alexandra, "Mercenaries," in *Encyclopedia of War*, ed. G. Martel (Hoboken, NJ: Wiley-Blackwell, 2011), available at http://onlinelibrary.wiley.com/doi/10.1002/9781444338232.wbeow397/pdf; Howard, *War in European History*, esp. chaps. 2 and 4; M. Mallett, *Mercenaries and Their Masters: Warfare in Renaissance Italy* (London: Bodley Head, 1974); G. Trease, *The Condottieri: Soldiers of Fortune* (London: Thames & Hudson, 1970); Todd S. Milliard, "Overcoming Post-Colonial Myopia: A Call to Recognize and Regulate Private Military Companies," *Military Law Review* 176 (June 2003): 1–95.

5 See Alexandra, "Mercenaries"; Howard, *War in European History*.

6 *Decree of 23 August 1793*, in John Hall Stewart, *A Documentary Survey of the French Revolution* (New York: Macmillan, 1951), 473.

7 Elliot Cohen, *Citizens and Soldiers* (Ithaca, NY: Cornell University Press, 1985).

8 The military of a number of other liberal democracies, such as the U.K. and Australia, were of similar composition.

9 See the discussions of nineteenth-century Prussia in U. Frevert, *A Nation in Barracks* (Oxford: Berg, 2004); and of Russia in J. A. Sanborn, *Drafting the Russian Nation: Military Conscription, Total War, and Mass Politics, 1905–1925* (DeKalb: Northern Illinois University Press, 2003).

10 Following Max Weber, a monopoly on the use of violence is commonly taken to be one of the defining marks of the modern state. This cannot mean, of course, that the state is the only agent that does, or even legitimately can, exercise violence. Many states, for example, allow (up to a point) the use of violence by parents against their children, and by the law-abiding against criminals. What it does mean is that the state claims (and largely must be able to enforce) the right to decide the terms under which non-state actors can use violence. So understood, there is no necessary incompatibility between the state's monopoly of violence and its employment of private

military forces. Similar points can be made about the claim that the exercise of military force is an "inherently governmental function." See, e.g., John R. Luckey, Valerie B. Grasso, and Kate M. Manuel, *Inherently Governmental Function and Department of Defense Operations: Background Issues, and Options for Congress* (Washington, DC: Congressional Research Service, 2009). Here, we should distinguish between functions that are *necessarily* governmental, in that they are partially constitutive of governing (such as legislating) and others that are *contingently* governmental. Arguably, functions such as deciding whether and how wars are to be fought are necessarily governmental. On the other hand, the actual fighting of such wars cannot be a necessarily governmental function, because, as a matter of fact, it is one that has often been undertaken by private forces. Of course, it may still be a contingently governmental function.

11 The term "civilian control" as it is used in discussions of the relationship between the military and society is ambiguous, since it can refer, on the one hand, to the effective subordination of the military by political leaders and, on the other, to genuine responsiveness to the wishes of the people. In the first sense, civilian control is compatible with lack of genuine political accountability to the populace in whose name the military is supposedly operating.

12 Gil Merom points to a number of cases (such as the Vietnam War, the Algerian War of Independence, and the Israeli invasion of Lebanon) in which democratic states were unable to prevail in wars they prosecuted with citizen armies (all of which included conscripts) despite having a persisting material and military advantage over their foes. This is, Merom argues, because of the loss of the domestic political support that made continuing deployment of troops impossible once public opinion decided that these wars were incurring costs disproportionate to their supposed benefits. Gil Merom, *How Democracies Lose Small Wars* (Cambridge, UK: Cambridge University Press, 2003).

13 Cheyney C. Ryan, *The Chickenhawk Syndrome: War, Sacrifice, and Personal Responsibility* (Lanham, MD: Rowman & Littlefield, 2009), 135.

14 J. Howorth, "The Transformation of European Military Capability, 1989–2005," in *Service to Country: Personnel Policy and the Transformation of Western Militaries*, ed. C. L. Gilroy and C. Williams (Cambridge, MA: MIT Press, 2006), 37.

15 David M. Halbfinger and Steven A. Holmes, "A Nation at War: The Troops; Military Mirrors a Working-Class America," *New York Times*, March 30, 2003; Pew Research Center, "War and Sacrifice in the Post-9/11 Era: The Military-Civilian Gap," October 2011, available at http://www.pew-socialtrends.org/2011/10/05/war-and-sacrifice-in-the-post-911-era/?src=prc-headline; Peter D. Feaver and Richard H. Kohn, *Soldiers and Civilians: The Civil-Military Gap and American National Security* (Cambridge, MA: MIT Press, 2001); Ryan, *Chickenhawk Syndrome*, esp. chap. 2.

16 Feaver and Kohn, *Soldiers and Civilians*, 286.

17 Pew Research Center, "War and Sacrifice in the Post-9/11 Era," chap. 5.

18. For evidence regarding the numbers granted waivers, see Lolita C. Baldor, "Army More Selective on Recruits, Re-enlistments," *Army Times*, May 22, 2012, available at http://www.armytimes.com/news/2012/05/ap-army-more-selective-recruits-reenlistments-052212/. For discussion of the initiatives taken to stimulate recruiting, see Ryan, *Chickenhawk Syndrome*, 44–46.

19 Ryan, *Chickenhawk Syndrome*, 44–46.

20 Pew Research Center, "War and Sacrifice in the Post-9/11 Era," chap. 2.

21 Peter W. Singer, "Corporate Warriors: The Rise and Ramifications of the Privatized Military Industry," *International Security* 26, no. 3 (2001/02): 186–220.

22 Peter W. Singer, *The Regulation of New Warfare* (Washington, DC: Brookings Institution, 2010), available at http://www.brookings.edu/opinions/2010/0227_defense_regulations_singer.aspx; Moshe Schwartz, *Security Contractors in Afghanistan: Background, Analysis, and Options for Congress* (Washington, DC: Congressional Research Service, 2011).

23 Office of the Deputy Assistant Secretary of Defense, "Contractor Support of U.S. Operations in the USCENTCOM Area of Responsibility," October 2011, available at http://www.acq.osd.mil/log/PS/CENTCOM_reports.html

24 See International Committee of the Red Cross, *International Humanitarian Law—Treaties and Documents* (Geneva: ICRC), available at http://www.icrc.org/ihl.nsf, esp. *Convention (IV) relative to the Protection of Civilian Persons in Time of War. Geneva, 12 August 1949*, available at http://www.icrc.org/ihl.nsf/FULL/380?OpenDocument

25. Unless they are in the special category of "civilians accompanying the armed forces."

26 Protocol Additional to the Geneva Conventions of August 12, 1949, and relating to the Protection of Victims of International Armed Conflicts (Protocol I), June 8, 1977. Art. 51.3 (available at http://www.icrc.org/ihl.nsf/7c4d08d9b287a42141256739003e636b/f6c8b9fee14a77fdc125641e0052b079). What counts as direct participation? The Third Geneva Convention explicitly excludes certain authorized "persons who accompany the armed forces without actually being members thereof, such as civilian members of military aircraft crews, war correspondents, [and] supply contractors" from being seen as directly participating in hostilities in virtue of their role. It also implies that other persons undertaking similar functions should also be excluded. The International Committee of the Red Cross has provided a cumulative set of criteria for direct participation: Nils Melzer, *Interpretive Guidance on the Notion of Direct Participation in Hostilities under International Humanitarian Law* (Geneva: ICRC, 2009). In this document it is asserted that "the great majority of private contractors … under the IHL generally come within the definition of civilian," though it also notes that personnel carrying out such functions as "denying the adversary the military use of certain objects, equipment and territory, guarding military personnel," could count as directly participating in hostilities, and of course these are just the kinds of functions that are now often undertaken by contractors (42). For a useful critical discussion of the inadequacies of the criteria that the *Interpretive Guidance* uses to attempt to define direct participation, see Michael N. Schmitt,

"Deconstructing Direct Participation in Hostilities: The Constitutive Elements," *NYU Journal of International Law and Politics* 42 (2010): 697.

27 See Michael N. Schmitt, "Humanitarian Law and Direct Participation in Hostilities by Private Contractors or Civilian Employees," *Chicago Journal of International Law* 5 (2005): 511–46, esp. 523–24.

28 Peter W. Singer, *Corporate Warriors: The Rise and Fall of the Privatized Military Industry* (Ithaca, NY: Cornell University Press, 2004), 88–100.

29 Elke Krahmann, "Controlling Private Military Companies in the UK and Germany: Between Partnership and Regulation" (2003), 6, available at http://www.mercenary-wars.net/private-military-companies/index.html

30 Protocol I, Art. 43.3.

31 See, e.g., Joint Chiefs of Staff *Doctrine for the Logistic Support of Joint Operations* 2000, 13.b, available at www.bits.de/NRANEU/others/jp-doctrine/jp4_0(00).pdf

32 John Whiteclay Chambers II, "Combat Support," in *The Oxford Companion to American Military History* (New York: Oxford University Press, 2000), available at http://www.highbeam.com/doc/1O126-CombatSupport.html

33 With a few insignificant exceptions, such as chaplains.

34 Joint Chiefs of Staff, *4-0 Doctrine for Logistics Support of Joint Operations,* V-1(d) (2000), 64–65, emphasis added, available at http://www.aschq.army.mil/gc/files/JP4-0.pdf

35 Jeremy Scahill, *Blackwater: The Rise of the World's Most Powerful Mercenary Army* (New York: Nation, 2007), 109.

36 Ibid., 125.

37 Dana Priest, "Private Guards Repel Attack on U.S. Headquarters," *Washington Post*, April 6, 2004.

38 See the estimates and discussion at http://www.unknownnews.net/casualties.html

39 Joe Burgess et al., "An Account of the Shootings at Nisour Square," *The New York Times,* September 21, 2007, available at http://www.nytimes.com/interactive/2007/09/21/world/middleeast/0921-blackwater-nisour-square.html; David Johnston and John M. Broder, "FBI Says Guards Killed 14 Iraqis Without Cause," *The New York Times*, November 14, 2007, available at http://www.nytimes.com/2007/11/14/world/middleeast/14blackwater.html?ex=1352696400&en=4d3e7a7a4fbc5721&ei=5088&partner=rssnyt&emc=rss

40 Scott Horton, "Getting Closer to the Truth About the Blackwater Incident," *Harpers*, November, 2007, available at http://harpers.org/archive/2007/11/hbc-90001669

41 Quoted in Scahill, *Blackwater*, 73.

42 Ibid., 74.

43 "Interview: Marine Col. Thomas X. Hammes (Ret.)," *Frontline*, June 21, 2005, available at http://www.pbs.org/wgbh/pages/frontline/shows/warriors/interviews/hammes.html

44 Ibid.

45 But see the concerns about the possible lack of validity and effectiveness of that amendment in David L. Snyder, "Civilian Military Contractors on Trial: The Case for Upholding the Amended Exceptional Jurisdiction Clause of the Uniform Code of Military Justice," *Texas International Law Review* 44, no. 1 (2008): 65–97, esp. 68.

46 Army Regulation 530-1, *"Operations Security"* (Washington, DC: Department of Army, 2007), para. 2.1.

47 Notably, the 2009 *Montreux Document on Pertinent International Legal Obligations and Good Practices for States Related to Operations of Private Military and Security Companies During Armed Conflict*, available at http://www.eda.admin.ch/etc/medialib/downloads/edazen/topics/intla/humlaw.Par.0078.File.tmp/Montreux%20Broschuere.pdf; and the 2010 *International Code of Conduct for Private Security Service Providers*, available at http://www.news.admin.ch/NSBSubscriber/message/attachments/21143.pdf

Unaccountable: The Current State of Private Military and Security Companies

MARCUS HEDAHL*

The current accountability system for private military and security contractors (PMSCs) is woefully inadequate, and mere enhancements in oversight cannot hope to remedy that failing. I contend that once we recognize the kind of accountability required of PMSCs, we will realize that radical changes in the foundational relationship between PMSCs and the state are required. More specifically, in order to be appropriately accountable, members of PMSCs must become a part of or, at the very least, directly responsible to the legitimate authoritative military or police structures, and there must be a clear and precise delineation of responsibility among public officials for holding individual members of PMSCs criminally liable.

Unaccountable (adj.): not to be held liable, not to be called to answer for a failing.
Unaccountable (adj.): extraordinary or baffling, not explainable.

This essay advances a simple thesis: the current accountability system for private military and security contractors (PMSCs) is woefully inadequate; radical revisions in oversight, regula-

Marcus Hedahl was a major in the U.S. Air Force. He served as an assistant professor of philosophy and ethics at the U.S. Air Force Academy and as a program manager for the National Reconnaissance Office. He is completing his PhD in philosophy from Georgetown University.

tion, and integration are required. This thesis, however, may seem an insufficient response to the very real and significant ethical dangers created by the mere existence of PMSCs. As someone who once claimed that the presence of PMSCs turns soldier and employee alike into a potential mercenary, while making the military's uniforms, medals, and codes of honor into "anachronistic window dressing," I am, perhaps, an unlikely candidate to be considering regulation and accountability rather than elimination.[1] I might seem to be the type of person who those within the private security profession would label part of the "ill informed . . . 'fire them all' crowd."[2]

There is, in fact, a deep tension between the possibility of increasing and improving the oversight of PMSCs and the possibility of eliminating them. This tension is evident in public debates between those who focus on the historical, theoretical, and pragmatic reasons that PMSCs are acceptable, if appropriately regulated, and those who focus on the long-term ethical issues inherent in their very existence. Yet once the questions of accountability are satisfactorily answered, very little remains to separate those who argue in favor of elimination and those who advocate enhanced oversight. Once properly regulated, PMSCs could cease to exist. The end of PMSCs, however, would not occur because they are driven out of business, or because the current employees of PMSCs would find themselves out of work or suddenly drafted as members of the Armed Forces. The end of PMSCs would occur because the changes required to attain sufficient accountability are so severe as to warrant the end of PMSCs as we know them today.

Consider, for example, a proposal from one of the staunchest supporters of PMSCs. Shawn Engbrecht considers the possibility that the best way to improve PMSC account-ability is by transforming U.S. PMSCs into an in-house security force for the U.S. State Department's Bureau of Diplomatic Security.[3] Whatever one thinks of this proposal, one thing is clear: it would no longer be appropriate to consider this force a *private* military and security contractor.

Against that backdrop, this essay considers the question of appropriate PMSC accountability. In the first section, I argue that once we recognize the type of accountability required for PMSCs, we will realize that mere enhancements in oversight can never be sufficient—*radical changes will be required*. In the second half of the paper, I argue for three such changes. First, there must be a clear and precise delineation of responsibility for holding individual members of PMSCs criminally liable. Second, members of PMSCs must become a part of or, at the very least, responsible to the legitimate authoritative military or police structures. Third, there have to be radical changes in the government's acquisition oversight structure focusing on personnel contracts in general and PMSC contracts in particular. These three changes may not on their own entail that an accountable PMSC would no longer be a *private* military and security contractor, but even these changes will require members of PMSCs to become more like public employees—and these changes clearly are not the only ones required.

The Problem of Divergent Interests

Some have argued that PMSCs *are* accountable through their contracts. Tim Spicer, head of Aegis, a PMSC based in London, responds to the claim that PMSCs are not accountable by asking a series of rhetorical questions: "Not accountable to whom? World opinion? Outside politicians? I can only speak for [my own company] but we were always accountable, to our own policies and ethos, and to our client government with whom we always have a binding contract."[4] The claim is that such men and women are, in fact, accountable, just through their contract rather than through an oath. PMSC accountability is *contractual accountability*, and contractual accountability is sufficient.

One common reply to this objection is to focus on what I will refer to as *the problem of divergent interests*. Allison Stanger, for example, responds to Spicer's argument by conceding that "Spicer does have a point: in most conflict situations, [loyalties to the mission] will carry the day."[5] She merely worries that this will not always be the case, contending that, "in a multi-polar environment, things may be different."[6] The point is clear. Members of PMSCs will conduct themselves well if they view themselves *as* military professionals, responsible to the same codes of conduct as their military brethren. The problem is that a company's interests can diverge from the interests of the public.[7]

P. W. Singer locates the issue of effectiveness in the problem of divergent interests. "Those ... doing escort duty are going to be judged by their bosses solely on whether they get their client from point A to B, not whether they win Iraqi hearts and minds along the way."[8] He quotes Ann Exline Starr, a former Coalition Provisional Authority adviser. According to Singer, Starr reports that the members of DynCorp told her: "Our mission is to protect the princi-

pal at all costs. If that means pissing off the Iraqis, too bad."[9] If Singer is correct, then, although the problem of PMSC effectiveness and proportionality can be alleviated by better communications, it cannot be eliminated. According to Singer, the profit motive of a PMSC is inherently at odds with good military effectiveness.

The problem of divergent interests can also lead to fraud, waste, and abuse. According to the Commission on Wartime Contracting in Iraq and Afghanistan, somewhere between one in six and one in three dollars spent on contracting in Iraq and Afghanistan has been lost to waste and fraud.[10] The numbers may be less surprising when coupled with information regarding the extreme lack of oversight of PMSCs. In fact, the owner and employees of an American playhouse face more legal inspection and accountability than those of a private military firm.[11] During the Coalitional Provisional Authority, for example, the U.S. shipped, on average, a ton of U.S. currency per day to Iraq.[12] I should make it clear that this does not mean the U.S. shipped *a lot* of U.S. currency to Iraq, nor does it mean that the U.S. shipped the *equivalent* of a ton of U.S. currency per day to Iraq. It means the U.S. shipped 2000 pounds of U.S. currency ... on pallet upon pallet ... in C-130s ... every day ... for a year. In fact, the U.S. frequently made multi-million-dollar cash payments to PMSCs during 2003 and 2004.[13] It is not surprising that this situation, which made oversight of fiscal spending virtually impossible, fostered a culture of fraud, waste, and abuse.

One part of the problem is that the U.S. acquisition force is simply too meager to provide the proper oversight.[14] While the number of contracts has ballooned exponentially in the last 20 years, the total number of acquisition professionals in the U.S. government has decreased by 40% or more.[15] Another part of the problem is that the U.S. acquisition process, particularly the Defense Department process, centers on the acquisition of hardware and software: tanks, satellites, intelligence software, planes, and so forth. When the U.S. acquisition system works, it works because of the regimented controls of such acquisitions: requirements reviews, design reviews, detailed cost-schedule reports, and so forth. Systems contracting has milestones, defined decision points, and a well-established and clearly defined management structure with program offices. No such structure exists for services and personnel contracting.[16] Yet today, more than half of the Defense Department's contract spending is for service and personnel.[17] In Iraq and Afghanistan, 66% of contract spending is for people and services.[18] However, the U.S. government's processes remain focused on the systems acquisition process.[19]

The problem of divergent interests is significant, and I do not mean to belittle efforts to try to better align the interests of companies with the public interests. In fact, *merely* implementing the changes outlined by the Commission on Wartime Contracting would constitute changes of unparalleled scope. However, smart acquisition folks in any field will recognize the problem of divergent interests as a fact of any contractual arrangement. If the problem of divergent interests were the only problem, then we ought to seek to align these divergent interests through smarter contracts (for example, a better award fee structure), more traditional oversight (for example, a larger acquisition force), and perhaps the creation of a few new regulations.

The problem of divergent interests is, in one sense, a reply to the claim of those in the industry that PMSCs and their members are appropriately accountable. Given the inappropriate contracts and the lack of sufficient oversight, PMSCs are not appropriately accountable. However, just as significantly, the problem of divergent interests does not undermine the central claim of the original argument: if current contractual accountability is insufficient, then the problem is with the current contractual arrangement. Contractual accountability *could* be sufficient, even if it is not currently so. Thus, the common refrain from the PMSC industry: "If you don't like something, all you need to do is change the contracts."

The Accountability Problem: More than Divergent Interests

Focusing solely on the problem of divergent interests makes the same mistake as Spicer's original argument: both mistakenly conflate the issue of accountability with related ethical concerns, such as, "What's in the interests of PMSCs?" or "Will PMSCs do the right thing?" By doing so, both approaches miss the central and significant point: contractual accountability can *never* provide the appropriate kind of accountability.

Let me be clear. I have no doubt that many members of PMSCs view themselves as soldiers do—as agents sacrificing for a common good. Many are willing to do the right thing for their mission and their nation, even in the face of great personal cost and risk. Most members are, in fact, highly talented former soldiers, sailors, marines, or airmen. Additionally, my point is not a question of profits, motives, or the problem of divergent interests. In fact, focusing solely on the problem of divergent interests overlooks a significant fact: most members of PMSCs are motivated by more than profit alone.

Accountability, however, is not synonymous with doing the right thing; accountability is a *response* to right and wrong actions. However noble some members of PMSCs may be, some will fail to do as they ought—just as some soldiers will fail, and just as some government officials will fail. Accountability is required in those cases in which agents fails to do as they ought, not in those in which they succeeds. The question of PMSC accountability is not about whether they can or even how often they do what morality requires; it is a question about what happens when they do not take the moral high ground. It is not merely a contingent fact that contractual accountability does not currently provide the right kind of accountability. By itself, it can *never* capture the proper type of accountability. Let me explain.

First, contractual accountability is insufficient because it makes the members of PMSCs accountable to the wrong people. Accountability is inherently an interpersonal relationship; one is not merely accountable, one is accountable *to another*. Consider again Springer's original argument: PMSCs, in his words, "were always accountable, to our own policies and ethos, and to our client government with whom we always have a binding contract."[20] The first thing to note is that there is an important ambiguity here in the use of the term "we." Contract employees are accountable to their company. The company, in turn, is accountable to the client government. However, this does not imply that the employees themselves are accountable to the client government. Accountability is a relational property.[21] If B is accountable to A to φ, and C is accountable to B to ψ, it is not the case that C is necessarily accountable to A, even if C's ψing is required for B's φing. The friends of my friends are not necessarily friends of mine. Accountability is similarly a non-transitive relationship. For example, if I loan Becky $50, Becky is accountable to me to repay that debt. If Becky then loans $35 to Sally, Sally is not accountable to me; Sally is accountable to Becky. I cannot demand as my due that Sally repay the debt to Becky, even if that debt is required for Becky to repay me.

This need not necessarily be a drawback for contractual accountability. In fact, at times it can be beneficial to contractual arrangements for goods and services. If my toaster breaks down while under warranty, I want to be able to hold the company accountable to repair or replace it. I do not want to figure out which part needs repair, nor am I particularly interested in holding the vendor accountable. In such cases, I want *one-shop accountability*.

The same is true for more complex contractual arrangements. I do not care who cleans my suit, so long as it gets clean. I want to hold the company accountable for cleaning my suit, regardless of who actually cleans it, and regardless of whom the company fires or promotes based on that person's ability or lack thereof to clean my suit. I do not require the employees, in such cases, to be accountable to me; I require the company to be accountable to me. So long as the company meets that criterion, I do not care about the arrangement between the company and its employees.

Of course, we could change the case and require Sally to be directly accountable to me. Such further accountability, however, is not by itself a *necessary* feature of any given contractual arrangement. Members of PMSCs are accountable to their company through their contract with the company. This fact does not entail that they are accountable to anyone else, including the country with which their company has a contract.

In the case of PMSCs, some further accountability is clearly required. One-shop accountability is insufficient for members of PMSCs operating in war zones and in contingency operations. At the contract level, we would most likely consider only one crime committed by only one member of a PMSC a success; or, more appropriately, it would demonstrate that the PMSC is not likely to be responsible for a systemic failing or for its failure to ensure good order and discipline. Nonetheless, we would want to hold violators *individually* and *criminally* accountable for their actions. Furthermore, we require members of PMSCs to be *personally* accountable for their ac-

tions and *personally* accountable to those responsible for broader security and policing concerns within a given nation. Employees of PMSCs must be accountable to more than their employers, and they must be accountable as more than mere employees. Contractual accountability is insufficient, first and foremost, because it makes the members of PMSCs accountable to the wrong people. If we believe that members of PMSCs *ought* to be so accountable to others, something must be added above and beyond the contract between the contracting nation and the company.

Consider another analogy. If I build you a house, I am accountable to you; however, I also must adhere to building codes that govern the minimum standards that such structures must meet. These standards do much more than lay out the minimum requirements to which you and I must agree. They make me, the builder, accountable to whomever is harmed by my failure to meet that code. If the building codes were removed, and you and I agree that I will build you a house conforming to the codes as they previously existed, the content of my duties is unchanged. I have a duty to build a house that meets those specifications. However, considerations of accountability have changed dramatically: I am accountable to you, and you alone. That contract is a private matter between consenting private individuals. Although I may be accountable to anyone, due to the consequences of *negligence*, I am not accountable to others merely for *my failure to meet the code*, even if my failure to do so causes them harm.[22]

Here, the question of contractual accountability reaches its limits; some further mechanism is required.

Individual agents could set up contracts granting further accountability to specific, named individuals. An agent could buy a house for her mother, and could specify that the builder be accountable to *her directly* in addition to being accountable to the purchasing agent. One also could set up contractual mechanisms to ensure the transfer of such accountability to specific individuals in specific roles. In this case, one could stipulate that the builder is accountable to any new owner, a move that could facilitate the eventual sale of the house.

One cannot, however, set up a contract granting accountability to whomever might be harmed by the builder's failures, because the contracting parties simply lack the constitutive authority to grant the universal authority to hold others accountable for their failures. This fact is true even when one of the contracting parties is the government itself, because the body doing the contracting (the executive) lacks the necessary legislative authority to require such universal accountability.

The lesson is clear: regardless of the strict nature of PMSC contracts, they merely make the contracting company accountable to the contracting nation. Barring some measure, such as the U.K. requirement to enlist members of PMSCs into the Reserves, members are not directly accountable *to* their contracting nations. Furthermore, regardless of the stringent nature of these contracts, PMSCs and their members could never be accountable to the people in the countries in which they are operating. Contractual accountability is insufficient because it makes PMSCs and their members accountable to the wrong people.[23]

Second, contractual accountability cannot provide the appropriate kind of accountability because it is the wrong *kind* of accountability. Legally, one is not obligated to fulfill a contract; rather, one is legally bound to fulfill *or* compensate for a breach. Contracting parties are permitted—some even argue obligated—to breach contractual arrangements whenever performance becomes too expensive or a better opportunity comes along, so long as they compensate the other party for the failure to fulfill the contract.[24] The theory of efficient breach, prevalent in contractual accountability, is clearly insufficient for members of PMSCs operating in combat zones or other contingency operations.

Consider the mathematics of PMSC profits in 2004. Contractors could bill $1200 per person, per day, for security work in Iraq. Even if employers could replace workers almost immediately (within weeks), firing a reckless and unskilled team of 12 would cost $175,000, not including travel costs. Contrast that with the U.S. policy to compensate victims of "accidental shootings" or, more appropriately, victims of *reported* "accidental shootings"—$1000—and there is a huge financial incentive to keep substandard, trigger-happy employees where they are.[25] However, we cannot believe it to be acceptable either to follow the dictates of the principles of noncombatant immunity and proportionality *or* to compensate the families of victims. Contractual accountability simply provides the wrong kind of accountability.

Finally, an important relationship also exists between *being held accountable* and *being accountable*. One must be held accountable on more than token occasions in order to be truly accountable. Some will argue that holding others accountable for their failures and being held accountable by others for one's own failure is an essential part of the moral stance inherent in the notion of accountability.[26] Others will focus on the consequences of not holding others accountable. In such cases, more violations are likely to occur.[27] Whatever the theoretical justification, to *be accountable*, one must *be held* accountable on more than token occasions.

By any plausible standard, we can conclude that PMSCs and their members are not being held adequately accountable. This claim holds true for all contractors, including PMSCs, serving in places such as Iraq and Afghanistan. In order to support that claim, it will be helpful to consider two different comparison classes: the first, a group of people with similar incomes; the second, a group of people with similar occupations who find themselves in similar situations.[28] The average income for contractors is equivalent to the average income for those living in the affluent Connecticut suburbs, so I will follow Peter Singer's lead in comparing the crime rates for contractors in Iraq to the crime rates for Westport, Connecticut. Some have questioned the utility of such a comparison, noting the radically different work environments for members of PMSC's and the typical citizen of Westport, so I will augment the first

comparison with one that compares the crime rates for members of PMSC's and the crime rates for members of the U.S. Army.

Let us begin by considering the crime rates for Westport, Connecticut. As Singer notes, if the crime statistics for contractors were consistent with Westport, we would expect reports of 121 assaults a year, 406 burglaries a year, and 1958 thefts a year just for contractors operating in Iraq.[29] Even more telling is the second comparison class. If the prosecution statistics were consistent with those of U.S. Army personnel, we would expect to see 663 courts martial a year in Iraq alone.[30] Yet the actual number of reported crimes by and prosecution of contractors each year across the world falls short of these predictions by orders of magnitude.[31] The token prosecutions over nearly a decade are the exception that proves the rule: contractors, including PMSCs, are not held accountable for their failings. Either we have stumbled upon Kant's angels, with no need for the moral law, through the miraculous workings of the private market, or we have to admit that contractors, including PMSCs, operating in contingency operations are not being held accountable when they fail.[32] Given the history, the former option, already theoretically impossible, somehow seems even more implausible.[33]

A New Accountability for PMSCs

So what changes are required to make PMSCs accountable? In this section, I argue in favor of three

modifications. First, there must be a clear and precise delineation of responsibility for criminality among individual PMSCs. Second, PMSCs at a collective level, and members at an individual level, must be accountable to the legitimate authoritative directives of the local security, whether in the form of local police or a military command structure. Third, there have to be radical changes in the government's acquisition oversight structure, focusing on personnel contracts in general and PMSC contracts in particular.

Let me begin with the issues of responsibility and criminality. Members of PMSCs must be individually accountable for their failures to protect non-combatants from unnecessary suffering. In straightforward terms, to hold members of PMSCs appropriately accountable, someone must have the authority to do so. Recently, the U.S. government has sought to enact some important legal measures in an effort to close the personal accountability gap. In 2000, Congress enacted the Military Extraterritorial Jurisdiction Act (MEJA), which authorized domestic prosecution of Department of Defense contractors under U.S. criminal law for felonious acts committed abroad.[34] Even more significantly, in late 2006 Senator Lindsay Graham inserted a clause into the 2007 Defense Authorization Act that changed the requirement of when contractors could be subject to the Uniform Code of Military Justice (UCMJ). Since 2007, UCMJ has been applicable to persons serving with or accompanying U.S. Armed Forces in the field during a declared war or "a declared contingency operation."[35] Many called for this change long before it was enacted, and many more, including this author, hailed it as an improvement in PMSC accountability.

These changes have led to some important prosecutions (for example, *U.S. v. Christopher Drotleff, et al.*, and *U.S. v. Jorge Thornton*)[36] as well as other legal proceedings that are perhaps more questionable (ironically, the first use of UCMJ authority was against one of the few contractors of Iraqi citizenship after the Iraqi government had decided against prosecution).[37] Yet, the number of reported crimes and prosecutions of contractors remains near zero. Why are they still not held accountable?

Although many critics have considered the problems of MEJA,[38] the limitations of the UCMJ are more nuanced and interesting. Military commanders have been given the authority to investigate, apprehend, arrest, and temporarily detain a contractor when there is probable cause that the employee in question has committed a covered offense. However, military commanders received no additional resources with which to pursue these actions—a particularly striking feature, since the change was made through the yearly defense authorization bill. Imagine if we doubled the size of the Armed Forces but did not change the size of the security police, investigators, or prosecutors. The problems, though, go far beyond the number of people charged with holding members of PMSCs accountable.

We have created, unintentionally, a collective action problem. Although many have the authority to hold members of PMSCs accountable, no one is responsible for doing so. Consider the fundamental difference between the civil and military justice systems. Soldiers are accountable to, and held accountable by, their commanding officer (CO)—that is a central point of the UCMJ. Soldiers are accountable to their commander to conduct themselves honorably, whether they get lost and wanders into the territory of another commander, and whether they are in England, Iraq, or the State of Nature. A CO, in turn, is responsible for holding soldiers accountable. A CO is not responsible when soldiers fail to do as they ought, but the CO is responsible for good order and discipline—the latter of which will require holding soldiers accountable when they fail to do as they ought.

Therefore, for members of PMSCs to be held individually and criminally accountable, there must be a clear and precise delineation of responsibility for PMSC individual criminal liability. In the case of UCMJ, commanders need to receive the delineated responsibility for holding PMSC employees accountable. The most important and significant changes will be in situations in which local security, law, and order has yet to be established or is maintained by a military organization. In such cases, specific contractors need to be assigned to specific local commanders in order to operate.

Those commanders, in turn, must take on the responsibility of ensuring order and discipline among the PMSC members for whom they are responsible, and they must have sufficient investigative, policing, and judicial assets to fulfill that responsibility. If no one is responsible for holding members of PMSCs accountable when they go astray, no one will do so—except, perhaps, in the most disturbingly egregious cases. Unfortunately, this lack of clearly delineated oversight will make violations more likely and

may create a self-sustaining cycle of dysfunctional accountability.

The second reform that I advocate requires that PMSCs themselves must be collectively accountable for their failures to protect non-combatants from unnecessary suffering. The UCMJ is built on the foundational assumption that those subject to it are members of a unified command structure. The order of a superior commissioned officer, or the instructions of a superior non-commissioned officer, has the force of law. This feature is important for enforcing order and discipline, but it also has important ethical dimensions: it helps to prevent wars from becoming more violent and destructive than they otherwise need to be.

Consider the problem of effectiveness, an issue that plays directly into the concern of preventing wars from becoming unnecessarily violent and destructive. I must admit that I found the sentiment that many consider so worrisome in the PMSC force—for example, "Our mission is to protect the principal at all costs. If that means pissing off the Iraqis, too bad."—rather prevalent among active duty personnel during my time in the service. *Our* mission is what mattered, and we understood *our* mission in a very local, unit-level way. Sentiment ran along the lines of, "*We*, in this unit, get the mission done regardless of what those Jagholes in [insert some other "competing" unit] think of it." In fact, the Marines rather famously are loyal first to their unit then to the Corps; loyalty to country comes fourth.

This attitude appears to be permissible, perhaps even desirable, when expressed by uniformed personnel; yet the sentiment is deeply troubling, perhaps even immoral, when expressed by members of PMSCs. The difference lies in the way in which their respective missions are modified. If the way in which one Armed Forces unit fulfills its small piece of the larger mission impedes some other unit's ability to carry out its mission, or the larger collective mission, then, in a well-functioning military, the small mission—or at the very least the Rules of Engagement (ROEs) and standing orders—will change. For military members, those changes have the full force of law. A military commander, well-functioning or not, at least has the authority to make such changes for the subordinate units under her command. Contrast that situation with the one for PMSCs. It would be bad enough if a local military commander had to coordinate with the Under-Secretary of Defense for Acquisition, or the equivalent in the Department of State. Since these are contracts, however, unless such changes are authorized beforehand, they must not merely be coordinated—they must be negotiated.

Now, some may argue that PMSCs need not respond to changes in the local ROEs and standing orders. In this volume, for example, Doug Brooks and Hanna Streng correctly note that PMSCs follow Rules on the Use of Force (RUFs) rather than ROEs and standing orders. The RUFs in Iraq are typical of those elsewhere: members of PMSCs can use force only (a) in self-defense, (b) in the defense of persons specified in the contract, (c) in defense of civilians against life threatening circumstances, or (d) in defense of Coalition-approved property specified in the contract. Furthermore, Brooks and Streng point out that unlike RUFs, ROEs can provide 'the legal

basis for the military to proactively engage with lethal force when it is deemed appropriate to achieve [the] mission.'[39] This is all true. The problem is that when one juxtaposes ROEs and RUFs in this manner, it implies that there is no need to bring contractors under ROEs—after all, PMSCs are already under RUFs, and the military's ROEs can be more lenient than RUFs. Why argue that PMSCs have to be responsive to ROEs, when they are already bound by "more stringent" RUFs?

The reason is easy to miss when comparing the entire class of ROEs with the entire class of RUFs: ROEs can be, and in fact often are, *more stringent* than RUFs. ROEs often *prohibit* the use of force *even when* there is a threat to oneself or one's fellows. In fact, one sees this phenomenon most often in policing actions and contingency operations precisely because the continual use of force in similar situations will have unnecessarily detrimental impacts on the overall level of destruction *and* on mission effectiveness—even if use of force could be morally justified in each instance.

Consider an epistemic issue: when defending a checkpoint, there are times at which one would be reasonably justified in believing one's life is in danger; but the ROEs and standing orders still *prohibit* the use of force. Such limitations work to ensure a higher level of certainty that force is, in fact, required.

Consider, as well, limitations even without any epistemic issue: sometimes a changing operational environment will require limitations, even when soldiers are *certain* they are under attack. In 2010, a common standing order for military members in Iraq dictated that soldiers bypass or evade attackers rather than suppressing them, because military leaders considered unnecessary suppression detrimental to the larger, long-term military mission.[40] The common reputation of PMSCs as "shoot-em ups" and "cowboys" is not always because they violate the RUFs—more often it is because they are legitimated in using force in situations in which their military brethren would not be.

U.S. Army Colonel Peter Mansoor puts the point simply: if PMSCs "push traffic off the roads or if they shoot up a car that looks suspicious, whatever it may be, they may be operating within their contract"— and, we could add, *within the RUFs* —"to the detriment of the mission."[41] Therefore, in order to be appropriately and collectively accountable for their failures to protect non-combatants from unnecessary suffering, PMSCs must be responsive to authoritative directives from the appropriate military hierarchy. In fact, army doctrine requires this type of embedded integration of missions. Without this integration, military leaders deem victory extremely unlikely, perhaps impossible. One solution, favored by Mansoor, would be to place all PMSCs under a unified military chain of command. However, to respond to this particular requirement, PMSCs and their members need merely to be *responsive* to authoritative directives from those responsible for broader issues of local security.

These two changes in the integrated role that PMSCs must play in order to be appropriately accountable require a third modification, this one in how the government oversees such contracts. Even if the U.S. government had a well-functioning,

widely used system for managing service contracts, that system would not serve as a satisfactory oversight mechanism for PMSC contracts. As we have seen, these are mission and personnel contracts—not service contracts. We do not care merely that the job is done, we care *who* the people doing the jobs are, and *how* they do that job. Simply being honest about this difference allows us to see an important fact: although large contracts with numerous, complicated subcontractor relationships are necessary, even beneficial, for holding a company accountable for developing a satellite or for providing a service, such contracts are extremely detrimental to the development of contractual accountability for personnel contracts.

In order to develop a framework that allows for the proper oversight of such personnel and service contracts, strict regulations and guidelines regarding the qualifications of potential employees will have to be developed. The United Kingdom recently implemented the Security Industry Authority (SIA) in order to establish a minimum set of qualifications PMSC's employees must possess. The U.S. need not adopt the exact same standards, but a set of similar guidelines would likely include the following: restrictions on recruiting, perhaps including a requirement for criminal and psychological background checks, as well as a requirement of proof of citizenship; initial training requirements, perhaps including basic training and Specific Task Augmentation Readiness Training (START); and recertification requirements, perhaps including drug testing, physical fitness tests, weapons qualifications, and UCMJ training.[42] Furthermore, the oversight would need to take into account the types of missions PMSCs perform. In the current system, PMSCs are "loath to report shootings."[43] Therefore, audits must include both financial records *and* incident reports. These audits could be enhanced by requiring video monitoring systems for PMSCs on patrol, similar to those used by domestic police forces.[44] Such audits of the security activities must be tied to real and significant financial incentives. In short, proper accountability requires PMSCs to be subject to public inspections that would be unnecessarily intrusive in service or development contracts.

Conclusion

PMSCs are currently unaccountable in almost every way imaginable. The current lack of accountability can be summed up by considering a new interpretation of Paul Bremer's famous CPA Order #17, which dictated that contractors in Iraq could not be subject to prosecution. The directive has been defended by some[45] and vilified by many others.[46] However, to my knowledge, no one has yet considered the most worrisome possibility about CPA Order #17: it may have been superfluous. If there is no policing force and no investigative force with both the authority and responsibility for holding a group of agents accountable for their misdeeds, prosecutions will be few and far between. PMSCs, it turns out, need no immunity; they have been unaccountable for quite some time. Without any modifications to our current system, they will continue to be so for the foreseeable future.

Bloody Sunday occurred after Order #17 had expired. This incident is perhaps the most indelible image of the lack of contractor accountability. A traffic stop in Nisoor Square in 2007 ended in a hail of Blackwater gunfire and Iraqi outrage. Witnesses recounted how men, women, and children were shot and killed while attempting to flee. The melee finally ended, leaving 17 Iraqis dead and over 20 wounded. Yet the Blackwater personnel involved returned to the United States, and government officials do not intend to extradite them for trial in Iraq.[47] The Iraqi government did take action against the company itself. In response to the outrage of its citizens, the Iraqi government banned Blackwater outright and kicked them out of the country. Blackwater, however, was back to stay a mere four days later.[48] The United States simply cannot conduct contingency operations without them. One Iraqi put the matter succinctly: "The Iraqis despise [PMSCs] because they are untouchable.... They [are] above the law."[49]

To achieve proper accountability, at least three major types of changes will be required beyond mitigating the problem of divergent interests. First, there must be a clear and precise delineation of responsibility for the criminality of individual members of PMSCs. Second, PMSCs at a collective level, and members at an individual level, must be accountable to the legitimate authoritative directives of the local security, whether in the form of local police or a military command structure.

Third, there have to be radical changes in the government's acquisition oversight structure that focuses on personnel contracts in general and PMSC contracts in particular.

There are, however, several significant ethical issues not yet considered. The mere existence of PMSCs has the potential to alter radically *jus ad bellum* considerations. Given the right financial incentives, the days of PMSCs fighting each other may not be far off. Similar concerns can be found when considering the PMSC army currently being raised by the United Arab Emirates.[50] Although the United Arab Emirates probably has the right to raise an army, private or public, to defend itself,[51] the use of PMSC personnel for *internal* security brings with it concerns of oppression.[52]

There is also the problem of what accountability mechanism, if any, we as a nation have put in place to respond to the needs of PMSC personnel. The Army's services for PTSD, lost limbs, and ongoing medical treatment are often insufficient for Armed Services personnel and veterans, but such services are generally non-existent for members of PMSCs who served in Iraq or Afghanistan.[53] Although members of PMSCs are paid more and they are not explicitly acting directly on behalf of us as a nation, it is not clear to me that this absolves us of all responsibility to them when they are injured in places such as Afghanistan and Iraq.[54] In other words, my fears about the ethical hazards of reducing the relationship between nation and soldier to nothing more than a financial transaction between employer and employee are relevant to the parties on both sides of the bargaining table. Not only may members of

PMSCs fail to be accountable to us, we may fail to be accountable to them.

Perhaps the easiest solution to all the concerns raised in this paper is one similar to the proposal made in the introduction: slowly integrate current PMSCs into the public rather than private sector.[55] This need not be integration into the military itself, nor must such entities be made fully public. The Aerospace Corporation, RAND, and other not-for-profit, independent, federally funded research and development centers (FFRDCs) could serve as a model for the development of quasi-public, yet market-driven, security capabilities. This is, I believe, a possibility that has yet to be advanced in the discussion of PMSCs.

First established during World War II, FFRDCs—originally called Federal Contract Research Centers (FCRCs)—are semi-academic laboratories and research groups created by the federal government.[56] FFRDCs are unique, independent, nonprofit entities sponsored by the U.S. government to meet specific long-term needs.[57] Obviously, the focus of PMSCs is not research, and the rich history between FFRDCs and academic universities is of little use to PMSCs. Nonetheless, the framework of semi-public entities that compete with each other without a direct profit motive is, I believe, worth considering. What is important to keep in mind is that, although FFRDCs do not compete for federal contracts against non-FFRDCs, they *may* compete with other FFRDCs. In this system, since there is no profit motive or conflict of interest with the public good, an FFRDC can therefore function as an independent, trusted advisor and honest broker.[58] Yet, because there is some level of competition between these semi-public entities, such a framework can harness some of the financial benefits of a market-driven competitive system without sacrificing the concerns of accountability.

Even if PMSCs are not integrated into a public or even a quasi-public role, radical changes in accountability are required. Those radical changes will require members of PMSCs to become more like public employees—at a very minimum, they must be integrated into the public authoritative hierarchy and be personally accountable to that public authoritative structure. Furthermore, PMSCs must be subject to public inspections that would be considered intrusive in private sector exchanges. In offering these recommendations, I have proven the truth of an idea asserted at the outset: the difference between those who want to eliminate PMSCs and those who want to develop a system of PMSC accountability is much less significant than one might initially suspect.

Notes

1 Marcus Hedahl, "Blood and Blackwaters: A Call to Arms for the Profession of Arms," *Journal of Military Ethics* 8, no. 1 (2009): 33.

2 Shawn Engbrecht, *America's Covert Warriors: Inside the World of Private Military Contractors* (Washington, DC: Potomac Books, 2011), 197.

3 Ibid., 215–18.

4 Quoted in Allison Stanger, *One Nation Under Contract: The Outsourcing of American Power and the Future of Foreign Policy* (New Haven: Yale University Press, 1999), 28.

5 Ibid., 90.

6 Ibid.

7 P. W. Singer, *Corporate Warriors: The Rise of the Privatized Military Industry*, updated ed. (Ithaca: Cornell University Press, 2008), 151–52.

8 P. W. Singer, "Can't Win with 'Em, Can't Go to War without 'Em: Private Military Contractors and Counterinsurgency," *Brookings Institute*, Foreign Policy Paper Ser. #4 (September 2007), 6.

9 Ibid. Originally from Steve Fainaru, "Where Military Rules Don't Apply," *Washington Post*, September 20, 2007.

10 Commission on Wartime Contracting in Iraq and Afghanistan, Final Report to Congress, *Transforming Wartime Contracting: Controlling Costs, Reducing Risks* (August 31, 2011), 5.

11 Singer, "Can't Win with 'Em, Can't Go to War without 'Em," 11.

12 Engbrecht, *America's Covert Warriors*, 91.

13 Ibid., 92.

14 Singer, "Can't Win with 'Em, Can't Go to War without 'Em," 13.

15 Renae Merle, "Government Short of Contracting Officers: Officials Struggle to Keep Pace with Rapidly Increasing Defense Spending," *Washington Post*, July 5, 2007. I should note as well that I witnessed this change first-hand, starting my government acquisition career as one of 10 government personnel dedicated to a 100-million-dollar contract and ending it as one of two government personnel dedicated to a billion-dollar contract.

16 Commission on Wartime Contracting in Iraq and Afghanistan, *Transforming Wartime Contracting*, 117.

17 Ibid., 7.

18 Ibid.

19 Ibid., 6–8.

20 Stanger, *One Nation Under Contract*, 28.

21 R. A. Duff, "Answering for Crime," *Proceedings of the Aristotelian Society* 106 (2006): 87–113.

22 Discussions with Kristine Huskey and Benjamin Perrin were extremely helpful on this point. I should note, as well, that this point both supports and is supported by Perrin's argument for the importance of criminal liability, also in this issue.

23 If an agent has a duty to φ, one might wonder what difference it would make if she were accountable to A or to B. The short answer is that in standard cases the one to whom one is accountable has the Hohfeldian power to either waive or enforce compensation for violated duties. For more discussion on this point, see Wesley N. Hohfeld, *Fundamental Legal Conceptions, as Applied in Judicial Reasoning*, ed. W. W. Cook (New Haven: Yale University Press, 1919); H. L. A. Hart, "Legal Rights," *Essays on Bentham* (Oxford: Clarendon Press, 1982); and Gopal Sreenivasan, "Duties and Their Direction," *Ethics* 120, no. 3 (2010): 465–94.

24 Seana Valentine Shiffrin, "Promising, Intimate Relationships, and Conventionalism," *Philosophical Review* 117, no. 4 (2008): 486–508.

25 Engbrecht, *America's Covert Warriors*, 110–12.

26 For more discussion, see P. F. Strawson, "Freedom and Resentment," *Proceedings of the British Academy* 48 (1962): 1–25; R. Jay Wallace, *Responsibility and the Moral Sentiments* (Cambridge, MA: Harvard University Press, 1994); Gary Watson, "Two Faces of Responsibility," *Philosophical Topics* 24 (1996): 227–48; and Stephen Darwall, *The Second-Person Standpoint: Morality, Respect, and Accountability* (Cambridge, MA: Harvard University Press, 2006).

27. See, for example, Richard Brandt, "Blameworthiness and Obligation," in *Essays in Moral Philosophy*, ed. A. I. Meldon (Seattle: University of Washington Press, 1958).

28 I should be explicit from the start that the numbers presented here are for all contractors in Iraq, not only members of PMSCs. However, given the fact that PMSCs are a significant subset of that larger group (likely 10–20%), and given the staggering number of contractors in Iraq, the case against the larger set applies to the subset as well.

29 Numbers are based on data from 2008, using Michael Hurst's estimate of 180,000 contractors working in Iraq; and city-data.com's data on crime and population in Westport for the same year. For specifics, see Michael Hurst, "After Blackwater: A Mission-Focused Jurisdictional Regime for Private Military Contractors During Contingency Operations," *George Washington Law Review* 76, no. 5 (2008): 1310; "Westport, Connecticut," *city-data.com*, http://www.city-data.com/city/Westport-Connecticut.html (accessed January 12, 2012). Singer's original analogy can be found in *Corporate Warriors*, 251.

30 Numbers are based on data from 2008, comparing Hurst's estimate of 180,000 for number of contractors in Iraq against an active-duty army of 520,000, and applying that ratio against the number of army courts-martial in 2008. For specific figures, see Hurst (2008): 1310; "U.S. Army Personnel Tried in General, Special, and Summary Courts-martial, and Discharges Approved, by Conviction Status, United States, Fiscal Years 1997–2010," *Sourcebook on Criminal Justice Statistics*, http://www.albany.edu/sourcebook/pdf/t5802010.pdf (accessed January 12, 2012).

31 Unfortunately, one great demonstration of the near total lack of oversight lies in the fact that there is no good aggregate data regarding such questions. Although it would be false to say there were no such prosecutions, it is no stretch to claim that they are few and far between.

32 Singer makes a similar point. See Singer, *Corporate Warriors*, 251.

33 The cases have been well considered. Abu Ghraib: 100% of the translators and 50% of the interrogators at Abu Ghraib prison were private contractors, as documented in Singer, "Can't Win with 'Em, Can't Go To War without 'Em," 7. The U.S. Army concluded that contractors were involved in 36% of the proven abuse incidents at Abu Ghraib and that contractors were responsible for the most serious abuses. The Fay-Jones report identified six particular PMSC employees as being

culpable in the abuses, as documented in Major General George Fay and Lieutenant General Anthony Jones, "Investigation of Intelligence Activities at Abu Ghraib," U.S. Army Official Report (2004). Not one of the private contractors has been charged, prosecuted, or even punished, as documented in Rebecca DeWinter-Schmitt, "Six Years on Abu Ghraib Victims Still Fighting for Justice," *Amnesty International USA Circular* (April 29, 2009). In 1999, several DynCorps employees were implicated in buying and keeping women and girls as sexual slaves, some as young as 12. One site supervisor videotaped himself raping two young women. Yet, as documented in Singer, none of the individuals was prosecuted: Singer, *Corporate Warriors*, 222. Finally, DynCorps, far from being held collectively accountable, was awarded even larger contracts in the years that followed, as documented in *Corporate Warriors*, 13–14, 147.

34 MEJA, however, is tragically limited in its scope. The Department of Justice can bring charges against an individual only when it can prove that the defendant's employment "relates to supporting the mission of the Department of Defense overseas." Lanny Breuer, *Statement by Assistant Attorney General Lanny A. Breuer of the Criminal Division Before the Senate Judiciary Committee* (Washington, DC, May 25, 2011), available at http://www.justice.gov/criminal/pr/testimony/2011/crm-testimony-110525.html. Whether any particular defendant falls within the scope of MEJA, therefore, depends upon highly specific facts and circumstances relating to his or her employment. In the words of the Department of Justice itself, "Cases that would otherwise be straightforward can turn into complex investigations focusing not just on the underlying criminal conduct, but also on the scope of the defendant's employment, his or her specific work duties, and other jurisdiction-related facts." Breuer, *Statement by Assistant Attorney General*.

35 David Hammond, "The First Prosecution of a Contractor Under the UCMJ: Lessons for Service Contractors," *Professional Services Council* (Fall 2008): 33.

36 Breuer, *Statement by Assistant Attorney General*.

37 Hammond, "The First Prosecution of a Contractor Under the UCMJ," 33–34.

38 See, for example, Breuer, *Statement by Assistant Attorney General*.

39 Doug Brooks and Hanna Streng, "The Stability Operations Industry: The Shared Responsibility of Compliance and Ethics," in this issue, section on Terminology.

40 Personal interview with Captain Kevin Schieman, U.S. Army, November 17, 2011.

41 Quoted in Singer, "Can't Win with 'Em, Can't Go to War without 'Em," 7; originally in Nathan Hodge, "Revised U.S. Law Spotlights Role of Contractors on Battlefield," *Jane's Defence Weekly*, January 10, 2007.

42 Engbrecht, *America's Covert Warriors*, 209–11.

43 Ibid., 19.

44 Ibid., 211.

45 See, for example, Engbrecht, *America's Covert Warriors*, 212–14.

46 See, for example, Singer, *Corporate Warriors*, 256–58; and Katherin Chapman, "The Untouchables: Private Military Contractors' Criminal Accountability under the UCMJ" *Vanderbilt Law Review* 63, no. 4 (2010): 1047–80.

47 James Risen, "Ex-Blackwater Guards Face Renewed Charges," *New York Times*, April 22, 2011; Eugene Robinson, "A Whitewash for Blackwater?" *Washington Post*, December 9, 2008.

48 Singer, "Can't Win with 'Em, Can't Go to War without 'Em," 7.

49 Fainaru, "Where Military Rules Don't Apply."

50 Mark Mazzetti and Emily B. Hager, "Secret Desert Force Set Up by Blackwater's Founder," *New York Times*, May 14, 2011 (correction to article June 17, 2011).

51 See Andrew Alexandra's contribution to this volume for these types of considerations.

52 These concerns are exacerbated by the fact that the army is intentionally staffed with non-Muslims, precisely because they may be used to quell local protests.

53 Members of PMSCs are covered legally for such injuries under the Defense Base Act. As is the case with the question of whether our service men and women receive the care that is appropriately due to them, the question of our accountability cannot be settled by pointing out the fact that individuals are legally entitled to such care. The likelihood that those so entitled will actually receive such care, as well the machinations required to gain such care, are equally important considerations. By these more complex standards, our care for our veterans is often lacking but our care for members of PMSCs is non-existent. Thanks to Doug Brooks for helping me see the need to clarify the precise location of this issue.

54 There are also concerns about whether we are appropriately accountable to members of PMSCs in an operational setting: perhaps when members of PMSCs are caught in isolation scenarios, we are less likely to meet our duties to them. Although I cannot say with certainty that we are failing members of PMSCs in this way, three things make the possibility more likely. First, members of PMSCs are not legal combatants under the Geneva Conventions. Second, since they are not integrated into the local command structure, search and rescue attempts may in some cases be more difficult. Third, because they are not integrated, there is typically not the same "all hands on deck" response by members of the military to these scenarios.

55 Engbrecht, *America's Covert Warriors*, 215–18.

56 "Federal Funded Research and Development Centers," *Defense Acquisition University's Online Acquisition Encyclopedia*, https://acc.dau.mil/CommunityBrowser.aspx?id=434942 (accessed January 12, 2012).

57 Ibid.

58 Ibid.

Accountability for Private Military and Security Contractors in the International Legal Regime

KRISTINE A. HUSKEY*

The rapidly growing presence of private military and security contractors (PMSCs) in armed conflict and post-conflict situations in the last decade brought corresponding incidents of serious misconduct by PMSC personnel. The two most infamous events—one involving the firm formerly known as Blackwater and the other involving Titan and CACI—engendered scrutiny of available mechanisms for criminal and civil accountability of the individuals whose misconduct caused the harm. Along a parallel track, scholars and policymakers began examining the responsibility of states and international organizations for the harm that occurred. Both approaches have primarily focused on post-conduct accountability—of the individuals who caused the harm, of the state in which the harm occurred, or of the state or organization that hired the PMSC whose personnel caused the harm. Less attention, however, has been paid to the idea of pre-conduct accountability for PMSCs and their personnel. A broad understanding of "accountability for" PMSCs and their personnel encompasses not only responsibility for harm caused by conduct, but responsibility for hiring, hosting, and monitoring these entities, as well as responsibility to the victims of the harm. This article provides a comprehensive approach for analyzing the existing international legal regime, and whether and to what extent the legal regime provides "accountability for" PMSCs and their personnel. It does so by proposing a practical construct of three phases based on PMSC operations—Contracting, In-the-Field, and Post-Conduct—with which to assess the various bodies of international law.

Kristine A. Huskey is the director of the Anti-Torture Program at Physicians for Human Rights, an adjunct professor on national security law at Georgetown University Law Center, and a contributing author to the book, Multilevel Regulation of Military and Security Contractors: The Interplay Between International, European, and Domestic Norms *(2012).*

"It is not only what we do, but also what we do not do, for which we are accountable."

Molière

Introduction

With the proliferation of private military and security contractors (PMSCs) and their increased presence in places of armed conflict or post-conflict in the last decade came corresponding media attention to newsworthy misconduct by PMSC personnel. Examples of such misconduct are the Nisoor Square shooting involving Blackwater (now Academi) that left 17 civilians dead, and the torture and abuse of detainees at Abu Ghraib prison involving Titan and CACI personnel. At first, such incidents resulted in an intense focus on the criminal and civil accountability of PMSC personnel whose conduct harmed individuals. Along a parallel track, though with much less ado or public interest, scholars and policymakers have been examining the legal responsibility of states and international organizations for the conduct of PMSCs and their personnel. Both approaches have viewed "the problem" of private military and security contractors primarily with an eye toward post-conduct accountability: that is, who is accountable for the conduct of PMSC personnel that results in harm, or to whom (which state or entity) such conduct can be attributed.

This article attempts to provide a comprehensive analysis by using a practical three-phase construct through which to view and assess whether and to what extent the existing international legal regime provides "accountability for" PMSCs and their personnel. First, "accountability for" is meant in the broadest sense and is meant to address accountability more extensively than in just the post-conduct setting.[1] Second, the three-phase construct derives from the nature of PMSC operations and their respective relationships to the states with which they necessarily interact. It thus exposes weaknesses with a view to practice rather than law or policy. This article demonstrates that the current international legal framework does not provide a comprehensive system of accountability for PMSCs or their personnel.

Definitions

PMSCs. This article does not distinguish among PMCs (private military contractors), PSCs (private security contractors), and PMFs (private military firms), but uses the more encompassing term, PMSCs, which denotes all private military and/or security contractors. Indeed, the large and modern PMSC typically offers a spectrum of services that falls within and overlaps with various categories defined—sometimes differently—by scholars, international instruments, and domestic legislation.[2] With overarching goals of regulating, monitoring, ensuring compliance, and assigning accountability and responsibility in an international legal regime, PMSCs should be viewed as one group and held to the same standards.[3]

The State. This article uses the terms "Hiring State" to refer to the state that contracts for the services of PMSCs and its subcontractors; "Host State" to refer to the state in which the PMSC is operating; and "Home State" to refer to the state in which the PMSC is registered, incorporated, or, if different from the state of registration or incorporation, has its principal place of management.[4]

1. A Practical Construct

This article proposes a three-phase construct with which to assess the international legal regime and its ability to provide comprehensive accountability for PMSCs and their personnel. This three-phase construct offers a practical lens through which to view the larger notion of "accountability for" by examining PMSCs and personnel and their distinct relationships with the Hiring, Host, and Home States. Accordingly, the three phases make up the "life cycle" of a PMSC and its personnel in the context of those relationships: (1) the Contracting Phase; (2) the In-the-Field Phase (often referred to as "in theater" in places of armed conflict); and (3) the Post-Conduct Phase (that is, the period following action or inaction by PMSC personnel that harms or impacts an individual).

Contracting Phase

During the Contracting Phase, the Hiring State is of paramount importance as, during this stage, it is the primary enabler and gatekeeper. The Hiring State can determine:

- the scope of activities to be outsourced;

- who can be hired, including license requirements, and what screening, or vetting, mechanisms can be used;
- whether previous allegations/conduct/violations play a factor in the hiring process;
- and the scope of the contract (for example, location of contract performance).

For example, the Hiring State can determine that translation for interrogation (but not interrogation itself) can be outsourced, that PMSC X (but not PMSC Y) can be hired, that the contract performance is limited to military bases in Host State (and specifically prohibits accompanying military forces on a mission), that the PMSC activity must be conducted in the presence of military at all times, and that PMSC personnel are not permitted to carry firearms. At the same time, the Home State has the capability to determine the requirements for companies to operate in its state (for example, licensing structures) and may remove a PMSC's corporate status or suspend its operations based on various factors. Thus, because the Hiring and

Home States wield both the power and authority—though to different degrees—during the Contracting Phase to engage specific actors and define the terms of the engagement, it would be relevant to consider what laws and mechanisms in the international legal regime govern these states' decisions during this phase.

In-the-Field Phase

In this phase, the conduct of PMSC personnel has the greatest potential to impact the largest number of people, as they are potentially interacting with various individuals, such as military forces of the Hiring and Host States, other PMSC personnel, civilian nationals and local police of the Host State, and other nationals in the territory of the Host State. Here, the Host and the Hiring States may have overlapping, or competing, interests in regulating PMSC personnel. Both states, however, may face substantial obstacles to effective regulation, such as limited resources or a failed infrastructure. Less obvious, but potentially significant, is the degree of the Home State's ability to monitor the conduct of its PMSC personnel in the field and to penalize the companies for failing to comply with domestic laws or internal guidelines. During this phase, the relevant factors are:

- domestic and international laws, regulations, and codes of conduct applicable to PMSC personnel conduct in the field;
- monitoring mechanisms, and which state has responsibility to monitor and ensure compliance with such laws, regulations, and codes of conduct;

- and responsibility of other bodies (for example, international organizations) for monitoring and ensuring compliance with the same laws.

Post-Conduct Phase

This phase assumes that the conduct of PMSC personnel—a specific act or omission—has caused harm to an individual. Thus, the analysis focuses on the consequences of that conduct and potential outcomes, such as criminal accountability of the perpetrator and justice for the victim. The relevant factors are:

- applicable law or legal doctrines to determine who is accountable/liable (for example, PMSC, individual, state) for the relevant conduct, and to whom;
- applicable criminal laws and mechanisms, and which state or international body has responsibility to enforce such laws, or, if not currently existing, to enact them;
- applicable civil liability laws and mechanisms, and which state or international body has responsibility to enforce such laws, or, if not currently existing, to enact them;
- and responsibility to provide reparations to victims, independent of civil liability lawsuits.

Much criticism and scholarship has centered on the lack of criminal accountability for misconduct by individual PMSC personnel. Yet, as important—and perhaps a far more fertile area for international law—is the assignment of responsibility to provide redress to the victim.

The three-phase construct enables a practical assessment of the existing international legal regime by highlighting not only the applicable substantive law but the roles, relationships, and responsibilities of the relevant actors as well, during the distinct stages.

This article will address the relevant bodies of international law in the context of the three-phase construct in order to determine how the international legal regime addresses, or fails to address, broad accountability for PMSCs and their personnel. This article will then briefly address recent initiatives to assist in informing the primary analysis, concluding that the current international legal framework does not effectively provide broad accountability because it is either silent or lacks clarity regarding states' or other entities' legal responsibilities at key points during the three phases.

2. International Human Rights Law

Scholarship addressing PMSCs under international law has largely focused on international humanitarian law (IHL) (the laws of war) due to the fact that PMSC personnel often operate in situations of armed conflict and on account of the *lex specialis* status of IHL.[5] The application of international human rights law (IHRL) to PMSCs, however, should not be discounted. First, IHL does not apply in the absence of protracted armed conflict and PMSCs are "increasingly engaged in unstable areas where the violence does not amount to a conflict and their very presence may be indicative of the practice of foreign policy by proxy, suggesting a circumvention of IHL."[6] Second, even when arguably there is a protracted armed conflict, governments sometimes deny the existence of such a conflict, making IHL application difficult to address with relevant parties.[7] Third, the human rights law framework may provide a wider range of accountability mechanisms, including monitoring by United Nations special rapporteurs and field officers.[8] Finally, IHRL may be more expansive in scope than IHL because, unlike IHL, it gives individuals standing to petition for alleged violations and provides a remedial scheme with compensation for victims who have established a breach.[9] IHRL can be relevant, then, in substantive application with respect to monitoring of conduct and redress for individuals.

Viewing international human rights law through the lens of the three-phase construct—the Contracting, the In-the-Field, and the Post-Conduct Phases—IHRL can be highly germane to the second and third phases, but less so during the first phase. As will be demonstrated below during discussion of recent initiatives, current IHRL does not easily lend itself to application in the Contracting Phase because this stage focuses primarily on the Hiring/Home State-PMSC relationship and, currently, domestic laws and regulations more readily govern such relationships.

During the In-the-Field Phase, the main inquiry is whether IHRL is applicable and, if so, which states bear responsibility for ensuring compliance. First, as mentioned, IHRL would apply in situations of non-armed conflict, such as reconstruction or civil strife—scenarios in which PMSCs are often found. Second, some human rights are non-derogable and apply to the conduct of PMSC personnel under any circumstance, even when the individual is in a theater of war. For example, the International Covenant on Civil and Political Rights (ICCPR), while permitting derogation from some obligations in times of public emergency, does not permit derogation at any time from certain fundamental rights, such as the inherent right to life, freedom from torture, cruel, inhuman, and degrading treatment, freedom from slavery, and the right to recognition as a person before the law.[10]

The inherent right to life "is the supreme right from which no derogation is permitted even in time of public emergency which threatens the life of the nation."[11] Consequently, arbitrary deprivation of life is prohibited under any circumstance. With the realities of PMSC conduct in mind, non-arbitrary deprivation of life may occur when legal self-defense is used.[12] It may also occur in armed conflict, if an individual is considered a lawful combatant under applicable IHL.[13] However, whether a PMSC individual operates as a legal state agent, and not as a mercenary, requires a complex analysis that will be addressed briefly below. Notwithstanding that some PMSCs may be state agents with the right to kill during conflict, arguably many more are not, and thus the right to life under IHRL is relevant.

The prohibition against non-arbitrary deprivation of life is contained in the core human rights instruments—the Universal Declaration of Human Rights (UDHR), the United Nations Covenant on Civil and Political Rights (ICCPR), and the United Nations Charter, as well as in customary international law.[14]

The right to be free from torture and cruel, inhuman, and degrading treatment (CID) is another non-derogable right, and is explicitly detailed in the United Nations Convention Against Torture, Cruel, Inhuman and Degrading Treatment.[15] The potential that PMSC personnel have for violating this right is immediately obvious, as PMSC individuals are often hired to guard people and/or places, which may include detention centers and other places that put them in close contact with a vulnerable population. The most vivid demonstration of such violations involved Titan and CACI, private firms whose personnel were hired to provide interrogation and translation services to the U.S. Department of Defense at the Abu Ghraib prison. The contractors were accused of subjecting Iraqi detainees to a variety of abuses rising to the level of torture and CID, including beatings, excessive cold temperatures, depriving them of food, water, and sleep, threatening them with dogs, urinating on them, and forcing them to witness the rape, sexual abuse, beatings, and electrocution of other detainees.[16]

The UDHR, ICCPR, European Convention on Human Rights (ECHR), and the American Convention on Human Rights (ACHR) also contain provisions explicitly prohibiting torture and abusive treatment.[17]

As to derogable rights, the Human Rights Committee has made clear that derogations in time of public emergency are to be tightly circumscribed and must be of an "exceptional and temporary nature."[18] Even during armed conflict, measures derogating from the ICCPR are allowed "only if and to the extent that the situation constitutes a threat to the life of the nation."[19] Thus, many rights—though derogable—may still apply to regulate PMSC conduct, such as rights to physical and mental health, liberty and security, freedom of thought and religion, freedom of movement, use and enjoyment of one's own property, and the right to be free from racial discrimination.[20] IHRL also specifically protects women and children, two groups that are especially vulnerable in armed conflict and post-conflict situations.[21]

There are, however, significant weaknesses in applying international human rights law to PMSC conduct during the In-the-Field Phase, the derogation provisions being one.[22] A second weakness is that—even absent specific derogation—international humanitarian law, as *lex specialis*, may operate to override IRHL. Third, IHRL generally applies only if an individual is in the territory or jurisdiction of a state party to the instrument.[23] Thus, although states are required to prevent harms caused by acts not only of their agents but also of private persons and entities,[24] in the scenario in which a PMSC from Home State X, contracted by Hiring State Y, sends personnel to operate in Host State Z—a failed state that lacks capacity to protect—it is unclear which state has the legal responsibility to ensure human rights violations are not occurring in Host State Z. In light of the extraterritoriality restriction, arguably only State Z assumes such responsibility, thus leaving a significant gap in IHRL protections.

In response, as previously discussed, there are non-derogable human rights that would apply in any circumstances and, moreover,

derogation is tightly circumscribed. As I have also mentioned, PMSCs often operate either in areas of instability that do not rise to the level of armed conflict or in post-conflict situations, as in reconstruction efforts in Iraq.

The *lex specialis* and extraterritoriality challenges are not as onerous as they appear on the surface. Despite previous assertions by the U.S. that IHRL does not apply in the context of the "global war on terror"—an armed conflict[25]—it is well established in international law that the application of international human rights law is not confined to times of peace, and that a state of armed conflict does not justify the suspension of fundamental human rights protections.[26] Moreover, recently the United States has softened its stance, stating in its Fourth Periodic Report to the Human Rights Committee that, "[i]ndeed, a time of war does not suspend the operation of the Covenant to matters within its scope of application."[27] In the same report, the U.S. also coyly acknowledges that it is out of step with contemporary international law on the extraterritorial application of IHRL, noting three important international law sources that take the contrary view: the International Court of Justice, other states' laws and practices, and the HRC. That is, a state must uphold its obligations under international human rights law where it exercises jurisdiction extraterritorially, or with respect to anyone within the power or effective control of that state government even if not situated in the territory of the state government.[28] This view is supported by recent jurisprudence in the European Court of Human Rights regarding the application of the European Human Rights Convention in Iraq with respect to the conduct of military forces of the United Kingdom. In two cases, after an exacting factual analysis, the court essentially concluded that the UK, through its agents, exercised control and authority over the relevant individuals and was therefore under the obligation to secure the rights and freedoms of the EHRC to those individuals.[29]

With regard to the Post-Conduct Phase, because states, not individuals, are responsible for international human rights law breaches, similar problems present themselves. For example, under the ICCPR, state parties are required to take "appropriate measures or to exercise due diligence to prevent, punish, investigate or redress the harm caused by such acts by private persons or entities . . . [and] provide effective remedies in the event of breach."[30] Thus, the requirements of punishment and redress are left in the hands of the individual states. In other words, domestic laws could serve to punish the perpetrator and redress the victim, yet many domestic laws fail in both regards. There is simply no enforcement mechanism to make states comply in the event that they do not take appropriate measures to punish or redress. Further, although individuals whose rights under the ICCPR have been violated can petition the Human Rights Committee for redress, they can do so only if the harm is committed in the territory of a state that is

a party to the Optional Protocol to the ICCPR,[31] or if they are within the power, or under the effective control, of a state party to the Optional Protocol in a territory which is within the state's extraterritorial jurisdictional reach.

Thus, in the case of post-conflict Iraq, where the U.S. Department of Defense has deployed close to 150,000 PMSC personnel, with as many as 10,000 of them armed, some may argue the U.S. has no obligation to ensure that its contractors respect human rights law in Iraq, to punish personnel who violate human rights law, or to provide victims with some measure of redress in the case of violations.[32] First, the extraterritoriality and *lex specialis* restrictions— though the U.S. is softening its position—may limit the U.S.'s interpretation of its obligations under human rights instruments. Second, the U.S. is not party to the ICCPR Optional Protocol and thus individuals cannot petition the HRC for redress. Lastly, the protracted and disappointing results in the prosecution involving Blackwater contractors involved in Nisoor Square and the civil lawsuits involving Titan and CACI demonstrate the difficulties in implementing domestically the punish and redress requirements.[33]

Although it is an important piece in the international legal framework, IHRL alone cannot adequately address accountability for PMSCs, and it is particularly lacking in the Contracting Phase.

3. International Humanitarian Law

Despite the attention paid to international humanitarian law in the PMSC context, IHL is, in fact, somewhat limited in its ability to address issues of regulation and accountability. As will be demonstrated, IHL tends to fall short during each of the three phases—the Contracting, the In-the-Field, and the Post-Conduct Phases.

As a preliminary matter, IHL is not applicable in all situations involving PMSCs, such as outside of an ongoing armed conflict. As an illustration, "armies" of private security contractors have been hired by governments to guard natural resource facilities in areas of unrest by the local population.[34]

Assuming, however, the existence of an armed conflict, other than explicitly assigning to states certain activities, such as exercising the power of the responsible officer over prisoners of war or internment camps, IHL offers little guidance in defining state obligations during the Contracting Phase.[35] It is left to states to determine what can be outsourced, whether to use screening and licensing mechanisms, and the scope of the contract. IHL is not concerned with the exercise of due diligence during the Contracting Phase as a matter of state responsibility, but rather with whether a state is responsible for acts committed by private entities in violation of IHL either directly or by failing to use due diligence to prevent and punish violations appropriately.[36]

IHL can provide the substantive applicable law in the In-the-Field Phase, but does so with great difficulty due to the complex nature of how PMSC personnel operate. The premise of IHL lies in the "status" of an individual—whether violator or victim—which then determines the protections and rights of the individual, as well as assignments of individual and state responsibility. Thus, status is especially critical when PMSC personnel violate a law of war, yet assigning a workable

status to such an individual can be a tremendous challenge. PMSC personnel perform a vast array of functions—from transporting food and medicine to designing precision weaponry—such that the "sole commonality is the sale of services within the military domain."[37] PMSCs are hired by governments as well as by international organizations and private business entities.[38] These complicating factors are further exacerbated by technological advancements in warfare which have blurred the lines of "the battlefield." It is generally accepted that the majority of modern-day PMSC individuals are not mercenaries, who are prohibited per se.[39] However, scholars are otherwise divided about the status of PMSCs under IHL.[40] Thus, PMSC personnel do not fall under a single status determination; rather, status is a case-by-case analysis of time, place, and manner.[41] Accordingly, while existing IHL is useful in providing standards regarding the In-the-Field Phase activities of PMSCs, it is difficult in application.

IHL is mostly silent with respect to PMSC personnel during the Post-Conduct Phase, though it may address state responsibility for state organs in the Fourth Hague Convention and Protocol I to the Geneva Conventions.[42] One must refer to the International Law Commission's (ILC) Articles on Responsibility for States for Internationally Wrongful Acts[43] in order to make determinations of state responsibility for violations of IHL by non-state actors.[44] The ILC initiates the responsibility of states for private entities when they are "empowered by the law of that State to exercise elements of governmental authority" or are de facto acting on its instructions or under its direction and control.[45] The example of U.S. private military security contractors who provided security services in Iraq demonstrates a tension. In the civil litigation involving accusations against Blackwater for various arbitrary killings and injuries, including the Nisoor Square deaths, the U.S. appeared as an "interested party" to assert that the PMSC defendants were not acting as employees of the U.S. and that Blackwater management oversaw the day-to-day operations of its employees.[46] In other words, in the view of the U.S., its responsibility was not engaged under the ILC Articles because Blackwater personnel were neither exercising governmental authority nor acting under its control or supervision.

On providing redress to victims, IHL is silent. Like IHRL, IHL does not provide a comprehensive regime of accountability for PMSCs even in the limited context of armed conflict.

4. International Criminal Law

International criminal law (ICL)[47] gives authority to international human rights and humanitarian law by making certain violations of those laws criminal offenses.[48] ICL derives from treaties, customary international law, and the jurisprudence of international criminal tribunals, including the International Criminal Court (ICC).[49] Although robust, ICL is narrowly focused on achieving criminal accountability of individuals during the Post-Conduct Phase.

The ICC is the universally recognized international court for prosecuting "the most serious crimes of concern to the international community": genocide, crimes against humanity, war crimes, and the crime of aggression. Two of these crimes are likely to arise in the PMSC context: war crimes and crimes against humanity.[50] Yet the ICC faces certain hurdles in prosecuting even these two crimes. The ICC has jurisdiction to prosecute war crimes only "when committed as part of a plan or policy or as part of a large-scale commission of such crimes."[51] Moreover, some scholars have suggested that it is debatable whether PMSC personnel could commit "war crimes," due to the requirement under IHL that alleged perpetrators be members of the armed forces of either party to the conflict, that their acts are attributable to either party, that they are exercising public authority, or that they are de facto representing the government to support the war effort.[52] "Crimes against humanity" requires that the attacks are directed against a civilian population as part of a "widespread or systematic practice" and that the attack be "pursuant to or in furtherance of a State or organizational policy."[53] Given the nature of PMSC operations and the often-attenuated control states have over PMSC personnel operations, ICC jurisdiction does not seem easily obtained.

Further, while the ICC has international legal authority and can exercise its powers on the territory of any state party or other states with permission, it can only exercise jurisdiction if the accused is a national of a state party, the crime occurred in the territory of a state party and after the state party joined the Rome

Statute, or the U.N. Security Council has referred the case to the ICC prosecutor and the case has not been and is not being investigated by a state that has jurisdiction.[54]

These restrictions present challenges to PMSC accountability, particularly the required nexus to a state party. Although a number of states have ratified the Rome Statute, 33 countries have signed but not ratified it and at least 44 member states of the U.N. have neither signed nor ratified the instrument.[55] Moreover, PMSC individuals are of many different nationalities. A recent U.N. report indicated that 89% of private contractors working under U.S. Department of Defense contracts in Iraq were neither American nor Iraqi but were from a range of countries, including Fiji, Nepal, South Africa, Sri Lanka, Uganda, Peru, and other South American countries.[56]

Finally, the ICC depends on the cooperation of state parties and other states in order to effectively investigate and prosecute alleged international crimes. For example, the ICC does not have its own police force. Victor Peskin's vivid account of the ICC prosecutor's shift from cautionary to confrontational with the Ugandan and Rwandan governments in pursuing investigations of their nationals demonstrates both the necessity of state cooperation and the substantial challenges thereof.[57]

Additional Challenges in International Criminal Law

Domestic courts are the primary venue for criminal accountability, including for international crimes, and, thus, the ICC and other international criminal tribunals depend on states to share the burden of trying international crimes. Unfortunately, effectiveness is questionable due to gaps in jurisdiction and enforcement and the problem of immunity agreements. For example, divergent interpretations of ICL issues, lack of incentive due to state complicity or the view that international criminal law norms are illegitimate, and lack of capacity—particularly in countries that have recently experienced mass atrocities—present severe challenges to enforcement by states.

Interstate immunity agreements present another obstacle to effective prosecution. In the case of the Nisoor Square shootings, the Iraqi government expressed intent to prosecute the PMSC employees who allegedly participated in the incident; however, the highly criticized immunity agreement between the U.S. and Iraq granted U.S. contractors immunity from Iraqi prosecution.[58]

Lastly, there is no mechanism under international criminal law to prosecute PMSCs in their corporate capacity.

5. Recent Developments in the International Legal Framework

In early 2004, two highly graphic events involving PMSCs in the Iraq conflict occurred within a span of three days: the disclosure of widespread torture and abuse of detainees by U.S. forces and private security contractors at Abu Ghraib prison, and an incident in Fallujah involving the public deaths, burning, and dismemberment of four Blackwater contractors.[59] The following year, two international initiatives addressing the use and conduct of private military and security contractors were set in motion. These initiatives were prescient, as the Nisoor Square massacre in 2007—which would bring PMSCs into the public spotlight—had yet to occur.[60] Numerous other incidents involving PMSCs in Iraq and Afghanistan and allegations of killings, torture, rape, arbitrary detention, trafficking, and other human rights violations have been documented over the last several years.[61] Calls for more regulation, and better monitoring, enforcement, and accountability have been sounding domestically and internationally. Though some may argue otherwise, there are indeed gaps in the international legal regime for ensuring broad accountability for PMSCs and personnel, as this article has demonstrated. At best, the legal regime is fragmented and lacks clarity, particularly with the assignment of responsibility to whom and at what stage.

Two recent international initiatives (Montreux and the U.N. Draft Convention) attempt to address this particular problem, among others. This article does not try to explain these initiatives in detail, as their provisions and related issues are addressed by other contributors in this issue.[62] Rather, it will employ the initiatives in the context of the three-phase construct in order to highlight the previously identified gaps in the current international legal regime.

The Montreux Document and the U.N. Draft Convention on Private Military and Security Contractors

The Montreux Document, which addresses "pertinent international legal obligations and good practices for States related to operations of private military and security companies during armed conflict," contains two parts.[63] The first part reiterates existing international law obligations of the states with which PMSCs and their personnel interact.[64] Montreux refers to these states as the Contracting, Territorial, and Home States.[65] The second half of the document sets out "good practices" for each of the three categories of states in the discharge of their international law obligations.[66]

Montreux makes a significant and unique contribution in its approach to law and practice from the perspective of each of the three relevant states—Contracting, Territorial, and Home (this article uses the terms Hiring, Host, and Home States). In Part One of Montreux, this approach goes far in attempting to clarify two concepts that are fairly murky in traditional international humanitarian law and international human rights law: "state responsibility" and "due diligence." In other words, Montreux endeavors to provide precision as to which state is responsible for discharging the relevant legal obligation and on what basis. However, the three-phase construct—Contracting, In-the-Field, and Post-Conduct—reveals that simply knowing each state's responsibility does not illuminate the "when" aspect of the obligation: at what stage in the life cycle of a PMSC is the state legally responsible for regulating, monitoring, and penalizing or providing redress? Montreux does not assist in this regard.

The "good practices" in Part Two of Montreux provide "guidance and assistance" to states in implementing their obligations under IHL and IHRL, as well as "promoting responsible conduct in their relationships with PMSCs operating in areas of armed conflict."[67] Setting forth these "good practices" through the perspective of each of the three participating states (Contracting, Territorial, and Home) enables legal parties to identify with specificity how a state—given its particular relationship to the PMSC—can appropriately carry out its international legal obligations. This approach, more so than any existing international law, underscores the necessity of domestic or national legislation as a complementary part of the international legal framework.

The Montreux Document and its unique state-perspective approach, together with the three-phase construct, highlight the gaps in the international legal regime and the need for domestic legislation. The most significant gap is the inability of international law to address the pivotal role that the Hiring State can play in the Contracting Phase. Montreux illustrates this myopic approach. In Part One, the section addressing the Hiring/Contracting State is largely concerned with the In-the-Field and Post-Conduct Phases as it aims toward preventing, suppressing, investigating, and prosecuting violations of international humanitarian law and human rights law, and providing remedies for "misconduct."[68] Montreux contains one paragraph specifically addressing the Hiring State's legal obligations during the Contracting Phase—namely, not to outsource that which is prohibited under international law. But as mentioned above, IHL speaks very little to this issue and IHRL not at all.[69]

In contrast, Montreux's "good practices," which are not legal obligations, include extensive paragraphs on Determination of Services (that is, what can be outsourced), Procedure for the Selection and Contracting of PMSCs, Criteria for the Selection of PMSCs, and Terms of Contract with PMSCs.[70] For example, "good practices" include the need for transparency and public disclosure of the contracting process, regulations, specific contracts, reported incidents, and oversight mechanisms.[71] There are two lessons to be gleaned from this comparison: (1) international law currently does not legally obligate states to any particular responsibilities in the Contracting Phase; and (2) domestic legislation may be the only realistic avenue for ensuring the articulation of these obligations.

Although Montreux is not binding law and does not set forth any new legal obligations, the U.N. Draft Convention on Private Military and Security Companies ("Draft Convention")[72] attempts quite the opposite—to establish a wholly new framework of international legal obligations for addressing PMSCs and personnel. The Draft Convention does this by setting forth obvious state responsibilities under existing international law and new formulations of international legal obligations that explicitly require national legislation on various aspects of PMSC operations. Further adding to its breadth, it is applicable at all times—not just during armed conflict, as in Montreux—and to international organizations.

As demonstrated, existing international law does not go far enough in the Contracting Phase, or the Post-Conduct Phase, to prevent and account for misconduct by PMSCs personnel. Moreover, existing international law is murky, or unsatisfactory at best, during the In-the-Field Phase with respect to which state or entity has responsibility for regulating PMSC conduct.

First, there are no binding standards or international laws articulating state obligations or responsibilities with respect to what can be outsourced, to whom, and how.[73] The current international law regime speaks very little to the matter of reparations to victims of PMSC misconduct and is far from clear in articulating state responsibility and due diligence in the context of violations of international law. The Draft Convention ambitiously attempts to fill these gaps by way of a new international legal framework and, in doing so, illustrates just how rife with holes the current international regime is.

The Contracting Phase—an area particularly silent in international law—is addressed by the Draft Convention in various ways. With respect to the outsourcing questions, the Draft Convention defines "inherently state functions" very broadly to include:

[D]irect participation in hostilities, waging war and/or combat operations, taking prisoners, law-making, espionage, intelligence, knowledge transfer with military, security and policing application, use of and other activities related to weapons of mass destruction, police powers, especially the powers of arrest or detention including the interrogation of detainees and other functions that a State Party considers to be inherently state functions.[74]

The Draft Convention not only prohibits the delegation and/or outsourcing of inherently state functions but it also requires state parties to define and limit the scope of activities of PMSCs and to adopt legislation and other measures to prohibit the delegation of military or security services.[75]

On the one hand, the Draft Convention does what no other international instrument has done, which is to require—in no uncertain terms—states to pass national legislation aimed at providing substance to the phrase "inherently governmental function" and then similarly to require prohibiting legislation. However, in providing substance by deeming several activities inherently state functions, it arguably goes too far with its definition by prohibiting the outsourcing of such a broad range of activities, including, for example, espionage and intelligence. An illustrative example is the United States, known for its large share of the PMSC industry as well as its lack of support for the Draft Convention. First, the U.S. has struggled to define "inherently governmental function" with more uniformity and clarity as required by domestic legislation enacted in 2009.[76] Second, it is no secret that the U.S. outsources its spying and intelligence activities and in considerable numbers—as much as 30% of the workforce in U.S. intelligence agencies are private contractors.[77] It is not surprising the U.S. has not been an ardent supporter of a convention that prohibits the outsourcing of intelligence activities. These tensions reflect the realities on the ground, some of which seem to be ignored by the Draft Convention.

The Draft Convention also addresses other aspects of the Contracting Phase, requiring that PMSC personnel be trained in and respect IHRL and IHL. Significantly, it makes clear that both the Hiring and Home States are responsible for implementing legislation and/or regulations that ensure such training.[78] It requires state parties to take other measures to establish criteria for screening PMSC firms and individuals, to establish licensing schemes that take into account reports of human rights violations, and to establish legal requirements concerning PMSC personnel training and experience.[79] These types of obligations and the degree to which they are detailed in the Draft Convention are simply not articulated in existing international law.

The Draft Convention is similarly outstanding because it provides shape and form to the substantive international law that would apply during the In-the-Field Phase and clarifies certain state responsibilities and obligations of due diligence during the same phase. For example, Article 18 requires state parties to enact legislation or take other measures regarding the use of force and firearms, going into great detail as to when and how PMSC personnel should use firearms.[80] On the issue of state responsibility, it makes clear that Host and Home States have responsibilities for the military and security activities of PMSCs registered or operating in their jurisdiction.[81]

The Draft Convention is likewise ambitious in its attempt to assign obligations to state parties with respect to the Post-Conduct Phase when PMSC conduct harms an individual in the course of the PMSC operations in the Host State. It makes clear that state parties have an obligation both to punish PMSC personnel when their conduct harms others and to provide redress to victims of such conduct. For example, Article 19 requires state parties to make carrying out inherently state functions punishable as criminal offenses under national law and to ensure that individual criminal responsibility is established for violations of the law, and that "no recourse is taken to immunity agreements."[82] With respect to victims of PMSC misconduct, state parties are required to establish legislation or other measures to ensure that "effective remedies," which include restitution, are provided to victims and to ensure that individuals who are found liable, in addition to being subject to "effective, proportionate and dissuasive sanctions," also have the obligation to provide restitution or compensation to victims.[83]

The Draft Convention goes quite far in every aspect of the three phases—Contracting, In-the-Field, and Post-Conduct—by not only detailing prohibited and required conduct, but also by explicitly requiring states to enact legislation that prohibits certain actions and requires certain affirmative conduct by PMSCs and personnel. Although it is not unusual for human rights instruments to require states to ensure rights and protections through domestic measures, the Draft Convention provides form and substance to those rights and protections and requires states to implement domestic legislation that provides the same form and substance. Its breadth may be both its victory and its downfall.

Conclusion

The existing international legal regime does not adequately provide broad "accountability for" PMSCs and personnel. This article has demonstrated such inadequacy by viewing the relevant bodies of law through the lens of the three-phase construct—the Contracting, In-the-Field, and Post-Conduct Phases. Most important is the inability of international law to assign responsibility to states and other entities at significant points of PMSC and personnel interaction with states and individuals. Montreux and the Draft Convention—neither of which is currently binding—illuminate these gaps, among others, and highlight the need for more comprehensive international and domestic law if full accountability in all three phases is to be achieved. The Draft Convention leaves one imagining an international legal regime that can be the primary body of law for ensuring the fullest accountability for PMSCs and personnel. On the other hand, its breadth leaves one wondering whether international law can provide only a scant framework, as the Montreux Document suggests, and states must be left to engage in "good practices," or pass legislation requiring such practices, on their own accord.

Notes

[The author would like to thank Rachel Evans for her substantial and outstanding work on this article.]

1 "Accountability" is defined as "liability to be called on to render an account" or "the state of being accountable"; "answerability" is provided as a synonym. See *Merriam-Webster Dictionary*, "accountability," Merriam-Webster.com, http://www.merriam-webster.com/dictionary/accountability (accessed September 25, 2011).

2 See Peter Singer, *Corporate Warriors: The Rise of the Privatized Military Industry* (Ithaca, NY: Cornell University Press, 2003), 88 (identifying three categories of PMFs—military support firms, military consulting firms, and military provider firms). The United Nations Draft Convention separates PMSCs into two categories—military and security services, defining "security services as armed guarding of things or people, knowledge transfer with security/police applications, development and implementation of informational security measures and other related activities." Draft of a possible Convention on Private Military and Security Companies (PMSCs) for consideration and action by the Human Rights Council, art. 2(a)–(b), U.N. Doc. A/HRC/15/25, Annex (July 2, 2010) (hereinafter *Draft Convention*). The Montreux Document includes armed guarding and protection of persons and objects, prisoner detention, advice to the training of local forces and security personnel, and activities relating to weapons systems. Montreux Document on pertinent international legal obligations and good practices for States related to operations of private military and security companies during armed conflict, pmbl. sec. 9, U.N. Doc. A/63/467, Annex (September 17, 2008) (hereinafter *Montreux Document*). U.S. legislation defines a "private security function" as the guarding of personnel, facilities, or properties and other activity for which contractors are required to be armed. National Defense Authorization Act for Fiscal Year 2008, PL 110–181, § 864(a)(5), January 28, 2008, 122 Stat. 3 (2008) (codified as amended 10 USCA § 2302 [2011]).

3 See also Amol Mehra, "Bridging Accountability Gaps—The Proliferation of Private Military and Security Companies and Ensuring Accountability for Human Rights Violations," *Pacific McGeorge Global Business and Development Law Journal* 22 (2010): 323, 324–25.

4 See *War By Contract*, ed. Francesco Francioni and Natalino Ronzitti (New York: Oxford University Press, 2011), chaps. 3, 5, 6, 7.

5 See, e.g., Won Kidane, "The Status of Private Military Contractors under

International Humanitarian Law," *Denver Journal of International Law and Policy* 38 (2010): 361, 365. *Lex specialis* is the principle that the governing law is that which concerns a specific subject matter, deriving from the legal maxim, *lex specialis derogat legi generali*, meaning special law prevails over general law. In the context of this discussion, international human rights law is considered general law (*lex generalis*).

6 Hin-Yan Liu, "Leashing the Corporate Dogs of War: The Legal Implications of the Modern Private Military Company," *Journal of Conflict and Security Law* 15 (2010): 141 n. 122.

7 Andrew Clapham, "Human Rights Obligations of Non-State Actors in Conflict Situations," *International Review of the Red Cross*, no. 863 (2006): 491, 503, available at http://www.icrc.org/eng/assets/files/other/irrc_863_clapham.pdf

8 Ibid.

9 Liu, "Leashing the Corporate Dogs of War," 141 n. 122, citing Yoram Dinstein, *The Conduct of Hostilities Under the Law of International Armed Conflict* (Cambridge, UK: Cambridge University Press, 2004), 20.

10 The International Covenant on Civil and Political Rights (hereinafter *ICCPR*), art. 4, 6, 7, 8, 16, December 9, 1966, 999 UNTS 171 (ratified June 8, 1992).

11 See U.N. Human Rights Committee (hereinafter HRC), CCPR General Comment No. 6, *The Right to Life*, sec. 1 (April 30, 1982), available at http://www.unhchr.ch/tbs/doc.nsf/0/84ab9690ccd81fc7c12563ed0046fae3

12 See Francesco Francioni, "The Role of Human Rights in the Regulation of Private Military and Security Companies," in Francioni and Ronzitti (eds), *War By Contract*, 61.

13 Ibid.

14 See ibid.

15 U.N. Convention Against Torture and Other Cruel, Inhuman or Degrading Treatment or Punishment, GA Res. 39/46, U.N. Doc. A/RES/39/46 (December 10, 1984).

16 *Saleh v. Titan Corp.*, 580 F.3d 1, 2–5 (DC Cir. 2009) *cert. denied*, 131 S. Ct. 3055 (2011).

17 Universal Declaration of Human Rights, art. 5, GA Res. 217 A(III), U.N. Doc. A/810 (1948) (hereinafter *UDHR*); ICCPR; European Convention for the Protection of Human Rights and Fundamental Freedoms, art. 3, November 4, 1950, 213 UNTS 221 (hereinafter *ECHR*); Organization of American States, American Convention on Human Rights, November 22, 1969, 9 ILM 217, art. 5, (1970).

18 See HRC, CCPR General Comment No. 29, "States of Emergency," (July 24, 2001): sec. 2, available at http://www.unhchr.ch/tbs/doc.nsf/898586b1dc7b4043c1256a450044f331/71eba4be3974b4f7c1256ae200517361/$FILE/G0144470.pdf

19 Ibid., sec. 3.

20 Francioni, "The Role of Human Rights in the Regulation of Private Military and Security Companies," 64–76 (citing various international human rights instruments).

21 Convention on the Elimination of All Forms of Discrimination Against Women, art. 3, GA Res. 34/180, 34 U.N. GAOR Res. Supp. (No. 46) 194, U.N. Doc. A/34/46, Annex, art. 4(1) (1979); United Nations Convention on the Rights of the Child, art. 3(2), GA Res. 44/25, U.N. Doc. A/RES/44/25 (November 10, 1989).

22 See, e.g., ICCPR, art. 4(1); ECHR, art. 15(1). It should be noted that many of the derogated rights under IHRL are replaced by protections in IHL and, accordingly, the ability to derogate does not necessitate a blanket-type gap in the international legal regime without closer analysis of specific provisions. See Liu, "Leashing the Corporate Dogs of War," 163.

23 See, e.g., ICCPR, art. 2; ECHR, art. 1.

24 See HRC, General Comment no. 31[80], "The Nature of the General Legal Obligation Imposed on States Parties to the Covenant," secs. 16, 18–20, U.N. Doc. CCPR/C/21/Rev1/Add13 (May 26, 2004). See also Nigel D. White's discussion of state responsibility and due diligence, in this issue.

25 See Second and Third Periodic Report of the United States of America to the U.N. Committee on Human Rights Concerning the International Covenant on Civil and Political Rights (October 21, 2005), sec. 130, available at: http://www.state.gov/j/drl/rls/55504.htm; see also "Response of the

United States for Request for Provisional Measures—Detainees in Guantanamo Bay, Cuba," submitted to Inter-American Human Rights Commission in *Coard et al. v. United States*, Case No. 10.951 (April 12, 2002), 15, 20–21, on file with author.

26 See Silvia Borelli, "Casting Light on the Legal Black Hole: International Law and Detentions Abroad in the 'War on Terror,' " *International Review of the Red Cross* 87, no. 857 (March 2005): 53–55, available at: http://www.icrc.org/eng/assets/files/other/irrc_857_borelli.pdf; International Court of Justice, "Legal Consequences of the Construction of a Wall in the Occupied Palestinian Territory," Advisory Opinion, July 9, 2005, par. 106.

27 Fourth Periodic Report of the United States of America to the U.N. Committee on Human Rights Concerning the International Covenant on Civil and Political Rights, (December 30, 2011), sec. 506.

28 Ibid., sec. 505; ICJ, "Legal Consequences of the Construction of a Wall in the Occupied Palestinian Territory," 136 at par. 111; HRC, General Comment No. 31, sec. 10.

29 See *Al-Skeini v. United Kingdom* [GC], no. 27021/08, European Court of Human Rights (July 7, 2011), sec. 150; *Al Jedda v. United Kingdom* [GC], no. 55721/07, European Court of Human Rights (July 7, 2011), sec. 86.

30 HRC, General Comment No. 31, sec. 8.

31 Optional Protocol to the International Covenant on Civil and Political Rights, GA res. 2200A (XXI), 21 UN GAOR Supp. (No. 16) at 59, U.N. Doc. A/6316 (1966), 999 UNTS. 302, *entered into force* March 23, 1976.

32 The United States has made payments under the Foreign Claims Act to victims in Iraq and Afghanistan who have suffered an injury caused by U.S. personnel, but denied a similar claim against PMSC personnel on the ground that the private contractor was not a "government employee" as required by the Foreign Claims Act. See documents released to the ACLU in a Freedom of Information Act request at www.aclu.org/natsec/foia/log.html

33 See *United States v. Slough*, No. 1:08-cr-00360-RMU, Slip Op. at 114 (DDC, December 31, 2009) (dismissing criminal case); but see *United States v. Slough*, No. 10-006, 2011

WL 1516148 (DC Cir. April 22, 2011) (reversing and remanding to trial court to reconsider its decision to dismiss). *Saleh v. Titan*, 14–16, and *Al Shimari v. CACI Premier Technology, Inc.*, 657 F.Supp.2d 700 (ED Va. 2009) (dismissing Alien Tort Statute claims).

34 See José L. Gómez del Prado, "A United Nations Instrument to Regulate and Monitor Private Military and Security Contractors," *Notre Dame Journal of International, Comparative, and Human Rights Law* 1, no. 1 (2011): 1, 11–12.

35 Emanuela-Chiara Gillard, "Private Military/Security Companies: The Status of their Staff and their Obligations Under International Humanitarian Law and the Responsibilities of States in Relation to their Operations," *International Review of the Red Cross*, no. 863 (January 16, 2006), 8–11, available at http://www.eda.admin.ch/etc/medialib/downloads/edazen/topics/intla/humlaw.Par.0071.File.tmp/Presentation%20PMSC%20and%20Int.%20Hum.%20Law.pdf

36 See Alexandre Faite, "Involvement of Private Contractors in Armed Conflict: Implications Under International Humanitarian Law," *Defence Studies* 4, no. 2 (2004): 166, 175–79.

37 Liu, "Leashing the Corporate Dogs of War," 142.

38 See Faite, "Involvement of Private Contractors in Armed Conflict," 166–67.

39 See U.N. International Convention against the Recruitment, Use, Financing and Training of Mercenaries, art. 1(2), (December 4, 1989), U.N. Doc. A/RES/44/34 ("A mercenary is also any person who … (d) [h]as not been sent by a State on official duty"); Protocol Additional to the Geneva Conventions of August 12, 1949, and Relating to the Protection of Victims of International Armed Conflicts, June 8, 1977, 1125 UNTS 3, art. 47 (hereinafter *Additional Protocol I*).

40 See, e.g., Richard Morgan, "Professional Military Firms Under International Law," *Chicago Journal of International Law* 9 (2008): 213, 218; Kidane, "Status Of Private Military Contractors Under International Humanitarian Law," 391–403; Faite, "Involvement of Private Contractors in Armed Conflict," 5–6.

41 Kidane, "Status Of Private Military Contractors Under International Humanitarian Law," 413.

42 Convention (IV) Respecting the Laws and Customs of War on Land, October 18, 1907, art. 3, 36 Stat. 2277; Additional Protocol I, art. 91.

43 International Law Commission (hereafter ILC), Draft Articles on Responsibility of States for Internationally Wrongful Acts, art. 1, U.N. GAOR, 56th Sess., Supp. No. 10, U.N. Doc. A/56/10 (2001).

44 See Nigel D. White's contribution on the ILC Articles on State Responsibility, in this issue.

45 ILC, Articles on Responsibility of State for International Wrongful Acts, arts. 5, 8, U.N. GAOR, 56th Sess., Supp. No. 10, U.N. Doc. A/56/10 (2001).

46 *In re Xe Services Alien Tort Litigation*, 665 F. Supp. 2d 569 (ED Va. 2009).

47 See Benjamin Perrin's contribution on international crimes, in this issue.

48 Chia Lehnardt, "Individual Liability of Private Military Personnel Under International Criminal Law," *European Journal of International Law* 19 (2008): 1015, 1016.

49 See, e.g., Allison Marston Danner, "When Courts Make Law: How the International Criminal Tribunals Recast the Laws of War," *Vanderbilt Law Review* 59 (2006): 1, 3 (discussing International Criminal Tribunal for the Former Yugoslavia and International Criminal Tribunal for Rwanda jurisprudence as codified into the ICC and playing an important role in developing international criminal law norms).

50 Rome Statute of the International Criminal Court, July 17, 1998, U.N. Doc. A/CONF 183/9, arts. 1, 5(1); reprinted in 37 *International Legal Materials* [ILM] 99 (1998) (hereinafter *Rome Statute*).

51 *Rome Statute*, arts. 7–8.

52 Lehnardt, "Individual Liability of Private Military Personnel Under International Criminal Law," 1017–18 (citing jurisprudence in the International Criminal Tribunal for Rwanda).

53 *Rome Statute*, art. 7.

54 Ibid., arts. 4(2), 11–12; ICC, "Jurisdiction and Admissibility," available at: http://www.icc-cpi.int/Menus/ICC/About+the+Court/ICC+at+a+glance/Jurisdiction+and+Admissibility.htm

55 U.N., Chapter XVIII: Penal Matters: Rome Statute of the International Criminal Court, U.N. Treaty Collection, available at http://treaties.un.org/Pages/ViewDetails.aspx?src=TREATY&mtdsg_no=XVIII-10&chapter=18&lang=en

56 Report of the Working Group on the use of mercenaries as a means of violating human rights and impeding the exercise of the right of peoples to self-determination, Mission to Iraq, sec. 21, U.N. Doc. A/HRC/18/32/Add.4 (August 12, 2011).

57 Victor Peskin, "Caution and Confrontation in the International Criminal Court's Pursuit of Accountability in Uganda and Sudan," *Human Rights Quarterly* 31 (2009): 655, 656–59.

58 Sabrina Tavernise and Graham Bowley, "Iraq to Review All Security Contractors," *New York Times*, September 18, 2007, available at http://www.nytimes.com/2007/09/18/world/middleeast/18cnd-iraq.html. See also Coalition Provisional Authority Order 17 (Revised), Status of the Coalition Provisional Authority, MNF – Iraq, Certain Missions and Personnel in Iraq, sec. 2, CPA/ORD/27 (June 2004).

59 See, e.g., Sewell Chan, "U.S. Civilians Mutilated in Iraq Attack," *Washington Post*, April 1, 2004, available at http://www.washingtonpost.com/ac2/wp-dyn?pagename=article&node=&contentId=A40722-2004Mar31&notFound=true; Julian Borger, "U.S. Military in Torture Scandal," *Guardian*, April 30, 2004, available at http://www.guardian.co.uk/media/2004/apr/30/television.internationalnews; Eric Schmitt, "Inquiry Ordered into Reports of Prisoner Abuse," *New York Times*, January 17, 2004, available at http://www.nytimes.com/2004/01/17/world/inquiry-ordered-into-reports-of-prisoner-abuse.html?ref=abughraib

60 See James Glanz and Alissa J. Rubin, "From Errand to Fatal Shot to Hail of Fire to 17 Deaths," *New York Times*, October 3, 2007, available at http://www.nytimes.com/2007/10/03/world/middleeast/03firefight.html?pagewanted=all

61 Prado, "A United Nations Instrument to Regulate and Monitor Private Military and Security Contractors," 17–23.

62 See Nigel D. White's contribution regarding the Montreux Process and the U.N. Draft Convention and José L. Gómez del Prado's contribution regarding the U.N. Draft Convention, in this issue.

63 Permanent Representative of Switzerland (Peter Maurer) to the U.N., Letter, October 2, 2008, addressed to the Secretary-General of the Security Council, U.N. Doc. A/63/467-S/2008/636 (October 6, 2008). See Switzerland Federal Ministry of Foreign Affairs, "The Montreux Document on Private Military and Security Companies", available at http://www.eda.admin.ch/eda/en/home/topics/intla/humlaw/pse/psechi.html

64 *Montreux Document*.

65 Ibid.

66 Ibid. See James Cockayne, "Regulating Private Military and Security Companies: The Content Negotiation, Weaknesses, and the Promise of the Montreux Document," *Journal of Conflict and Security Law* 13 (2008): 401, 402 (noting "good practices" drafted with reference to codes of conduct, domestic legislation, regulations, and political statements).

67 *Montreux Document*, Part Two.

68 Ibid., Part One, secs. 1, 3(c), 4, 6, 8; see also secs. 3(b), 5, 7.

69 Ibid., Part One, sec. 2.

70 Ibid., Part Two, sec. A, I–IV.

71 Ibid., Part Two, sec. A, II.4. See Allison Stanger's contribution regarding transparency as a mechanism of compliance, in this issue.

72 U.N. Human Rights Council, Report of the Working Group on the use of mercenaries as a means of violating human rights and impeding the exercise of the right of self-determination, July 2, 2010, U.N. Doc. A/HRC/15/25, Annex ("Draft of a possible Convention on Private Military and Security Companies (PMSCs) for consideration and action by the Human Rights Council").

73 The Geneva Conventions explicitly assign to state agents the responsibility of guarding prisoner of war camps and civilian internees. See *Montreux Document*, Part One, sec. A, sec. 2.

74 *Draft Convention*, arts. 2(i), 9.

75 Ibid., arts. 4(3), 4(5), 9.

76 See Duncan Hunter National Defense Authorization Act for Fiscal Year 2009, Pub. L. No 110-417, par. 321 (2008).

77 See Kristine Huskey and Scott Sullivan, "United States: Law and Policy Governing Private Military Contractors After 9/11," in *Multilevel Regulation of Military and Security Contractors*, ed. Christine Bakker and Mirko Sossai (Oxford, UK: Hart, 2011), 331, 339–41.

78 *Draft Convention*, arts. 4(2), 15(1)(ii), 14(3), 17(2)–(3), 18(3), 20(1).

79 Ibid., arts. 14(3), 16(1)(b).

80 Ibid., art. 18.

81 Ibid., art. 4(1).

82 Ibid., art. 19.

83 Ibid., arts. 19(4), 20(4); see also art. 23(1).

Mind the Gap: Lacunae in the International Legal Framework Governing Private Military and Security Companies

BENJAMIN PERRIN*

This article examines the common claim that there are gaps in international law that undermine accountability of private military and security companies. A multi-actor analysis examines this question in relation to the commission of international crimes, violations of fundamental human rights, and ordinary crimes. Without this critical first step of identifying specific deficiencies in international law, the debate about how to enhance accountability within this sector is likely to be misguided at best.

Benjamin Perrin is an associate professor at the University of British Columbia, Faculty of Law, and a faculty associate at the Liu Institute for Global Issues. Professor Perrin holds a Master of Laws (with honours) from McGill University, a Juris Doctor from the University of Toronto, and a Bachelor of Commerce (with distinction), specializing in international business, from the University of Calgary. He was a law clerk at the Supreme Court of Canada, and judicial intern at the International Tribunal for the former Yugoslavia

I. Introduction

This article investigates the frequently made claim that there are "vacuums" or "gaps"[1] in the legal framework governing private military and security companies (PMSCs)[2] that have given rise to a "regulatory problem, namely, the violation of human rights and noncompliance with international humanitarian law (IHL) by the global security industry."[3] Through a rigorous step-by-step analysis, this article aims to identify precisely where gaps in international law arise with respect to the commission of international crimes, violations of fundamental human rights, and ordinary crimes. It does not delve deeply into enforcement issues, but rather focuses on the preliminary issues of the formal existence of relevant substantive law and jurisdiction, and some ethical ramifications of these legal findings.

The focus of this article is on the extent to which international law currently provides substantive norms and confers jurisdiction to enforce norms that are most relevant to PMSCs. The methodology for analysis is described and then applied to identify specific lacunae in the international legal framework and accountability mechanisms governing alleged misconduct by PMSC employees. Gaps related to criminal liability and state responsibility that are identified herein may be addressed through a variety of approaches, but without this critical first step of identifying specific deficiencies, the debate about solutions is likely to be misguided at best.

2. Methodology

For the purposes of the legal analysis that follows, I use the generic term "incident" to refer to an act or omission by an individual employee or employees working for a particular PMSC. To streamline analysis, incidents are considered in the following categories (this classification is introduced with the understanding that there is a certain degree of overlap among these categories):

(1) International crimes (specifically, genocide, crimes against humanity, and war crimes);
(2) International human rights violations (e.g., preventing the right to peaceful assembly, arbitrary detention, and degrading treatment); and
(3) Ordinary crimes (e.g., murder, sexual assault, theft, and dangerous use of a firearm).

Although an individual employee or employees bring about an incident, multiple actors may be held legally responsible. The following types of actors will, therefore, be considered in the analysis that follows to determine the extent of any gaps in the international legal framework governing PMSC activity more broadly:

A. Employee(s) of the PMSC who directly caused the "incident";
B. PMSC (including supervisors, and the officers and directors of the company);
C. Client of the PMSC (which may be a contracting state or a non-state client);
D. Territorial State (i.e., the country in which the incident took place);
E. Home State (i.e., the country in which the PMSC is registered or incorporated); and
F. Nationality State (i.e., the country of nationality of the PMSC employee).

It is important to note that the analysis in this paper on the existence of gaps in the international legal framework governing PMSC activity is a legal analysis focusing on perceived substantive and jurisdictional gaps. In other words, it primarily seeks to analyze the state of the law rather than the political will to enforce the law.

3. International Crimes

A. Employees

PMSC employees who commit genocide, crimes against humanity, or war crimes may be criminally prosecuted pursuant to international law. At least with respect to these most serious of crimes, there is no "gap" in the international law governing accountability for PMSCs. Genocide, crimes against humanity, and war crimes are international crimes of universal jurisdiction. This means that under customary international law, perpetrators may be prosecuted by any state in their national courts.[4]

Genocide, crimes against humanity, and war crimes committed by employees of PMSCs may also be prosecuted before the International Criminal Court (ICC), if the conditions for exercising jurisdiction are met. A key jurisdictional requirement is that either the incident took place in the territory of a state party to the Rome Statute, or was committed by a national of a state party to the Rome Statute. In either case, the state party must be found to be either unwilling or unable genuinely to investigate and prosecute the perpetrator.[5] The ICC may also hear cases that have taken place in a situation that has been referred to it by the United Nations Security Council (UNSC) acting under Chapter VII of the UN Charter.[6] In all cases, the incident must be sufficiently grave for the ICC to exercise jurisdiction.

Despite the theoretical availability of national courts, specialized international courts and tribunals, and in some cases the ICC, to prosecute employees of PMSCs for international crimes, the substantive definition of each of these crimes includes onerous elements that are likely to be met in only the most egregious cases of gross misconduct. Most notably, a genocide conviction requires the special "intent to destroy, in whole or in part, a national, ethnical, racial or religious group, as such."[7] Establishing special intent can be an arduous task. With respect to crimes against humanity, it is insufficient that an employee of a PMSC engaged in an isolated act of murder, extermination, forcible transfer, torture, rape, or other inhumane act. For a crime against humanity to exist, the incident must have been "committed as part of a widespread or systematic attack directed against a civilian population" and, further, "[t]he perpetrator [must have known] that the conduct was part of or intended . . . to be part of a widespread or systematic attack against a civilian population."[8] Many of the more egregious allegations of misconduct by employees of PMSCs appear to be "isolated or sporadic events"[9] that would prevent them from being classified as crimes against humanity.

Finally, of the three international crimes under review, war crimes are arguably the least onerous to establish. Unlike genocide, there is no special intent requirement for a war crime and, unlike crimes against humanity, a war crime can comprise a single incident. The *chapeau* element for war crimes is instead the "nexus requirement," namely that the incident "took place in the context of and was associated with an . . . armed conflict" and that the "perpetrator was aware of factual circumstances that established the existence of an armed conflict."[10] In other words, a war crime can take place only during an international or non-international armed conflict, or belligerent occupation. Thus, it is impossible for an incident to be classified as a war crime unless international humanitarian law is applicable at the time and in the territory that the incident occurred. Although many PMSCs operate in conflict or post-conflict zones in which IHL would apply, others instead operate in fragile, failed, or failing states where IHL would not apply.

To sum up, though there is no formal substantive gap in the international legal framework with respect to individual employees of PMSCs committing genocide, crimes against humanity, or war crimes, there is likely to be very limited recourse to the ICC as a forum. In addition, there is inherent difficulty in establishing the special elements of each of these grave crimes. As with other alleged international criminals, the primary responsibility for prosecution lies with national courts. Due to universal jurisdiction over these crimes, any state may exercise jurisdiction.

B. PMSC

In addition to holding individuals who are the direct perpetrators of international crimes liable, there is a growing interest in also ensuring that if employees are acting on behalf of a company, the legal entity of the firm should also be held responsible. This may take place most commonly through private lawsuits, but some states also allow companies to be criminally charged. Although a legal entity obviously cannot be imprisoned, the gravity of a criminal conviction is significant due to the reputational impact and potential harm to future business interests (for example, investors and joint ventures falling through). Sentencing can also carry significant consequences with orders to pay substantial fines or restitution to victims.

There are several reasons why human rights advocates (in particular) pursue corporate criminal liability. To begin with, individuals rarely act alone in committing international crimes. Other agents, employees, representatives, or superiors in the company may have been complicit in the crime. Additionally, corporate liability is often favored due to corporate deep pockets, making it more likely that fines or restitution orders to victims in criminal cases can compensate for the harm caused. It is also believed that the mere ability to hold a company responsible in law for the conduct of its employees will incentivize better behavior on its part, as part of a preventative approach to crime reduction.

International criminal law has favored individual criminal responsibility for natural persons rather than collective criminal responsibility (that is, crimes committed by states or other legal entities). Most notably for the present analysis, states party to the Rome Statute made a deliberate decision during the Rome Conference negotiations that the ICC would not have jurisdiction to prosecute corporate entities as such.[11] However, at the ICC and under international criminal law more generally, individuals holding leadership responsibilities within a corporation may be held liable, inter alia, for ordering, planning, or instigating international crimes,or for the international crimes committed by their subordinates under the doctrine of superior criminal responsibility. This approach has the advantage of incentivizing individuals in leadership positions within corporations to take preventative action to ensure their subordinates are neither directly committing nor otherwise participating in such crimes. However, the company itself and its finances remain out of reach of the ICC.

Certain states may hold companies liable under their domestic law for international crimes committed by their employees. Rules of criminal attribution for corporate wrongdoing vary, based on national law. In my view, there is insufficient case law at the international level to recognize a settled standard of criminal attribution for corporate liability.

To sum up, though private military and security companies cannot be prosecuted for international crimes before the ICC, superiors within these companies may be held individually liable for ordering, planning, or instigating international crimes, or for failing to prevent or punish international crimes committed by their subordinates. Under national laws, the ability to hold a company as a legal entity criminally or civilly liable for international crimes varies widely.

C. Contracting State

The public international law doctrine on State Responsibility sets out the principles by which a state is responsible for internationally wrongful acts. Indeed, state responsibility is the dominant theme of the Montreux Document, which aims to clarify the primary means by which to address the accountability of PMSCs.

Under customary international law, states are responsible not only for violations that are committed by their armed forces and other governmental organs, but also for violations that occur in three other general instances. First, state responsibility arises for "violations committed by persons or entities it empowered to exercise elements of governmental authority," second, for "violations committed by persons or groups acting in fact on its instructions, or under its direction or control," and third, for "violations committed by private persons or groups which it acknowledges and adopts as its own conduct."[12] In the first instance, the question of what constitutes "governmental authority" is critical and has been discussed in the literature.[13] It is interesting to see that the UN Draft International Convention on the Regulation, Oversight and Monitoring of Private Military and Security Companies (UN Draft Convention) prohibits "governmental functions" from being carried out by PMSCs.[14]

The responsibility of a contracting state is independent from the obligation of the territorial state to prosecute perpetrators for committing genocide, crimes against humanity, and war crimes.[15] In other words, a contracting state would still bear legal responsibility for international crimes attributable to it when the territorial state has met its obligations to punish the perpetrators. This would hold true even where the contracting and territorial state are the same.

The primary limitation in holding a contracting state liable for international crimes committed by its PMSCs, beyond meeting these onerous attribution rules, is enforcement of these norms. Internationally wrongful acts of this nature would ordinarily be remedied on a direct-claim basis where an aggrieved state seeks redress directly from the contracting state. Without a supervening authority, the processing of the claim becomes largely a diplomatic matter. In certain instances, however, the International Court of Justice (ICJ) could have jurisdiction to adjudicate such a case. This would require special agreement by the aggrieved state and the contracting state, the contracting state having submitted to the compulsory jurisdiction of the ICJ or a binding international treaty that confers jurisdiction on the ICJ.[16] In most incidents, however, these jurisdictional requirements will not be met and the contracting state will not be held accountable for PMSC conduct.

D. Non-State Client

Non-state client organizations (i.e., corporations, non-governmental organizations, etc.) are essentially governed by the same legal principles as PMSCs themselves, as discussed above. In other words, these legal entities cannot be prosecuted before the ICC, but individuals in positions of authority within them may face prosecution for direct or indirect modes of criminal liability, including superior criminal responsibility under international criminal law. However, this particular mode of liability would require, inter alia,

a superior-subordinate relationship of effective control in order for an individual who is part of a non-state client organization to be legally responsible for the wrongful action of a PMSC employee. This is not dependent on the formal language employed in the contract for services between the PMSC and non-state client, but rather on the de facto powers that can be proven to have been held by the individual who is part of the non-state client organization.[17]

E. Territorial State

Even where a state does not contract for the services of a PMSC, it may still be responsible for the actions of PMSCs that operate on its territory. Scholars have argued that "a State that failed to exercise due diligence in preventing and punishing the unlawful actions of armed groups could be held responsible for such failure."[18] There is no principled basis on which to exclude PMSCs from this rule. In other words, a territorial state would be responsible for its failure to exercise due diligence through necessary regulation of PMSCs within its territory.[19] As discussed above with respect to contracting states, the primary obstacle to this form of liability is enforcement.

F. Home State

The home state of a PMSC whose employee(s) commit an international crime is not responsible under general rules of State Responsibility. In my view, neither is there an analogous obligation owed by home states, as is owed by territorial states, to exercise due diligence in regulating the conduct of PMSCs. This could be seen to be one of the greatest "gaps" in the international legal framework governing PMSCs—the presence of a significant disparity between the formal law and ethical precepts. It is particularly problematic because home states enjoy economic benefits from the PMSCs that are incorporated in their country, including through direct investment, employment, and tax revenues. This disconnect between accrued benefits to home states and lack of legal responsibility for the actions of PMSCs is at the root of a deficient international regulatory framework governing PMSCs, particularly given that most PMSCs originate in developed countries that have the ability to regulate them. This lack of accountability coupled with significant financial benefit actually creates a disincentive for home states to regulate PMSC conduct abroad, as they currently gain without any significant risk. This ethical gap is compounded by the fact that territorial states are invariably less equipped to develop, implement, and enforce regulations on PMSCs than home states, since the former are typically suffering from a breakdown of public institutions, thus creating a demand for private security, whereas the latter have stable public institutions that are attractive for investors. This disconnect between the legal responsibilities of home states and the ethical necessity to regulate PMSC conduct adequately represents a serious gap in PMSC accountability.

Much effort has been expended in the attempt to breathe life into the international obligation of states to "ensure respect" for IHL, as set out in Common Article 1 to the 1949 Geneva Conventions. Alexandre Faite, legal advisor to the International Committee of the Red Cross, has made the argument that home states have substantive obligations with respect to their PMSCs.[20] Unfortunately, the abstract and unspecified nature of the "ensure respect" obligation makes it implausible to read into the obligation more than a prohibition against states to condone, counsel, or assist in any way in the violation of IHL by its own organs, nationals, or PMSCs incorporated within its borders. It is certainly not a sufficient basis on which to assert a positive obligation on the part of home states to enact laws or regulations directed at securing the compliance of PMSCs with IHL or lesser standards.[21] Where home states have enacted laws to regulate PMSCs, they have done so largely for reasons unrelated to ensuring these companies and employees comply with IHL.[22] The United States provides the most notable example of extraterritorial regulations on PMSC activity, as discussed below.

Using a different example, it has been repeatedly noted that Canada, which is a minor home state, has no legislation that is specifically designed to regulate PMSCs while they are operating outside of Canada. Nevertheless, the combined effects of the Canadian *Criminal Code*[23] and *Crimes Against Humanity and War Crimes Act*[24] could be used to prosecute both Canadian nationals who are employees of PMSCs and the PMSCs themselves as corporate entities for genocide, war crimes, and crimes against humanity.[25]

There are issues, however, with the unilateral extraterritorial regulation of PMSCs by home states. First, it may impugn the sovereignty of territorial states by applying different or even conflicting standards. Second, some argue that it would be an unjustified and improper restraint on the legitimate exercise of commercial interests—and possibly even a violation of international trade in services agreements.

Several reasons have been offered in the literature for why home states are reluctant regulators. First, "charter shopping" is the concern that onerous regulations will simply cause PMSCs to relocate to states in which standards are less cumbersome and liability exposure is reduced.[26] Second, a conflict of interest arises where home states are also contracting states, as they may be "disinclined to act at the same time as effective regulators."[27]

G. Nationality State

Countries are not generally responsible for the international crimes committed by their nationals abroad. Thus, the nationality state of an employee of a PMSC is not legally responsible for any international crimes such individuals commit. Laws prohibiting a country's nationals from engaging in armed service for a foreign power often do not extend to PMSCs,[28] and the existence of such laws does not imply a corollary state responsibility with respect to the conduct of that state's nationals abroad. While this is a "gap" in the international regulatory framework governing PMSCs, it is not as significant as the gap discussed with respect to home states. Nationality states receive few benefits from the expatriate work of their nationals for PMSCs, particularly if they do not have a taxation regime based on worldwide income. Due diligence-style regulation of individuals, as opposed to companies, is also far less efficient and more difficult to enforce than regulation of the PMSCs by home states. Consequently, though it may be said that nationality states represent a "gap" in the international regulatory framework governing PMSC employees committing war crimes, it is not one that should be a priority to fill.

4. International Human Rights Violations

It is generally accepted that international human rights law recognizes rights held by individuals, secured as obligations against the state.[30] Violations of human rights may take place directly through the state's laws or the conduct of its public officials. The conventional view is, thus, that only states can violate international human rights, which is an inherent limitation in this body of law with respect to actions undertaken directly by non-state actors, such as PMSCs.

Although the state owes international human rights obligations to individuals within its jurisdiction, the actions of private actors may impugn these rights in several ways. First, as discussed above, a state may be responsible through the public international law doctrine of State Responsibility for the conduct of private actors in the following ways: for "violations committed by persons or entities it empowered to exercise elements of governmental authority," for "violations committed by persons or groups acting in fact on its instructions, or under its direction or control," or for "violations committed by private persons or groups which it acknowledges and adopts as its own conduct."[30]

Second, some commentators and courts have suggested that a state may be responsible for human rights violations that are directly caused by independent private actors, but in which the harm transpired due to of a "lack of protection by public authorities."[31] For example, in *X and Y v. the Netherlands*, the European Court of Human Rights (ECtHR) held that the Dutch government was responsible for a citizen's violation of a mentally handicapped citizen's human rights because of a statutory gap that would not allow the victim's father to file a criminal complaint for sexual assault.[32] The notion is that the state—through its inaction or omission—contributes to the violation of individual human rights. This view was reaffirmed in the *Case of Velásquez-Rodríguez v. Honduras*, in which the Inter-American Court of Human Rights stated that: "Where the acts of private parties that violate the Convention are not seriously investigated, those parties are aided in a sense by the government, thereby making the State responsible on the international plane."[33] This proposition hinged on a recognized duty under the American Convention on Human Rights that "States must prevent, investigate and punish any violation of the rights recognized by the Convention"[34] as part of their "due diligence to prevent the violation or to respond to it as required by the Convention."[35] The strongest support for this notion comes from the African Commission on Human and Peoples' Rights in *Social and Economic Rights Action Center v. Nigeria*, which explicitly states that "[g]overnments have a duty to pro-

tect their citizens, not only through appropriate legislation and effective enforcement, but also by protecting them from damaging acts that may be perpetrated by private parties."[36]

These decisions signify a shift toward increased state accountability for human rights and a growing willingness to recognize state responsibility for the acts of private entities. In my opinion, however, they do not demonstrate sufficient state practice and *opinio juris* to find that customary international law obligates such a state responsibility. This is even more doubtful when applied to human rights violations committed by private citizens of a home state in other jurisdictions, as all of the above case law has found state failure to protect its citizens only for acts that occurred within the territory of the state.

Remedial action with respect to violations of international human rights law depends largely on treaty-based enforcement mechanisms, which can include access to international or national courts, human rights tribunals, monitoring and complaint committees, and other such bodies.

In contrast to the conventional state-centric view of international human rights, commentators like Andrew Clapham advance the view that non-state actors are bound to a minimum standard of adherence to human rights. Clapham highlights the concept of "general principles common to international human rights law,"[37] which were articulated by the Guatemalan Historical Clarification Commission as applicable to non-state actors. He also notes the findings of the Truth and Reconciliation Commission of Sierra Leone that a PMSC (Executive Outcomes) committed "human rights violations."[38] However, others, such as

Philip Alston, UN Special Rapporteur on Extrajudicial, Summary, or Arbitrary Executions, have not gone so far as to characterize non-state actors as having legal *obligations* with respect to human rights, but instead argue for "human rights expectations"[39] on non-state actors. But the term "expectations," with shadows of the common law of contracts, carries little strength in contrast to binding obligations.

Clapham also cites instances in which the UN Security Council has called on "various groups ... to formally assume international obligations to respect human rights,"[40] but those instances have been tied to armed groups with some degree of territorial control—something PMSCs invariably lack. Clapham's ambitious and admirable project to seek to extend international human rights law directly to non-state actors is at its high-water mark when the relevant non-state actor has effective control over some territory, and the situation is one of armed conflict. In such situations, certain obligations that could ordinarily be called human rights are mirrored in the overlapping IHL obligations that more clearly apply to non-state parties to armed conflicts.

The prevailing state of international law is unlikely to hold that PMSCs acting for non-state clients[41] are bound by international human rights law. The Montreux Document states that "PMSCs are obliged to comply with international humanitarian law or human rights law *imposed upon them by applicable national law.*"[42] This clarifies that international human rights law does not automatically apply to PMSCs absent national legislation. The contrast between the application of international humanitarian law and international human rights law (IHRL) to PMSCs could not be

clearer in the Montreux Document—they are bound by the former body of law, and only by the latter if they exercise governmental authority (at the behest of a state client):

26. *The personnel of PMSCs:*
a) are obliged, regardless of their status, to comply with applicable international humanitarian law;
[...]
d) to the extent they exercise governmental authority, *have to comply with* the State's *obligations under international human rights law*[43]

However, it bears noting that the UN Draft Convention on PMSCs seeks to develop international law by extending a range of international human rights law obligations as directly applicable to PMSCs, and the UN Working Group on mercenaries has already been tasked with monitoring the effects of PMSCs on human rights.[44]

We find ourselves, thus, at an interesting point in history where strict adherence to the conventional state-centric view of international human rights law is eroding, but not to a point that would enable an incident by a PMSC employee acting for a non-state client to be readily classified as a violation of international human rights law. This is despite efforts to encourage and monitor their compliance with those standards. Consequently, there can be said to be a gap in the international human rights law framework with respect to these incidents.

A. Employees

Holding individual employees of PMSCs responsible for violations of international human rights faces a double-hurdle that is inherent in this body of law: first, the actors themselves are individuals; and second, they are employed by a private organization. Hence, any attempt to hold individual employees directly accountable for international human rights violations is likely to fail, unless their conduct can be characterized as ordinary crimes. In the latter case, the forthcoming analysis on such incidents comes into play, with unique limitations as well.

B. PMSC

As noted above, since international human rights law secures rights against the state, violations of those rights by PMSCs are unlikely to result in direct responsibility for the companies. Indirect legal responsibility of PMSCs in such instances could take place on a civil basis if they act for a state client who sues the PMSC to indemnify them for violations that are attributable to the state in the unique circumstances contemplated below. Generally, however, as with employees of PMSCs, the PMSCs themselves are unlikely to be held responsible for international human rights violations committed by their employees unless the conduct can be characterized as ordinary crimes, subject to the analysis that follows below.

C. Contracting State

In the event of an incident in which a PMSC employee violates a person's international human rights, the public international law doctrine of State Responsibility, with its previously recognized limitations, may make the contracting state responsible for the following: "violations committed by persons or entities it empowered to exercise elements of governmental authority," "violations committed by persons or groups acting in fact on its instructions, or under its direction or control," or "violations committed by private persons or groups which it acknowledges and adopts as its own conduct."[45]

D. Non-State Client

An incident committed by a PMSC employee acting for a non-state client cannot be characterized as a violation of international human rights that could involve responsibility of the non-state client, due again to the private nature of the conduct and the inherent limitation of international human rights law in terms of rights of individuals owed by the state. In such a situation, the only party that could be held responsible under international human rights law could potentially be the territorial state, based on a somewhat tenuous "due diligence" argument, as discussed above.

E. Territorial State

The territorial state in which an alleged violation of international human rights law occurs may have specific obligations even when it is not the contracting state. However, this is at most a crystallizing area of custom. Again, the difficult case must be made that there was a lack of protection by public authorities, and, even if that is persuasively argued in the context of an incident involving a PMSC employee, there is the issue of an effective forum to adjudicate the claim and award a remedy. This varies based on the particular treaty that recognizes the particular right that has been violated. The issue of an effective forum and remedy for alleged international human rights violations is an issue that has plagued this body of law since its expansion after World War II.

F. Home State

It is unlikely that home states can be said to owe obligations under international human rights law to regulate their PMSCs operating abroad. International human rights law lacks the general admonition that states "ensure respect" for fundamental human rights.[46] The extraterritorial extension of state human rights obligations is at most an unsettled area of law. Although the European Court of Human Rights has occasionally recognized the extraterritorial application of state human rights obligations,[47] the method by which these obligations apply has appeared to fluctuate over time.

The most recent formulation in Al-Skeini requires that, if the state is to incur responsibility for human rights violations outside its own territory, it should exercise over the territory in question "some of the public powers normally to be exercised by a sovereign government." In this context, soldiers engaged in security operations exercise "authority and control over individuals killed in the course of such security operations."[48] This represents a combination of spatial and personal jurisdiction.

In contrast, Canadian courts have been willing to apply human rights obligations encapsulated in the *Canadian Charter of Rights and Freedoms* only if Canada had effective control *over the territory* in which a rights violation allegedly occurred.[49] In fact, in *Amnesty International v. Canada*, Desjardins, J. A., rejected application of the *Charter* in Afghan detention facilities under control of the Canadian forces in part because several international security forces shared those facilities.[50] Under the *Al-Skeini* test for jurisdiction, this factor would be irrelevant.[51] This inconsistent application of human rights documents coupled with the considerable likelihood that PMSC home states will never exercise public powers in the territory of PMSC operations abroad shows that home states are unlikely to be bound by human rights obligations for the acts of resident PMSCs.[52]

G. Nationality State

As with international crimes, nationality states have the weakest potential responsibility with respect to alleged violations of international human rights. Only with respect to violations of international human rights that are also characterized as international crimes (for example, torture) where there is an obligation to extradite or prosecute, are nationality states likely to have any obligation to act.

5. Ordinary Crimes

Even extremely serious "ordinary crimes," such as murder and rape, are generally considered to be within the ordinary jurisdiction of the territorial state in which they are committed.[53] International comity and the principle of non-interference generally prevent ordinary crimes from being prosecuted in non-territorial states. This substantially limits the role of international law in the proscriptive and enforcement aspects of ordinary criminal law, which is the bailiwick of national jurisdictions.[54]

One exception to this general rule of the territorial state being primarily empowered to enforce criminal law within its territory is with respect to members of its armed forces who are deployed abroad. Status of Forces Agreements are often entered into between the state in which the armed forces are operating and the state which is sending its armed forces. Such agreements specify rules about criminal and civil jurisdiction. National military law provides for procedures, most notably the court martial, to enforce the laws of the state of the armed forces throughout the world. These laws apply to so-called "ordinary crimes" as well as offenses that are particular to military service. The effect of these arrangements is that ordinary crimes committed by servicemen and servicewomen are frequently not subject to the ordinary jurisdiction of the territorial state in which alleged incidents are committed, but rather the home state of their armed forces. These time-honored arrangements have not been smoothly translated into the realm of PMSCs, giving rise to the greatest claims of impunity gaps.

A. Employees

The most notorious legal gap with respect to the commission of crimes by PMSC employees was one that was created by law. In occupied Iraq, Section 4(3) of Coalition Provisional Authority (CPA) Order No. 17 provided: "Contractors shall be immune from Iraqi legal process with respect to acts performed by them pursuant to the terms and conditions of a Contract or any sub-contract thereto . . ."[55]

In all situations in which either the law promulgated by an occupying power or a Status of Forces Agreement provides for immunity from local criminal jurisdiction for PMSC employees, there will be a gap in the regulatory framework with respect to the commission of ordinary crimes *unless* PMSC employees are working for a contracting state that has enacted special legislation subjecting them to the criminal jurisdiction of that contracting state.

For example, the national law of contracting states may provide that PMSC employees who are accompanying their armed forces abroad are subject to military disciplinary codes. Even in cases in which contracting states have such laws, they are customarily limited to those PMSC employees contracted to work directly for the armed forces. In other words, PMSC employees who work for non-state clients (for example, private companies and NGOs) and non-armed forces state clients (for example, embassies and development agencies) are typically not covered by such legislation. This infamous gap was exposed most prominently in Iraq with respect to criminal acts by PMSC employees working for the U.S. Department of State who enjoyed immunity from local prosecution under CPA Order No. 17, but who were not at the time subject to U.S. military discipline since they were not contracted to the U.S. Department of Defense. Controversy spurred several rounds of legislative reforms to attempt to fill this gap by extending the scope of U.S. military law to PMSC employees via the *Military Extraterritorial Jurisdiction Act*.[56]

Other countries have also been slow to react to this issue. Without explicitly mentioning PMSC employees, several Status of Forces Agreements entered into by Australia since 2003 may be seen as subjecting these individuals to either the concurrent or exclusive criminal jurisdiction of Australia.[57] Overall, it appears that insufficient attention has been paid to this issue and it should be expressly resolved prior to the deployment of PMSC personnel abroad.

B. PMSC

Many jurisdictions do not merely hold individuals responsible for ordinary crimes, but also have rules that attribute such criminal conduct to the organization that employs the principal offender as well. The rationale for corporate criminal liability was discussed above in the section dealing with international crimes, and it applies here as well. So, too, does the caution that national laws vary widely in the extent, if any, to which private corporations can be held criminally responsible for the conduct of their employees.

C. Contracting State

In certain instances, the previously discussed doctrine of State Responsibility may give rise to state responsibility for ordinary crimes committed by PMSCs acting for a contracting state. In many instances, however, the incident involving an ordinary crime may not be constituted as a "breach of an international obligation of the State,"[58] as required for State Responsibility to apply. It is more

likely that a contracting state implicated in an ordinary crime via the conduct of the PMSC employees that it hires could be seen to be in violation of the principle of non-interference in the domestic affairs of the territorial state.

D. Non-State Client

Party liability rules in national criminal law dictate the extent to which a non-state client may be held criminally liable for the ordinary crimes committed by PMSC employees. Depending on the applicable territorial state, the various modes of criminal liability may include aiding and abetting, incitement, planning, conspiracy, ordering, joint criminal enterprise/common intention, superior criminal responsibility, and so on.[59] Each of these modes of liability comes with its own unique requirements with respect to the prohibited conduct (*actus reus*) and the mental fault (*mens rea*) of the party. Hence, there are well-established legal rules and principles governing the attribution of party liability to a non-state client of a PMSC for ordinary crimes, but these are limited to enforcement in national courts of the territorial state, which may be unable or unwilling to pursue them.

An interesting question that has not yet been mooted is whether a non-state client may be held criminally responsible for an ordinary crime committed by its PMSC employees who have themselves been granted immunity from local prosecution by the territorial state. One view is that because there would effectively be no principal offender, there can be no party liability. Another view is that the immunity acts only to bar the prosecution of the principal offender, but does not prevent parties from being held liable because the immunity is an exception and applies only to those actors to whom it has been specifically granted. The latter view is more agreeable both as a matter of principle and law under most national systems. In principle, limitation of immunity enhances the accountability of non-state clients for the acts of contracted PMSCs, thus likely incentivizing those actors to seek the services of more prudent PMSCs. As a matter of law, most national systems interpret secondary modes of liability, such as aiding and abetting, as separate offenses to the principal crime that do not even require the apprehension or charge of a principal offender.[60] Immunities attach to the identities of principal offenders, excusing their individual acts, which would normally be criminal. Thus, since the aiding organization has committed a separate offense that does not require determination of the principal's identity, it is at the least arguable that the aider's offense will not be protected by the granted immunity. However, each state's national courts will address the issue from their own jurisprudence and legal traditions.

E. Territorial State

As discussed above, territorial states have the well-established jurisdiction under international law to proscribe, enforce, and adjudicate crimes committed within their territorial jurisdiction. However, this power itself does not create a corollary responsibility to investigate and prosecute ordinary crimes diligently, except insofar as international human rights law must be respected throughout the criminal justice process. The obligation of territorial states to extradite or prosecute individuals who commit ordinary crimes is limited to multilateral or bilateral treaties that exist with respect to specific serious crimes.

F. Home State

Because ordinary crimes fall within the plenary jurisdiction of the territorial states in which they are committed, there is no general obligation on home states of PMSCs to undertake any action whatsoever when an ordinary crime is committed by employees of a PMSC that is incorporated in their country.

G. Nationality State

Although some states with civilian legal traditions have laws that assert extraterritorial criminal jurisdiction over their nationals for very serious "ordinary crimes," there is no obligation under international law on the part of a state to prosecute one of its nationals for committing an ordinary crime abroad. The "gap" that is most significant with respect to nationality states is that though members of a national armed force operating abroad are invariably subject to military law, there is no general practice to subject members of PMSCs to military law. Nationality states may have certain treaty-specific obligations with respect to extradition, mutual legal assistance, and judicial cooperation when an ordinary crime is allegedly committed by a PSMC employee that is their national, but this depends on the existence of an applicable treaty dealing with criminal matters between the territorial and nationality state.

6. Conclusion

This essay has identified six significant gaps in the international legal framework governing PMSCs that should be of greatest priority to address:

(1) PMSCs as corporate entities are unlikely to face international criminal responsibility for international crimes due to the inability of the ICC to exercise jurisdiction over these legal entities, and uncertain rules for attribution of criminal liability to corporations under international law.

(2) Home states of PMSCs enjoy economic benefits, but lack a corresponding accountability under international law to proactively regulate the conduct of these firms abroad.

(3) Alleged international human rights law violations committed by PMSCs acting for non-state clients are unlikely to succeed in being characterized as international human rights violations, and thus go unaddressed under international law.

(4) Most international human rights treaties lack the specificity, or enforcement mechanism, to compel states to regulate PMSCs effectively. At this point in time, the legal responsibility of a state to exercise due diligence by enacting laws to regulate PMSCs extraterritorially is tenuous.

(5) Although PMSC employees are generally subject to the criminal jurisdiction of the territorial state, the territorial state may be unable or unwilling genuinely to investigate or prosecute the commission of ordinary crimes by such individuals.

(6) Where either the law promulgated by an occupying power or a Status of Forces Agreement provides for immunity from local criminal jurisdiction for PMSC employees, there will be a significant gap *unless* PMSC employees are working for a contracting state that has enacted special legislation subjecting them to the criminal jurisdiction of that state.

These findings are important in developing an agenda for law reform and accountability efforts at both the national and international levels. They also demonstrate the limitations of some current approaches to regulating PMSCs. For example, though the Montreux Document holds some promise, it is limited to the existing state of international human rights law and ordinary criminal jurisdiction, which are inadequate to govern PMSCs. Furthermore, focused as it is largely on State Responsibility, the Montreux Document provides little in terms of direct responsibility for PMSC perpetrators and the firms themselves. It is inadvisable to assume that enhanced state responsibility will lead to a trickle down to more effective national regulation of PMSCs, given that claims of state responsibility are few and far between. Furthermore, this approach to accountability is indirect.

In *Beyond Market Forces: Regulating the Global Security Industry*, the authors identify the problem to be "the lack of industry-wide standards to protect human rights and ensure respect for IHL, and effective arrangements for their implementation and enforcement."[61] However, the study assumes that national jurisdictions may be available to adjudicate "PMSC human rights violations,"[62] without grappling with the fundamental problem discussed in detail above—namely, the state-centric nature of international human rights law. As I have demonstrated here, the problem of PMSC accountability runs far deeper than a lack of industry-wide standards or willingness to prosecute suspects. Instead, it indicates inherent deficiencies in the applicability of international criminal law, international human rights law, and ordinary national criminal jurisdiction over allegations of misconduct by PMSC employees. Therefore, the long-term project required to regulate PMSCs effectively is far more ambitious, as it is the applicability of the legal norms themselves that is the threshold problem for achieving PMSC accountability.[63]

Notes

[This article is adapted from a paper presented at "Outsourcing Security: Private Military and Security Companies (PMSCs) and the Quest for Accountability" at John Jay College of Criminal Justice, City University of New York, October 7–8, 2011. The author is pleased to acknowledge research assistance from Jim Cruess and feedback on this paper from the conference organizers and participants. The views expressed in this article are those of the author alone.]

1 See, e.g., Alexandre Faite, "Involvement of Private Contractors in Armed Conflict: Implications under International Humanitarian Law," *Defence Studies* 4, no. 2 (2004): 166–83; P. W. Singer, "War, Profits, and the Vacuum of Law: Privatized Military Firms and International Law," *Columbia Journal of Transnational Law* 42 (2004): 521–50; David Antonyshyn, Jan Grofe, and Don Hubert, "Beyond the Law? The Regulation of Canadian Private Military and Security Companies Operating Abroad," *PRIV-WAR Report—Canada*, National Reports Series 03/09 (February 12, 2009): 33.

2 For the purposes of this article, the definition used is the one provided in *The Montreux Document on Pertinent International Legal Obligations and Good Practices for States Related to Operations of Private Military and Security Companies During Armed Conflict* (Montreux, Switzerland, September 17, 2008), 9; available online via the International Committee of the Red Cross, http://www.icrc.org/eng/assets/files/other/icrc_002_0996.pdf (accessed July 5, 2011): " 'PMSCs' are private business entities that provide military and/or security services, irrespective of how they describe themselves. Military and security services include, in particular, armed guarding and protection of persons and objects, such as convoys, buildings and other places; maintenance and operation of weapons systems; prisoner detention; and advice to or training of local forces and security personnel."

3 James Cockayne et al., *Beyond Market Forces: Regulating the Global Security Industry* (New York: International Peace Institute, 2009), 2.

4 However, absent particular legislation, PMSC employees are unlikely to fall within the jurisdiction of military courts and tribunals that are operational in conflict and post-conflict areas.

5 UN General Assembly, *Rome Statute of the International Criminal Court* (last amended January 2002), July 17, 1998, A/CONF. 183/9, Art. 17(1).

6 Ibid., Art. 13.

7 *Convention on the Prevention and Punishment of the Crime of Genocide*, Art. II, adopted by Resolution 260 (III) A of the U.N. General Assembly, December 9, 1948. Entry into force: January 12, 1951. *International Criminal Court Elements of Crimes* as reproduced from the *Official Records of the Assembly of States Parties to the Rome Statute of the International Criminal Court*, 1st session (New York, September 3–10, 2002), 2. United Nations Pub., No. E.03.V.2 and corrigendum, part II.B.

8 *ICC Elements of Crimes*, 5.

9 Antonio Cassese, *International Criminal Law*, 2nd ed. (Oxford: Oxford University Press, 2008), 98.

10 *ICC Elements of Crimes*, 15.

11 Rebecca Bratspies, " 'Organs of Society': A Plea for Human Rights Accountability for Transnational Enterprises and Other Business Entities," *Michigan State Journal of International Law* 13 (2005): 25–27.

12 Jean-Marie Henckaerts and Louise Doswald-Beck, *Customary International Humanitarian Law–Volume 1: Rules* (Cambridge: Cambridge University Press, 2005), 530. See also *Responsibility of States for Internationally Wrongful Acts*, Annex to GA Res 83, U.N. GAOR, 56th Sess., U.N. Doc A/Res/56/83 (2001).

13 James Cockayne, "Regulating Private Military and Security Companies: The Content, Negotiation, Weaknesses and Promise of the Montreux Document," *Journal of Conflict and Security Law* 13, no. 3 (2009): 410–11.

14 United Nations Office of the High Commissioner for Human Rights (UNHCR), Working Group on the Use of Mercenaries As a Means of Violating Human Rights and Impeding the Exercise of the Rights of Peoples to Self-Determination, *Draft International Convention on the Regulation, Oversight and Monitoring of Private Military and Security Companies* (final draft for distribution, July 13, 2009), Art. 2(k), 8, 31(5).

15 See Henckaerts and Doswald-Beck, *Customary International Humanitarian Law*, 531.

16 See, e.g., *Convention on the Prevention and Punishment of the Crime of Genocide*, Art. IX.

17 See Cassese, *International Criminal Law*, 247–49.

18 Henckaerts and Doswald-Beck, *Customary International Humanitarian Law*, 532.

19 See Louise Doswald-Beck, "Private Military Companies under International Humanitarian Law," in *From Mercenaries to Market: The Rise and Regulation of Private Military Companies*, ed. Simon Chesterman and Chia Lehnardt (Oxford: Oxford University Press, 2007), 20.

20 Faite, "Private Contractors in Armed Conflict."

21 Doswald-Beck, "Private Military Companies," 21.

22 See, e.g., Antonyshyn et al., "Beyond the Law," 9.

23 *Criminal Code*, RSC, 1985, c. C-46.

24 *Crimes Against Humanity and War Crimes Act*, SC 2000, c. 24.

25 See W. Cory Wanless, "Corporate Liability for International Crimes under Canada's Crimes Against Humanity and War Crimes Act," *Journal of International Criminal Justice* 7 (2009): 201–21.

26 See Benjamin Perrin, "Promoting Compliance of Private Security and Military Companies with International Humanitarian Law," *International Review of the Red Cross* 88, no. 863 (2006): 616; Antonyshyn et al., "Beyond the Law," 3.

27 Antonyshyn et al., "Beyond the Law," 3.

28 Ibid., 8.

29 Liesbeth Zegveld, *Accountability of Armed Opposition Groups in International Law* (Cambridge, UK: Cambridge University Press, 2002), 53.

30 Henckaerts and Doswald-Beck, *Customary International Humanitarian Law*, 530.

31 Anthony Aust, *Handbook of International Law*, 2nd ed. (Cambridge, UK: Cambridge University Press, 2010), 217.

32 *X and Y v. the Netherlands* (1985) 8 EHRR 235 at para. 23, 27–30.

33 *Case of Velásquez-Rodríguez v. Honduras* (1988), Judgment of July 29, 1988, Inter-

American Court of Human Rights (Ser. C) No. 1 at para. 177.

34 Ibid., para. 166.

35 Ibid., para. 172.

36 *The Social and Economic Rights Action Center v. Nigeria* (2001), African Commission on Human and People's Rights, October 27, 2001, Comm 155/96, para. 57.

37 Andrew Clapham, "Human Rights Obligations of Non-State Actors in Conflict Situations," *International Review of the Red Cross* 88, no. 863 (2006): 503; the Guatemalan Historical Clarification Commission conceived of this concept to encompass the "prohibition on torture, inhumane and degrading treatment, a prohibition on hostage-taking, guarantees of fair trial and physical liberty for the individual." See ibid., 504.

38 Ibid., 504.

39 Cited in ibid., 506.

40 Ibid., 507.

41 Even with state clients, the response to human rights violations by PMSC employees has been inadequate. See Clapham's discussion of the aftermath of the Abu Ghraib scandal. Ibid., 518.

42 *Montreux Document*, para. 22 (emphasis added).

43 Ibid., para. 26 (emphasis added).

44 For more on the U.N. Draft Convention, see José Gómez del Prado's contribution in this issue.

45 Henckaerts and Doswald-Beck, *Customary International Humanitarian Law*, 530.

46 The preamble of the U.N. General Assembly, *Universal Declaration of Human Rights*, December 10, 1948, 217 A (III) instead "proclaims... that every individual and every organ of society, keeping this Declaration constantly in mind, shall strive by teaching and education to promote respect for these rights and freedoms."

47 See, for example, *Pad v. Turkey* (dec.), No. 60167/00, June 28, 2007 (ECHR); *Isaak v. Turkey* (dec.), No. 44587/98, September 28, 2006 (ECHR); *Al-Skeini v. United Kingdom* [GC], No. 55721/07, Judgment of July 7, 2011.

48 *Al-Skeini*, paras. 149–50.

49 *Amnesty International Canada v. Canada (Chief of the Defence Staff)*, 2008 FCA 401, [2009] 4 FCR. 149 at para. 24, leave to appeal refused [2009] SCCA No. 63.

50 Ibid., para. 25.

51 In fact, in *Al-Skeini*, the U.K. was found responsible for failing to investigate the death of its prisoner in Iraq because it exercised authority and control over the individual and exercised some public powers normally to be exercised by a sovereign government. *Al-Skeini*, para. 150.

52 See, e.g., *Banković v. Belgium*, No. 52207/99, [2002] 123 ILR 94; *R. v. Hape*, 2007 SCC 26, [2007] 2 SCR 292; *Amnesty International Canada v. Canada (Chief of the Defence Staff)*.

53 Unless these crimes can be categorized as international crimes (i.e., murder as a war crime, which is murder with a nexus to an armed conflict; or rape that is widespread and systematic as a crime against humanity).

54 The role of international human rights law within the national criminal justice process (e.g., rights of accused) is not a feature of international law that affects the present analysis.

55 *Coalition Provision Authority Order Number 17 (Revised): Status of the Coalition Provisional Authority, MNF – Iraq, Certain Missions and Personnel in Iraq*, CPA/ORD/27 June 2004/17, s. 4(3), available at http://www.iraqcoalition.org

56 See, for example, Michael Hurst, "After Blackwater: A Mission-Focused Jurisdictional Regime for Private Military Contractors During Contingency Operations," *George Washington Law Review* 76 (2008): 1308.

57 Donald Rothwell, "Legal Opinion on the Status of Non-Combatants and Contractors under International Humanitarian Law," Australian Strategic Policy Institute, last modified December 24, 2004, available at http://www.aspi.org.au/pdf/ASPIlegalopinion_contractors.pdf (accessed August 30, 2011), 7.

58 International Law Commission, *Draft Articles on the Responsibility of States for Internationally Wrongful Acts*, November 2001, Supplement No. 10 (A/56/10),

chp.IV.E.1, art. 2(b), available at http://www.unhcr.org/refworld/docid/3ddb8f804.html (accessed 1 November 2012).

59 For an overview of these modes of liability, see Cassese, *International Law*, 187–252.

60 For example, France, South Africa, the United States, and the Netherlands do not require the perpetrator to be identified. It is necessary only that a crime has occurred. FAFO, "Assessing the Liability of Business Entities for Grave Violations of International Law," last modified September 2009, available at http://www.fafo.no/liabilities/index.htm (accessed January 26, 2011).

61 Cockayne et al., *Beyond Market Forces*, 4.

62 Ibid., 12.

63 For a critique of the Draft U.N. Convention, see Benjamin Perrin, "Searching for Accountability: The Draft U.N. International Convention on the Regulation, Oversight and Monitoring of Private Military and Security Companies," *Canadian Yearbook of International Law* 47 (2009): 299–317.

Due Diligence Obligations of Conduct: Developing a Responsibility Regime for PMSCs

NIGEL D. WHITE*

As non-state actors, PMSCs are not embraced by traditional state-dominated doctrines of international law. However, international law has itself failed to keep pace with the evolution of states and state-based actors, to which strong Westphalian notions of sovereignty are no longer applicable. It is argued that these structural inadequacies stand in the way of international regulation of PMSCs, rather than defects in international human rights and humanitarian law per se. By analyzing understandings of legal responsibility, where such structural issues come to the fore, it is argued that, rather than attempting to resolve the essentially ideological dispute about the inherent functions of a state, regulatory regimes should focus on the positive obligations of states and PMSCs, and the interactions between them. Applying the results of this analysis, current and proposed regulatory regimes are evaluated and their shortcomings revealed.

Nigel D. White is Professor of Public International Law at the University of Nottingham, formerly Professor of International Law at the University of Sheffield. He has held a Chair since 2000 and an academic post since 1987. He is author of a number of books including Democracy Goes to War: British Military Deployments under International Law *(2009). He is also editor and co-editor of a number of collections including* Counter-Terrorism: International Law and Practice *(2012). He is co-editor of the* Journal of Conflict and Security Law *published by Oxford University Press and in its 17th year.*

1. Introduction

This article puts forward an analysis of two main international legal approaches that are emerging as part of an effort to regulate the activities of private military and security companies (PMSCs). PMSCs are non-state actors that have an increasing role and impact on conflict and post-conflict zones around the globe.

One approach, the Montreux Process, is based on non-binding (soft law) international instruments:[1] the Montreux Document of 2008 applicable to participating states,[2] and the International Code of Conduct of 2010 applicable to PMSCs.[3] The second approach is based on the development of a hard (binding) law regime that would, if in force, be applicable to states and international organizations. This type of hard law is exemplified in the UN Working Group on Mercenaries' Draft Convention put before the Human Rights Council in 2010.[4] These regulatory initiatives are considered through the lens of the law of responsibility, an area of international law concerned with the "incidence and consequences of illegal acts, and particularly the payment of compensation" and other remedies for loss caused.[5]

Traditionally, international law has been concerned with legal responsibility for the internationally wrongful acts or omissions of states—the traditional actors in international relations. This article examines the responsibility of states, for example when they contract with PMSCs, but it also covers institutional as well as corporate responsibility for acts or omissions that violate international law. By covering these three actors—both state and non-state—the article investigates whether the Montreux Process (within which is included the International Code of Conduct) and the Draft Convention can work together in a complementary way as regards issues of responsibility and accountability. In so doing, it considers the law of state and institutional responsibility as developed by the UN's International Law Commission (ILC), which, though not formulated in treaty form, is customary binding law or has the potential to

become such. The article also considers the soft (non-binding) law of corporate social responsibility (CSR), particularly as developed by John Ruggie, former Special Representative of the U.N. Secretary-General on the issue of human rights and transnational corporations and other business enterprises.[6] Although customary and treaty law binds international legal persons—states and intergovernmental organizations—norms of CSR operate at the level of non-binding soft law directed at entities such as PMSCs that do not have international legal personality.

A note of caution: this article does not try to find unity where there is none. The author is well aware of the divisions that exist between those supporters of the Montreux Process and those of the Draft Convention,[7] but this does not necessarily mean that the outcomes of these two processes should automatically be in conflict with one another.[8]

The focus of the analysis will not be so much on mechanisms of accountability, though they will be mentioned, but on the issue of where legal responsibilities lie. Furthermore, rather than analyzing the criminal responsibility of an individual working for a PMSC, this article considers which entities are jointly or severally responsible for that wrong. Those in the frame for the purposes of this article are: the company or corporate actor itself, the state or organization that contracted with the PMSC, the state in which the PMSC is registered, or the state in which it is working. Of course a complete review of all forms of responsibility would include possible individual criminal responsibility of contractors,[9] but even robust and effective national and international mechanisms for determining individual criminal responsibility will not, by themselves, make up for the lack of accountability for violations of international law committed by those working for PMSCs. To build an accountability regime for PMSCs solely on the basis of individual criminal responsibility would be akin to relying on courts martial or criminal trials to address the responsibilities of the U.S. and the U.K. for prisoner abuse in Abu Ghraib and Basra during the military operations in Iraq, following the invasion of that country in March 2003. In the case of the U.K., the conviction of one soldier for war crimes in relation to the death of Baha Mousa in a British detention center in Basra was clearly inadequate to address the responsibility of the army and, ultimately, of the U.K., for prisoner abuse.[10] Such inadequacy is evidenced by the need for a public inquiry,[11] and by the proceedings against the U.K. before English courts for violation of the right to life and then before the European Court of Human Rights.[12] Compensation has also been paid by the U.K. government[13] and further criminal prosecutions may follow from the findings of the public inquiry.

Ethically speaking, though individual criminal responsibility can go toward satisfying the needs for retribution as well as deterrence, it fails to address fully the range of moral as well as legal responsibilities that arise from breaches of international law. For these reasons the iconic statement of the Nuremberg Tribunal in 1946—"crimes against international law are committed by men, not by abstract entities, and only by punishing individuals who commit

such crimes can the provisions of international law be enforced"[14]—oversimplifies, as Andre Nollkaemper argues, "the relationship between individual and state."[15] As regards the actions of individuals like Adolf Eichmann in Nazi Germany, such crimes occurred, and could only occur according to Hannah Arendt, within a "criminal state";[16] in other words, both individual and state bear responsibility for the sort of systematic and egregious crimes committed. The same analysis is applicable to human rights violations, and is reflected in the fact that human rights are embodied and protected in international law and are not necessarily guaranteed in the national legal systems of all states. Given that states (and international organizations) are committed to protect and uphold human rights at the international level, they must bear responsibility in international law when they are violated. Furthermore, as Nollkaemper notes, the "remedies for state responsibility and for individual responsibility are different," with the latter involving the punishment of individuals and the former involving reparations, though there can be overlaps between the two.[17]

In order to address the responsibilities of states, organizations, and corporations (in the form of PMSCs) this article initially considers how international law defines and delimits their responsibilities. In so doing, it highlights the substantive weaknesses of international law in attributing the wrongful acts of private actors to either the states or organizations employing them or otherwise having interaction with them. Furthermore, it highlights the structural weaknesses of international law in not imposing obligations directly on PMSCs as non-state actors. Given these circumstances, the article turns to consider whether the nebulous concept of due diligence, which applies in differing forms for the various actors, can provide a robust enough framework upon which accountability can be built. The article concludes by looking at whether the Montreux Process and the Draft Convention can work separately or together to develop responsibility and accountability of states, organizations, and PMSCs for internationally wrongful acts committed by PMSCs and their employees.

2. The Responsibility Matrix

Business corporations such as PMSCs, states, and international organizations are all, in a conceptual sense, corporate actors relying on individuals to carry out their will, and so all raise problems in attaching responsibility. Certainly there is difficulty in attaching criminal responsibility to these entities. The Rome Statute on the International Criminal Court covers neither corporations nor states, only "natural persons."[18] Although the notion of criminal responsibility is underdeveloped at the international level (apart from individual responsibility for certain core crimes), there are developed and developing rules on state and institutional responsibility. As international actors possessing international legal personality, states and intergovernmental organizations (formed by states) are responsible for wrongful acts committed by them or attributed to them. Unfortunately, when it comes to corporations, which are non-state actors established under national private law, international law does not generally recognize their responsibility, at least not in the same sense as state or institutional responsibility.

The U.N.'s International Law Commission (ILC) has produced sets of articles on state and institutional responsibility (the latter still in draft form). Unfortunately they are rather abstract and reveal inconsistencies and differences of approach. States and organizations are very different—organizations have neither territory nor population over which they have jurisdiction, and furthermore do not possess a monopoly on the use of force and the capacity to enforce it by police and military means.[19] This should signify that the rules as to when an organization is responsible should be different from those that apply to a state, but although there are differences between the two sets of articles (for example, on attribution of conduct), they do not fully reflect the differences between the two types of international legal persons. Setting aside these differences, the responsibility of states and organizations is conceptually of a different order from the notion of CSR that is being developed at both national and international levels.

2.1 State Responsibility

When considering the wrongful acts of PMSCs and the rules of state responsibility, the ILC's Articles on State Responsibility of 2001 indicate that the state is responsible for those wrongful acts in three possible separate circumstances. First, when PMSCs are incorporated into the armed forces, so becoming a part of a state organ (Article 4); second, if PMSCs were exercising elements of governmental authority (Article 5); or third, where, in the absence of the first or second circumstances, PMSCs act under the instructions, direction, or control of the state in carrying out that conduct (Article 8). The first two grounds are less likely to be applicable than the third— PMSCs are unlikely to be fully incorporated into the armed forces of a state since this would seem to negate the whole idea of outsourcing. Furthermore, there is an ideological dispute as to what are the inherent functions of a state. This dispute is revealed in the differences on permissible forms of outsourcing found between the Draft Convention and the Montreux Document.

The premise underlying the approach contained in the Draft Convention is that there are inherently governmental or state functions that should not be delegated or outsourced.[20] This is based on a certain understanding of the role of the state, a view that might not be shared by all governments, especially those with the most aggressive approaches to privatization. It contrasts with the Montreux Document, which identifies only prohibitions on contracting states outsourcing activities that international humanitarian law assigns to states (such as exercising the power of the responsible officer over prisoners of war or internment camps).[21] The Draft Convention defines inherent state functions broadly on the basis that they are "consistent

with the principle of State monopoly on the legitimate use of force," and cannot be outsourced or delegated to non-state actors. These functions include:

direct participation in hostilities, waging war and/or combat operations, taking prisoners, law-making, espionage, intelligence, knowledge transfer with military, security and policing application, use of and other activities related to weapons of mass destruction and police powers, especially the powers of arrest or detention including the interrogation of detainees.[22]

Although the Montreux Document views PMSCs as civilians and frowns upon them directly participating in hostilities (though not directly prohibiting them from so doing),[23] it assumes that all services, other than the ones assigned to states under international humanitarian law, can legitimately be performed by such actors. The Montreux Document states that

military and security services include, in particular, armed guarding and protection of persons and objects, such as convoys, buildings and other places; maintenance and operation of weapons systems; prisoner detention; and advice to or training of local forces and security personnel.[24]

Thus there are clear problems in compatibility between the Montreux Document and the Draft Convention as regards combat roles and other functions performed by PMSCs away from the front-line including detention.

The problems in determining the inherent functions of a state leave the "control test" under Article 8 of ILC's Articles as the most relevant and applicable one for attribution of PMSC conduct to a state. This test is said to be a strict one (requiring effective control of the conduct in question), and reflects the jurisprudence of the International Court of Justice in the Nicaragua case of 1986,[25] and the Bosnia case of 2007. In the latter case, the International Court dismissed lesser forms of control by saying that a state is "responsible only for its own conduct, that is to say the conduct of persons acting, on whatever basis, on its behalf."[26]

Assuming that a state contracts with a PMSC to perform functions such as escorting aid convoys and, furthermore, agrees with the PMSC that force can be used to protect those convoys, when lethal force is used it could be argued that the PMSC is acting under the instructions of the state, making the state directly responsible for the ensuing deaths. The doubt about this argument is in the formulation of the control test, which requires that the state has to be in effective control of the actual act, conduct, or operation in question. This is a high threshold to cross.[27] Although it may be argued that a contract for services should be construed as giving instructions to PMSCs, there could be doubt about whether those instructions were given in relation to the conduct or operation in question. Certainly in the Montreux Document, the participating states made it clear that, in their view at least, "entering into contractual relations does not itself engage" state responsibility; and that state responsibility would only be engaged if the PMSCs were part of the armed forces of the state, or were empowered to exercise governmental authority, or were "in fact acting on the instructions of a State (i.e. the State has specifically instructed the private actor's conduct) or under its direction or control (i.e. actual exercise of effective control by the State over the private actor's conduct)."[28] The Draft Convention simply refers to the ILC's Articles on State Responsibility of 2001 in its preamble, and so could be said to have incorporated the rules on attribution (including Article 8 on private conduct). This all suggests that there has been no loosening of the rules on attribution of private conduct to a state, making it very difficult in reality to establish that a contracting state is directly responsible for the wrongful acts of PMSCs. Given that this seems to be the position for the contracting state, it is even less likely that the home state or the host state will be in effective control of the PMSC conduct in question to allow for direct attribution of any wrongful conduct to those states.

2.2 Institutional Responsibility

Turning to an international organization's relationships with PMSCs, the latter could either be directly contracted with for services (for example, to provide humanitarian aid or even carry out peacekeeping functions) or may come within a peacekeeping operation when attached to a country's military or civilian component. Peacekeeping operations are normally composed of contingents from troop-contributing nations (TCNs), and some of those TCNs may well be supported by PMSCs under governmental contract.[29]

In these two different sets of circumstances attention should be paid to the ILC's 2011 Draft Articles on Institutional Responsibility.[30] In this document, the issue of attribution of the acts of private actors is somewhat different from the rules on state responsibility. Those PMSCs

directly contracted with by an organization could potentially fall under
draft article 5, which considers that
the conduct of an "organ" or "agent"
of the organization in performance of
its functions shall be an act of the
organization. Draft article 2's definition of "agent" was narrowed from
earlier versions to mean "an official
or other person or entity, other
than an organ, who is charged by
the organization with carrying out, or
helping to carry out, one of its functions, and thus through whom the
organization acts." The tightening of
the definition came after the U.N.
Department of Legal Affairs expressed concern that, without the
addition of a functional limitation,
the "definition of an agent could
have been perceived as being so
broad as to expose us to unreason-
able liability in respect of persons or
entities over whom we have little
or no control, and who do not carry
out the functions of the U.N.,
but rather provide goods and services which are incidental to our
mandated tasks," specifically referring to contractors.[31] This follows the
U.N.'s own internal law on contractors, which indicates that the UN
does not view them as "agents" of
the organization.[32]

In the case of PMSCs working for
TCNs within a peacekeeping operation, once again the draft articles
do not provide great clarity, even
though they adopt, in draft article 7,
an effective control of conduct test
for state organs (which would cover
national military contingents) placed
at the disposal of international organizations. This would suggest that
as an effective control test applies to
regular troops, the same would apply
to PMSCs. But again the issue has
not been settled because practice

indicates that the UN accepts responsibility for the conduct of peacekeepers even when it cannot be said
to be in effective control.[33] A looser
form of control for multinational
forces under UN mandate was—
albeit controversially—accepted by
the European Court of Human Rights
in the Behrami case of 2007. In its
decision, the court imputed responsibility to the U.N. for the conduct
of French troops in Kosovo on
the basis that the U.N. retained "ultimate authority and control" over the
operation.[34] Disputes in international
legal doctrine about the nature of the
control test for the attribution of acts
of private actors are set to continue
and reflect the failure of international law to keep pace with changes in the structure of states and
organizations.

2.3 Acts of State and Organizations in a Post-modern World

Thus—as with state responsibility,
according to the ILC Draft Articles
at least—attribution of the conduct of
PMSCs to an organization requires a
high threshold of control to be
crossed.[35] Though there are doubts
about the "effective control of conduct" test for attribution to states and
organizations,[36] the majority view
supports the effective control test
and dismisses any deviation from it
as wrong.[37] However, as well as
misrepresenting the way in which
organizations exercise authority, the
orthodox effective control test, as a
depiction of acts of state, is inaccurate. The orthodox doctrine of international law—that conduct can
constitute an act of state only if the
state is in effective control of such
conduct—arguably fails to understand how many post-modern states

currently operate. In such a state—
for example, the U.K.—many functions that were traditionally performed by organs and employees of
the state, such as running prisons,
prisoner escort, and protection services, are outsourced to private companies. Furthermore, in such states
there may be greater outsourcing and
privatization in some areas, such as
security, than in others, such as
health or education. Different speeds
of outsourcing are reflective of what
is achievable politically and ideolo-
gically, rather than what is ethically
acceptable. In areas in which outsourcing is deeply entrenched, and
applying the orthodox test, the government is no longer in effective
control of the conduct of private
companies and is therefore not responsible. The alternative view is
that the government, in the words
of the European Court in Behrami,
retains "ultimate authority and control" of these services, and should,
therefore, accept responsibility.

The prevailing orthodox view of
state responsibility is very much
based on the concept of a strong
sovereign state, one that retains a
firm grip if not monopoly on the
use of force. Though such states
clearly still exist, international
legal doctrine has failed to adapt to
the increasing variety of modern,
post-modern, and also pre-modern
states.[38] In this vein, Neil Walker has
cogently argued that within the European Union at least, a post-West-
phalian phase of sovereignty—what
he labels as "late sovereignty"—has
been reached. In this phase, sovereignty is "no longer so widely or so
confidently conceived of as part of
the meta-language of explanation
and political language"; rather, it

is "about a plausible and reasonably
effective claim to ultimate authority"
or a "representation of authority
made on behalf of a society which
is (more or less successfully) constitutive of that society as a political
society, or as a polity." Thus it should
be possible to "imagine ultimate
authority, or sovereignty, in non-
exclusive terms."[39]

In relation to developing states
in the context of colonialism and
decolonization, Antony Anghie has
argued that the "acquisition of sovereignty by the Third World was an
extraordinarily significant event; and
yet, various limitations and dis-
advantages appeared to be somehow
peculiarly connected with that sovereignty."[40] Anghie's compelling
thesis is that sovereignty in the Westphalian sense was not simply ex-
tended from European states to
newly decolonized states; rather, colonialism helped to shape a new form
of sovereignty for this new wave of
independent states, one that is "rendered uniquely vulnerable and dependent by international law."[41] Add
to this Gerry Simpson's powerful
analysis of the sovereign inequality
that exists between great power states
and "outlaw" states.[42] Thus current
thinking about sovereignty indicates
that it is not the construct upon which
international relations is conducted,
though unfortunately the repetition
of the Westphalian concept of sovereignty in legal doctrine signifies that
its influence remains in core areas
such as state responsibility.

The notion of what is "inherently
governmental" has been hollowed
out by certain key states,[43] rendering
the orthodox test rarely applicable
to them, though unsurprisingly these
states continue to support such a test

as it effectively allows them to out-source their responsibility as well as their functions. The same argument can be applied to an international organization such as the U.N. where the level of control of its operations involving state and non-state actors rarely reaches the threshold required by the orthodox test.

Although it is possible to object morally to the reduction of a state's inherently governmental functions on the basis, for instance, that even a minimal state should provide security and not contract it out (as this may lead to some citizens, or areas, within a state not being covered by security arrangements),[44] the fact of governmental hollowing out has been clearly established in the case of the U.S.[45] This has resulted in a reduction in democratic accountability (for example, little attention is paid in democracies to the loss of life of private military or security personnel, in contrast to loss of regular soldiers) and corresponds to an increase of corporate influence in government.[46] Not conceding that the moral argument has been irre-vocably lost, this article argues that even in such a weakened condition the state still has positive obligations to prevent human rights abuse by corporate actors it contracts with, or those which are based or operating within its jurisdiction.

2.4 Corporate (Social) Responsibility

It is unsurprising that just as inter-national legal doctrine has failed to keep pace with the changing nature of sovereignty of the main actors (states), it has also failed to fully accommodate non-state actors within the subjects of the international legal

order. International organizations are the exception in this regard, for though they are non-state actors, they are formed by states, and states often dominate their institutional structures. Nevertheless, the separate international legal personality of in-tergovernmental organizations has been grudgingly accepted by states.[47] Individuals have acquired derivative rights under international human rights law, though the applicability and enforcement of those rights remain problematic. Furthermore, duties have been imposed on indivi-duals under international criminal law.

Corporations, despite the huge power and influence of multinational corporations especially in the era of economic globalization, are in many ways barely touched by international law at least directly in the form of binding treaty or customary obliga-tions. The U.N. Sub-Commission on Human Rights' "Norms on the Responsibilities of Transnational Cor-porations and other Business Enter-prises with Regard to Human Rights" of 2003 were ultimately rejected be-cause they purported to impose ob-ligations on corporations under international law. John Ruggie, then Special Representative of the U.N. Secretary-General on business and human rights, dismissed the Norms' assertion of obligatory force to cor-porations as having "little authorita-tive basis in international law—hard, soft or otherwise."[48] Interestingly, there has been a more recent attempt to revive the possibility of legally binding corporations. An earlier ver-sion of the Draft Convention on PMSCs would have enabled corpora-tions to have become parties to it, but the version that finally saw the light of day before the Human Rights Council in 2010 would be open only to states and organizations (a major breakthrough in itself if accepted) but not PMSCs.[49]

This limitation is despite the fact that states and private companies have been intimately entwined since the days in which Hugo Grotius worked for the Dutch East India Company in the seventeenth century, a company that, along with the British East India Company, was responsible for establishing colonies on behalf of the state up until the end of the nineteenth century.[50] The presence of private corporations at the heart of empire-building states seems to have been forgotten in the history of international law, which sees the nineteenth century as the period of absolute state domination.[51] Antony Anghie writes that, "examined in the context of colonial history," the multinational corporations of the twenty-first century are "in many respects successors to entities such as the Dutch and British East India Companies which, after all, had been central to the whole imperial project."[52] Bearing in mind the global reach of companies such as G4S, with over half a million employees operating in 125 countries worldwide,[53] the impact they have on states, especially weak or post-conflict states, is considerable.

Although there appears to be no conceptual barrier to accepting corporations as having international legal personality and therefore being capable of having rights and duties, progress in establishing this has been limited.[54] Instead, a softer form of regulation has emerged, labeled "corporate social responsibility," which can be found in initiatives such as the U.N.'s Global Compact launched in 2000[55] and, more specifically, in the International Code of Conduct for Private Security Service Providers of 2010. John Ruggie has undertaken the conceptual and normative development of this form of responsibility.

Ruggie's "Guiding Principles on Business and Human Rights: Implementing the United Nations 'Protect, Respect and Remedy' Framework,"[56] endorsed by the U.N.'s Human Rights Council in June 2011,[57] represents the culmination of his work on this matter. Ruggie's Framework has three pillars. The first "protect" pillar refers to the state's due diligence obligations under the international law discussed below, namely its "duty to protect against human rights abuses by third parties, including business enterprises, through appropriate policies, regulation and adjudication." The second pillar (the "respect" pillar) refers to CSR—that is, a corporation's own due diligence obligations arising from the expectation that responsible corporate actors "should act with due diligence to avoid infringing the rights of others and to address adverse impacts with which they are involved." The third pillar (the "remedy" pillar) is the "need for greater access by victims to effective remedy, both judicial and non-judicial."[58] Ruggie states that each pillar is an

essential component in an inter-related and dynamic system of preventative and remedial measures: the State's duty to protect because it lies at the very core of the international human rights regime; the corporate responsibility to respect because it is the basic expectation society has of business in relation to human rights; and access to remedy because even the most concerted efforts cannot prevent all abuse.[59]

Essentially Ruggie's Framework works within the structures and strictures of international law[60] as currently understood, by recognizing that proper accountability for human rights abuse will work only if a regime of CSR is underpinned by states fulfilling their duties under international law. As Sorcha MacLeod observes, Ruggie's "position is that only states are required to protect human rights while business actors are expected to respect human rights standards and to utilize due diligence in their commercial activities to ensure that the standards are observed."[61] In effect, Ruggie's approach could be summed up in simple terms of states being required to fulfill their due diligence obligations under human rights law to ensure that corporations within their jurisdiction, with whom they contract or otherwise control, operate with due diligence to avoid violating human rights and other applicable international laws. An elaboration of the different due diligence obligations of states, organizations, and corporations will be provided below, before analyzing the Montreux Process and Draft Convention to see if they could provide the combination that Ruggie identifies.

3. Due Diligence

Given the weaknesses of international law in imposing direct responsibility on states, organizations, or corporations for the wrongful acts of individuals working for the latter, the specter is raised of a legal black hole in which PMSCs operate with impunity despite the existence of human rights law and international humanitarian law.[62] The solution may take the form of due diligence, by which these actors have obligations to try to prevent misconduct. As Susan Marks and Fiorentina Azizi have written: "especially in the context of human rights, it is often the State's failure to act—its failure to ensure protection, including protection against invasions of human rights by non-State actors—that is the problem."[63] Due diligence obligations are of conduct rather than result, meaning that the actors in question have to "deploy their best efforts to achieve a desired outcome (which might be to prevent a given event), even if that outcome need not be ensured."[64] This gives the actors in question certain latitude in how to fulfill these obligations.

In the case of states, the different perspectives of home state (where the PMSC is based), host state (where the PMSC operates), and contracting state (which is purchasing PMSC services) need separate consideration.[65] In general, much of Ruggie's first pillar (the protect pillar) is directed at the state's duty to "prevent, investigate, punish and redress private actors' abuse." Ruggie explains that though states "generally have discretion in deciding upon these steps, they should consider the full range of permissible preventative and remedial measures, including policies, legislation, regulations, and adjudication."[66] Thus, in discussing the positive obligations of different states, and later organizations and PMSCs, there is a fair degree of leeway in how due diligence should be implemented.

3.1 Home States

Developing the general principle of international law identified by the International Court of Justice in the Corfu Channel Case in 1949,[67] the home state in which the PMSC is based should be responsible for knowingly allowing its territory to be used for unlawful acts against or in other states. Francesco Francioni cogently argues that the home state

is in a good position to prevent human rights violations arising from the commercial export of security services because it is able to regulate the PMSC 'at the source' by virtue of the effective control it exercises over the centre of management of the company.

This strongly supports the need for both a licensing and a monitoring system to be established by the home state.[68]

Unfortunately, there are common misunderstandings concerning the obligations of the home state. Ruggie's statement that states are not "required under international human rights law to regulate the extraterritorial activities of businesses domiciled in their territory and/or jurisdiction"[69] misses the point that though the direct provisions of national human rights law and criminal law may not apply extraterritorially (depending upon a particular state's approach to jurisdiction), this does not absolve the state from ensuring, within its territory and jurisdiction, that corporate actors fulfill their human rights obligations. This could be achieved through proper training, impact assessment, and so forth. Thus although it is accurate to say that states have no obligation under international law to apply and enforce their laws extraterritorially (unless they exercise control over

another state's territory or citizens), they still have due diligence obligations within their own jurisdictions to ensure that corporations based there (including ones such as PMSCs that operate overseas) are human rights compliant.

3.2 Host States

In international human rights law, cases such as the Velasquez Rodriguez case before the Inter-American Court of Human Rights (IACtHR) and subsequent ones developed by other human rights institutions[70] have confirmed that the host state, in which private actors operate, has an obligation to exercise due diligence to protect anyone within its jurisdiction from human rights abuse, whether committed by state agents or private actors. As the IACtHR has stated,

an illegal act which violates human rights and which is ... not directly imputable to a State (for example, because it is the act of a private person or because the person responsible has not been identified) can lead to international responsibility of the State, not because of the act itself, but because of the lack of due diligence to prevent the violation or to respond to it as required by the Convention.[71]

Undoubtedly, many host states will be in a weak conflict or post-conflict condition, but they must not turn a blind eye to human rights abuses by private actors within their territory and therefore must try to bring the perpetrators to justice with the resources available to them. In addition, Ruggie suggests that where the host state is weak and unable adequately to protect human rights, the home state of any transnational corporation involved should also endeavor to ensure that the corporation is not involved in human rights abuse.[72]

3.3 Contracting States

In addition to the possibility of directly imputable conduct discussed above, contracting states also have due diligence obligations. Ethically, it is the positive act of contracting for services with PMSCs that leads to wrongful acts being committed by their operatives; thus contracting governments should arguably bear responsibility above the home state, and certainly above the host state. Ruggie strongly argues that "states do not relinquish their international human rights law obligations when they privatize the delivery of services that may impact upon the enjoyment of human rights."[73] His Framework lays down two principles that support this. Principle 5 declares that states "should exercise adequate oversight in order to meet their international human rights obligations when they contract with ... business enterprises to provide services that may impact upon the enjoyment of human rights"; and Principle 6 declares that "states should promote respect for human rights by business enterprises with which they conduct commercial transactions."[74]

There is jurisprudence from the various international and regional human rights systems to support the application of due diligence obligations to contracting states.[75] If a state is going to contract with a PMSC to help its troops in a foreign country, it should be prepared to ensure to the best of its ability that those contractors do not commit human rights abuses in that country. It is argued

that due diligence obligations are necessary particularly when the contracting state does not itself assert effective national jurisdiction over such actors, beyond the enforcement of its contractual rights. This obligation would be strengthened further when the contracting state knows that the host state has a weak judicial system and enforcement mechanisms. Given that it is the contracting state that is responsible for the presence of PMSCs on the territory of another state, it would be incongruous for it not to have due diligence obligations when both the home and host state do. It might be argued further that, before it contracts with a PMSC for services to be rendered in the host state, the contracting state has a duty to ensure that the host state has satisfactory laws, courts, and enforcement mechanisms for holding PMSCs to account for human rights abuse if it is not prepared to assert jurisdiction over them itself. If such criteria are not met then the state should not contract with the PMSC in question. In this way it is contended that a contracting state has a positive obligation to undertake a human rights impact assessment of its decision to contract services to PMSCs or, alternatively, it has to have in place processes that give it confidence that the PMSC itself will undertake its own full impact assessment.

3.4 International Organizations

As an international legal person, bearing rights and duties under international law,[76] an international organization such as the U.N. or EU—that either contracts with a PMSC for the delivery of services, or mandates and commands a peacekeeping force consisting of TCNs with PMSC support—cannot deny that it owes due diligence obligations under customary international law to ensure that the private actors it has contracted with or mandated either directly or indirectly do not violate human rights or international humanitarian laws. For example, the U.N. could achieve this through its own accountability mechanisms such as the Office of Internal Oversight Services (OIOS) in relation to directly contracted PMSCs;[77] or through its agreements with TCNs; or through the U.N. Secretary-General as commander of peacekeeping forces in relation to PMSCs working within U.N. mandated and commanded peace operations.

3.5 PMSCs

Although the due diligence obligations of states and organizations are binding customary obligations in international law, because corporations are not subjects of international law, any due diligence commitments they may have are non-binding outcomes of exercises in CSR. Although they are not subject to direct obligations under international law, corporations will be governed by national laws adopted by states in fulfillment of their human rights obligations to ensure that private actors within their jurisdictions do not violate human rights law. In this sense corporations would be wise, and would be expected, to respect human rights. This sense of CSR is the one used in Ruggie's Framework—for instance, in Principle 11, which states that "business enterprises should respect human rights," meaning that "they should avoid infringing on the human rights

of others and should address adverse human rights impacts with which they are involved."[78] According to Ruggie, the relevant human rights standards are to be found in the Universal Declaration, the International Covenants and eight core ILO Conventions.[79] As explained above, although these standards are not binding directly on corporations under international law, such actors are expected to comply if they want to avoid adverse publicity and reputational consequences, as well as government action against them under applicable national laws.

The nature of corporate due diligence is illustrated by the International Code of Conduct for Private Security Service Providers of 2010. In subscribing to the International Code companies recognize that they must act "with due diligence to avoid infringing the rights of others."[80] More specifically on this requirement, the International Code provides that signatory PMSCs will

exercise due diligence to ensure compliance with the law and with the principles contained in this Code, and will respect the human rights of persons they come into contact with, including, the rights to freedom of expression, association, and peaceful assembly and against arbitrary or unlawful interference with privacy or deprivation of property.[81]

The due diligence requirement emphasized in the code of conduct is not by itself a binding obligation on PMSCs[82]—this is in contrast to the due diligence obligations placed on states and organizations by international law. This significant limitation is made clear in the International Code of Conduct when it states that it "creates no legal obligations on the Signatory Companies, beyond those which already exists under national or international law. Nothing in this Code shall be interpreted as limiting or prejudicing in any way existing or developing rules of international law."[83] In a way this is akin to the Montreux Document, which is not a binding treaty and creates no new obligations on states. However, unlike the International Code of Conduct, the Montreux Document is based on an understanding of existing international legal obligations on states[84] whereas there are no such underpinning obligations on corporations in international law.

Nevertheless, Ruggie's Framework of 2011 contains a number of principles that help to flesh out the components of a corporate human rights due diligence process, which "should include assessing actual and potential human rights impacts, integrating and acting upon the findings, tracking responses, and communicating how impacts are addressed."[85] More specifically, according to Ruggie, corporate due diligence should cover human rights impacts caused by businesses through their activities or directly caused by their operations. In addition:

- it should be an ongoing process that varies with the size and type of business;
- it should draw on internal and external human rights expertise and should involve meaningful consultation with potentially affected groups;
- it should involve the effective implementation of the findings of any human rights impact assess-

ment by assigning responsibility within the business but also by ensuring that decision-making and oversight mechanisms are designed to respond to such impacts;
- it should include proper verification that human rights impacts are being addressed by businesses in tracking the effectiveness of their responses to impacts on individuals and groups, which can be done by obtaining feedback and by using indicators, surveys, and audits;
- and, finally, it should include effective communication by corporations of how they address human rights impacts—meetings, online dialogues, consultation, and formal reports are all suggested.[86]

Although responsible corporations are expected to fulfill these requirements, states are required by their positive obligations in international law to ensure their fulfillment. In these terms this binary form of responsibility—corporate social responsibility and state responsibility—has certain structural weakness arising out of its dependency upon states having the primary legal obligation to ensure corporations act responsibly. This premise means that if a state is weak, or simply fails to recognize its obligations, the framework is undermined unless there is a mechanism at the international level that could help ensure that states take action to ensure that PMSCs do not violate human rights. With that in mind, this analysis turns to the current international regulatory initiatives.

4. The Montreux Process

This section contains an examination of the provisions of the Montreux Document and the International Code of Conduct (together forming the Montreux Process) to see how they address issues of responsibility, especially in furthering the due diligence obligations outlined above. The article will then turn to see how the Draft Convention would work if it came into force within the context of the existing Montreux Process.

In many ways, and despite leading analysis to the contrary,[87] the Montreux Document of 2008 is quite strong on due diligence content in the form of identifying obligations and good practices for states. In its first part, the document affirms the legal obligations, including ones of due diligence, under international humanitarian law and international human rights law, of home states, host states, and contracting states.[88] In addition to identifying "hard" laws binding under custom or treaty, the Montreux Document also lists "soft standards" in the form of 73 "good practices." These good practices are detailed in the document's second part, and this list may lay the foundations for the regulation of PMSCs through contracts, codes of conduct, national legislation, regional instruments, and international standards.[89] In many ways the second part of the Montreux Document provides flesh to the due diligence bones of the first part, but its formulation in the form of good practices could be seen as recognition of the fact that due diligence standards may vary from state to state depending on their relationship to PMSCs.

What the Montreux Document does make clear in the first part is that all three types of states—home, host, and contracting—owe due diligence obligations to ensure respect for international humanitarian law by PMSCs and to give effect to their human rights obligations by taking appropriate measures to prevent, investigate, and provide effective remedies for PMSC conduct.[90] The second part then provides some detail of how these might be honored by states and here there is some variation, as expected, between the different types of state (though there is a large element of overlap in matters such as training). For contracting states, as well as indicating the procedures and criteria for selection of contractors, there is the expectation that the contract will include clauses and performance requirements to ensure respect for humanitarian and human rights law, and a stipulation that lowest price should not be the only criterion for selection.[91] For host and home states, good practice would require them to authorize PMSCs operating or based on their territories by having systems of licenses to be granted only after vetting of PMSCs as regards their policy statements, track records, monitoring and accountability systems, and training provision.[92]

Although it can readily be construed as a significant contribution to recognizing the due diligence obligations of states, the Montreux Document has several weaknesses. First, it is not by itself obligatory for states. Although it invokes a mixture of hard and soft international law applicable to states, the Montreux Document itself is not in the form of a treaty and, as recognized in its preface, is therefore "not a legally binding instrument and so does not affect existing obligations of States under customary international law or under international agreements to which they are parties."[93] Second, it is directed at states. The international law obligations identified and good practices proposed in the Montreux Document are mainly applicable to states, and, although PMSCs and their personnel do not completely escape from those provisions,[94] the document does not attempt to regulate the industry. Rather, it serves to remind states of their obligations when engaging PMSCs or allowing them to operate from or in their territories. Third, though human rights obligations are included, the focus of the Montreux Document is on the application of international humanitarian law to PMSCs in situations of armed conflict, when it is arguably more likely that PMSCs will be more readily deployed to post-conflict situations in which international human rights law is applicable.

Although the Montreux Document encourages national monitoring and supervision by home, host, and contracting states (including through licensing and accountability mechanisms), it does not itself establish any international mechanism for regulation of the due diligence obligations of either states or PMSCs. The Montreux Process has led to the development of the International Code of Conduct of 2010, which is premised on the creation of an oversight mechanism for corporations,

but not for states, and thus may remedy the second of the weaknesses listed above.

The International Code of Conduct for Private Security Service Providers builds on the Montreux Document although the latter was directed at states. The Code of Conduct is directed at businesses, and is essentially an exercise in CSR as reflected in the preamble which refers to the "Protect, Respect, and Remedy" human rights framework for business developed by Ruggie. As explained earlier, in subscribing to the Code of Conduct companies recognize that they must act with due diligence.[95] More generally, in signing the code, PMSCs "commit to the responsible provision of Security Services so as to support the rule of law, respect the human rights of all persons, and protect the interests of their clients."[96]

The purpose here is not to go through all the Code of Conduct's provisions and consider whether they completely fulfill the due diligence requirements identified earlier. In a sense that is not possible, given that due diligence is not by any means a precise science, but the indications are that the code has strengths in CSR terms. On applicable human rights standards, the code does have well-developed and quite specific rules on the use of force and on detention as well the following prohibitions:

- on torture or other cruel, inhuman or degrading treatment;
- on sexual abuse and gender based violence;
- on human trafficking;
- on slavery and forced labor;
- on child labor;
- and on discrimination.[97]

All of these deepen the Code of Conduct's human rights coverage. Arguably, though, the code should have covered all human rights standards, or at least those most applicable to PMSCs. The absence of any economic, social, or cultural rights is of concern because, for instance, the activities of a PMSC may well impact on cultural rights. The preamble to the Code of Conduct identifies the importance of PMSCs "respecting the various cultures encountered in their work,"[98] but does not develop due diligence standards in this regard. The code is explicitly stated to be the beginning of a process, the "founding instrument," that will be built on by the development of "objective and measurable standards for providing security services."[99] In developing standards for assessing human rights impact, cultural rights could and should be included.

The Code of Conduct requires signatory companies to exercise due diligence in the selection of personnel, which will include checks on the criminal and military records of individuals as well as reviewing their fitness to carry weapons.[100] Due diligence extends to the selection, vetting, and ongoing review of subcontractors, in relation to which the PMSC undertakes to take reasonable and appropriate steps to ensure that subcontractors select, vet, and train their personnel in accordance with the requirements of the code.[101] Signatory companies also agree on the training of personnel in "all applicable international and relevant national laws, including those pertaining to international human rights law, international humanitarian law, international criminal law and other relevant criminal law."[102] Although

there are also requirements for reporting of incidents of abuse,[103] there is little on PMSCs undertaking a proper assessment of their likely human rights impact, except for a very general statement that signatory companies "take steps to establish and maintain an effective internal governance framework in order to deter, monitor, report, and effectively address adverse impacts on human rights."[104] Thus not all the due diligence obligations of corporations identified above in section 3.5 and contained in Ruggie's Framework are covered in the code.

In addition to management and training requirements, signatory companies agree to establish grievance procedures to address claims alleging failure to respect the principles contained in the Code of Conduct. Such procedures must be "fair, accessible and offer effective remedies."[105] However, the creation of what is essentially a non-binding set of standards, one that businesses can choose to sign up to, can be labeled only as a means of self-regulation. All remedies will be at the whim of businesses, unless there is some form of supervision of the Code of Conduct either by an oversight body set up within the code itself or by states in fulfillment of their obligations under international law (a number of which are identified in the Montreux Document). Preferably, it would be both. Furthermore, in order to ensure that states fulfill their due diligence obligations, another level of supervision is required at the international level, established by states for states. Before looking at the proposal for this in the Draft Convention, we must first consider the oversight mechanism for the industry as envisaged in the Code of Conduct.

The code, as originally adopted in 2010, is surprisingly light on regulation, though in the preamble an "independent governance and oversight mechanism" is envisaged, and a Steering Committee—consisting of a small group of stakeholders drawn from the industry, states (the U.S. and U.K.), and civil society—was established to develop such an oversight mechanism by November 2011.[106] The Steering Committee produced a Draft Charter for the oversight mechanism in January 2012[107] that envisaged a 12-strong executive board with equal numbers of members from industry, civil society, and states participating in the Montreux Process. This body would have competence over the oversight process to be operated by a secretariat including a chief of performance assessment (CPA). The CPA would have oversight over participating companies, including instances when a PMSC has committed a serious violation of the Code of Conduct. In such a case, the CPA would have responsibility for the development of a remediation plan. In-field as well as remote oversight and monitoring of PMSC compliance is envisaged. Sanctions for non-compliance are limited to suspension and expulsion by the board following a report from the CPA.[108] The strengths and weaknesses of the Draft Charter are readily apparent, especially the danger of the board being dominated by a small section of states and industry representatives. Furthermore, the sanctions at its disposal have not been proven to be effective in other codes of conduct. Nevertheless, the operation of the Draft Charter, assuming it comes into force, will determine whether it is a robust mechanism of oversight and accountability, or more of a symbolic form of CSR.

5. The Draft Convention

If the development of a regulatory regime for PMSCs were to stop at the Montreux Document and the International Code of Conduct, then, no matter how robust the CSR element, the state responsibility (SR) element would be inadequate, relying purely on states taking their due diligence obligations seriously. The current very limited regulatory regime put in place in the U.K., for example, where a large number of PMSCs are based, does not suggest that this will happen without some form of international regulation of states.[109]

Although the Draft Convention on Private Military and Security Companies is a long way from seeing the light of day as a binding international treaty, this section contains an overview of some of its provisions in order to see how they address issues of responsibility and accountability. The Draft Convention was put forward by the U.N. Working Group on Mercenaries to the Human Rights Council in July 2010. The Draft Convention itself recognizes the value of codes of conduct, but declares that these are, by themselves not enough.[110] The rationale for some form of treaty regime is clear—that without proper supervision of states' positive obligations at the international level, there will not be a robust framework within which PMSCs will act in accordance with their due diligence obligations.

In general, the Draft Convention is restrictive on the types of activities that can be carried out by PMSCs. State responsibility is engaged if PMSCs undertake functions that would either be inherently governmental[111] or if they perform legitimately outsourced activities that violate the standards of international human rights law or international humanitarian law.[112] State responsibility is established for "military and security activities of PMSCs registered or operating in their jurisdiction, whether or not these entities are contracted by the state." In addition to establishing the obligations of home and host state, the Draft Convention requires contracting states to "ensure that the PMSCs it has contracted are trained in and respect human rights and international humanitarian law."[113] Furthermore, it is clear from the formulation of many of the provisions that the form of state responsibility envisaged is largely for failure to exercise due diligence over the actual or potential conduct of private actors within the jurisdiction of states (and organizations) parties to the convention.[114] State parties are required to take such "legislative, administrative and other measures as may be necessary to ensure that PMSCs and their personnel are held accountable for violations of applicable national or international law."[115] Crucially, the Draft Convention requires that each state party "ensure that PMSCs and their personnel apply due diligence

to ensure that their activities do not contribute directly or indirectly to violations of human rights and international humanitarian law."[116]

The Draft Convention provides a number of techniques for state parties to fulfill their positive obligations to ensure that PMSC operate with due diligence. Basically, these involve the criminalization of certain activities, on the one hand, and the regulation of PMSC activities, on the other. With respect to the former, each state party is required to create national laws prohibiting acts carried out by PMSCs that are in furtherance of inherently state functions or that violate either international standards (under international human rights law, international criminal law, and international humanitarian law) or other provisions of the Draft Convention (such as those limiting the use of firearms). Furthermore, according to the Draft Convention, unlicensed or unauthorized PMSC activities should also be made an offense under national law.[117]

As well as mandating that states create legislation that can lead to punishment, the Draft Convention requires that state parties regulate the activities of PMSCs by adopting and implementing oversight laws.[118] The Draft Convention would require state parties to

establish a comprehensive domestic regime of regulation and oversight over the activities in its territory of PMSCs and their personnel including all foreign personnel, in order to prohibit and investigate illegal activities as defined by this Convention as well as by relevant national laws.

To facilitate this, state parties are required to establish a register and/ or a governmental body to act as a national center for information concerning possible violations of national and international law by PMSCs. State parties shall investigate reports of violations of international humanitarian law and human rights norms by PMSCs, ensure prosecution and punishment of offenders, as well as revoke licenses given under the national licensing system required by the Draft Convention.[119]

The Draft Convention envisages national licensing regimes[120] that should cover trafficking in firearms[121] as well as the import and export of military and security services,[122] but there is little detail in the convention on whether licenses should be general to companies or specific to individual contracts. In addition, although the implementation of due diligence obligations allows states some choice, it may be necessary in any final version—in order to avoid the development of vastly different national licensing regimes and consequent problems of forum shopping—to specify some minimal conditions that rule out the possibility of a company being granted an open-ended and unsupervised license.[123] Such conditions could be developed in the jurisprudence of the Convention's Oversight Committee (discussed below), which is required to be kept informed about licensing regimes by those parties that import or export PMSC services.[124] The requirements that state parties have a register of PMSCs operating within their jurisdiction, that they establish a governmental body responsible for the register's maintenance, and that they exercise oversight over PMSC activities[125] are equally lacking in detail and again could lead to a very weak system of registration and licensing.

Supervision of the positive obligations of state parties would fall to the proposed Committee on the Regulation, Oversight and Monitoring of Private Military and Security Activities (Oversight Committee) consisting of international experts.[126] This committee would receive reports from state parties on the legislative, judicial, administrative, and other measures they have adopted to give effect to the Draft Convention, and the committee would make observations and recommendations thereon.[127] There are two further proposed methods of supervision and accountability by the Oversight Committee—an inquiry procedure and a conciliation process.[128] Having a range of potential avenues for resolving disputes and claims may help to ensure that accountability is possible even in the most sensitive of situations. Unfortunately, however, the focus of the inquiry and conciliation processes seems to be solely on states, and not on the victims of violations.[129]

Having said that, in addition to a state complaints procedure[130]—which, if other human rights treaties are any guide, is unlikely to be used—the Draft Convention contains an individual and group petition procedure into which state parties may opt. Individuals or groups claiming to be victims of a violation of any of the duties contained in the Convention (by those state parties opting into the process) may bring a petition. This envisages complaints being brought against states for their failure to regulate and control PMSCs in fulfillment of their positive obligations under the Draft Convention.

The lack of direct forms of redress against PMSCs in the convention is remedied by the requirement that each party implements domestic legislation giving effect to the Draft Convention, thus giving complainants local remedies that must be exhausted before a petition is submitted to the Oversight Committee.[131] After considering petitions, the Oversight Committee shall forward its suggestions and recommendations, if any, to the state party concerned and to the petitioner.[132] Although the remedy seems weak, this is standard in this type of procedure, and, given the evidence from the various U.N. human rights committees, it can be successful if the Oversight Committee performs its tasks with impartiality and bases its decisions on accepted interpretations of international law. If the Oversight Committee manages to establish its legitimacy, its decisions will generally be accepted by state parties. It will then be the job of the governments of state parties to enforce these decisions against PMSCs based in or operating on their territory, or employed by them.[133]

6. Right To An Effective Remedy

The dual combination of state responsibility and corporate social responsibility outlined above would facilitate the provision of remedial mechanisms and therefore facilitate access to justice for individuals. Such a view is supported by Ruggie's Framework in the "Remedy" pillar. The principles contained in that document require that states provide those affected by business-related human rights abuse within their jurisdictions with effective remedies. These should include "apologies, restitution, rehabilitation, financial or non-financial compensation and punitive sanctions (whether criminal or administrative, such as fines), as well as the prevention of harm through, for example, injunctions or guarantees of non-repetition." Remedial avenues should take the form of both judicial and non-judicial mechanisms and fora—"courts (for both criminal and civil action), labor tribunals, National Human Rights Institutions, National [OECD] Contact Points, ... ombudsperson offices, and Government-run complaints offices."[134] In addition to these burdens placed on states in fulfillment of their due diligence obligations, Ruggie also includes "operational-level grievance mechanisms" provided by corporations that are "accessible directly to individuals and communities who may be adversely impacted by a business enterprise."[135]

The presence of fair and effective remedies available from PMSCs for human rights abuses would reduce the need for victims to go through state procedures and, ultimately, to resort to the international level. The Draft Charter for an oversight mechanism for the International Code of Conduct put forward for consultation by the Steering Committee in January 2012 does give some positive indications by providing for supervision of the obligations in the Code of Conduct that all participating PMSCs have internal grievance procedures, and by allowing for individuals to bring complaints to the oversight mechanism alleging violations of the code.[136] However, the Draft Charter's provisions are obscurely worded and seem to provide a great deal of leeway for PMSCs. In particular, the provisions present them with a chance, in the face of a complaint against them, to conduct an internal investigation and put forward proposals for remediation. Even more worryingly, it also allows the oversight mechanism itself to reject not only frivolous complaints but complaints that are too challenging due to the "difficulties in establishing facts in the context of activities that take place in complex environments."[137] A reluctance to consider, let alone investigate, complex cases is not encouraging evidence of the type of CSR remedial mechanism envisaged by Ruggie.

The Draft Convention, on the other hand, does in general oblige states to provide the sort of remedies and access to them required by the "Protect, Respect and Remedy" framework and, furthermore, provides oversight and remedial processes at the international level. As outlined above, the Draft Convention generally envisages that such remedies will be found in the national systems of the contracting parties,

with the Oversight Committee ensuring this through state reports and, where applicable, by allowing individual petitions. However, just looking at the international level, it is doubtful whether envisaging a right of individual petition to the Oversight Committee represents an "effective remedy." The Draft Convention's protection of the individual victim at the international level is premised on the traditional paradigm of gaining the consent of states to an optional petition procedure, which is a supplement to remedies that the victim should gain (if the Draft Convention is in force for the state in question) before national courts and mechanisms. As it is, there is a recognition in the Draft Convention that a further remedial mechanism may be required at the international level, but it takes the form of a weak provision that requires states to "consider establishing an International Fund to be administered by the Secretary General to provide reparation to victims of offences under this Convention and/or assist in their rehabilitation."[138]

7. Conclusion

The analysis in this article has shown that the Montreux Process and the Draft Convention (assuming the latter comes into being and enters into force) could either be rival or complementary regimes for the regulation of PMSCs. If rivals—each attracting a different set of stakeholders (states and non-state actors)[139]—it can be predicted that the Montreux Process will enhance the CSR of PMSCs whereas the Draft

Convention will harden the SR of states (and the institutional responsibility of organizations). However, it is only if they emerge as complementary regimes, with the majority of the same states signing up for both, that the CSR regime of the Montreux Process can be made more effective by the SR regime of the Draft Convention. By themselves, neither sufficiently encompasses both CSR and SR elements. More particularly, neither fully addresses the relationship between these elements, which is necessary for a legitimate and effective system of regulation that will deliver access to justice for victims of human rights abuse by PMSCs. Without a supervised treaty regime to ensure that states fulfill their due diligence obligations under SR, there can be no assurance that states will ensure that corporations fulfill their due diligence obligations under CSR.

Until corporations are recognized as subjects of international law against which direct enforcement can be taken, any CSR regime for PMSCs, no matter how successful in its own terms, will not fully deliver justice and accountability for the simple reason that voluntary self-regulation (even with oversight) will primarily cover the good citizens of the corporate world and not the bad. Ensuring that states have strong national systems of accountability applicable to PMSCs, and providing international accountability mechanisms against states, is necessary to ensure that states fulfill these obligations. But, of course, this ultimately comes up against the weaknesses in all international regulation—that even though treaties provide for binding commitments for states, it is a decision of each state whether to become a party. Little can be done to change this given that a mandatory legislative decision of the U.N. Security Council on this matter is very unlikely and, in any case, is a hugely problematic way of making legitimate international law.

There is a great deal of work to be done, both to persuade those states that are behind the Montreux Process

that an international treaty along the lines of a Draft Convention is necessary (and the recent meeting of the open-ended intergovernmental working group established by the Human Rights Council in 2010 shows how difficult this is going to be),[140] and to make the provisions of the Montreux Process and the Draft Convention compatible—for instance, in achieving clarity (via compromise) on what can and cannot be outsourced to PMSCs. Rather than the current approach adopted in the Draft Convention of prohibiting the outsourcing of inherently governmental functions, a compromise would be to recognize that certain functions such as combat, arrest, detention, interrogation, and intelligence gathering, are acts of states no matter who performs them. They therefore give rise to state responsibility. Under this approach the outsourcing of state functions is permitted but the outsourcing of state responsibility is not. If this agreement can be achieved, further work will still be required to ensure that the Montreux Process and the Draft Convention provide clear and interlocking due diligence obligations on all three actors—states, organizations, and PMSCs. One method of achieving this would be to bring the Draft Convention's due diligence obligations closer to the "good practices" detailed in the second part of the Montreux Document. The overriding purpose of any such developments must be to provide comprehensive provision for effective access to justice, through judicial and non-judicial means, for victims of abuse at the hands of PMSCs at both national and international levels.

Notes

1 This article follows the orthodox legal distinction between hard law as legally binding and soft law as not legally binding, though this author recognizes the more subtle analysis of the differences located in non-legal literature. See, for example, Kenneth W. Abbott and Duncan Snidal, "Hard and Soft Law in International Governance," *International Organization* 54 (2000): 421–56.

2 Montreux Document, U.N. Doc. A/63/467-S/2008/636, October 6, 2008; (hereinafter "Montreux Document").

3 International Code of Conduct for Private Security Service Providers 2010, http://www.icoc-psp.org/uploads/INTERNATIONAL_CODE_OF_CONDUCT_Final_without_Company_Names.pdf (accessed February 3, 2012) (hereinafter "International Code of Conduct").

4 In Report of the Working Group on the Use of Mercenaries as a Means of Violating Human Rights and Impeding the Exercise of the Right to Self-Determination, U.N. Doc. A/HRC/15/25, July 2, 2010 (hereinafter "Draft Convention").

5 Ian Brownlie, *Principles of Public International Law*, 7th ed. (Oxford: Oxford University Press, 2008), 434.

6 Last year, the Human Rights Council decided to establish a Working Group on this issue consisting of five independent experts. Human Rights Council, Resolution 17/4, *Human Rights and Transnational Corporations and Other Business Enterprises*, A/HRC/RES/17/4, July 6, 2011.

7 See the contribution by José L. Gómez del Prado, in this issue.

8 Nigel D. White, "The Privatization of Military and Security Functions and Human Rights: Comments on the UN Working Group's Draft Convention," *Human Rights Law Review* 11 (2001): 149–51.

9 See the contributions by Katherine Huskey and Marcus Hedahl, in this issue.

10 Gerry Simpson, "The Death of Baha Mousa," *Melbourne Journal of International Law* 8 (2007): 340.

11 Sir William Gage, "The Report of the Baha Mousa Inquiry," September 8, 2011, http://www.bahamousainquiry.org/report/index.htm (accessed February 3, 2012).

12 *Al-Skeini v. United Kingdom* (app. no. 55721/07), July 7, 2011.

13 Matthew Weaver and Richard Norton-Taylor, "MoD to Pay £3m to Iraqis Tortured by British Troops," *Guardian*, July 10, 2008.

14 International Military Tribunal, *The Trial of German Major War Criminals: Proceedings of the International Military Tribunal Sitting at Nuremberg, Germany*, August 22, 1946 to October 1, 1946, Part 22, 447.

15 Andre Nollkaemper, "Concurrence between Individual Responsibility and State Responsibility in International Law," *International and Comparative Law Quarterly* 52 (2003): 624.

16 Hannah Arendt, *Eichmann in Jerusalem: A Report on the Banality of Evil* (New York: Viking Press, 1963), 240.

17 Nollkaemper, "Concurrence," 636.

18 Rome Statute of the International Criminal Court 1998, Art. 25, U.N. Doc. A/CONF.183/9.

19 Nigel D. White, "Institutional Responsibility for Private Military and Security Companies," in *War by Contract: Human Rights, Humanitarian Law and Private Contractors*, ed. Francesco Francioni and Natalino Ronzitti (Oxford: Oxford University Press, 2011), 392.

20 See the preamble to the Draft Convention, which expresses concern about the "increasing delegation or outsourcing of inherently State functions which undermine any State's capacity to retain its monopoly on the legitimate use of force." See also Art. 1(1) of the Draft Convention.

21 Montreux Document, Part IA, para. 2.

22 Draft Convention, Art. 2(i).

23 Montreux Document, Part I, para. 25; Part II, paras. 1, 24, and 53.

24 Ibid., Preface, para. 9. The International Code of Conduct adopts a similar definition in section B—"guarding and protection of persons and objects, such as convoys, facilities, designated sites, property or other places (whether armed or unarmed), or any other activity for which the Personnel of Companies are required to carry or operate weapons in the performance of their duties."

25 *Military and Paramilitary Activities in and Against Nicaragua (Nicaragua v. United States of America)*, International Court of Justice Reports 1986, 62–64.

26 *Application of the Convention on the Prevention and Punishment of the Crime of Genocide (Bosnia and Herzegovina v. Serbia and Montenegro)*, International Court of Justice Reports 2007, 43 at para. 406.

27 Ibid., para. 402.

28 Montreux Document, Part I.A, para. 7.

29 For an overview of the U.N.'s engagement with PMSCs, see A. G. Ostensen, "UN Use of Private Military and Security Companies: Practices and Policies," DCAF, SSR Paper No. 3, 2011.

30 In ILC Report of the Work of its Sixty-Third Session, U.N. Doc. A/66/10 (2011), 52.

31 U.N. General Assembly, 66th Session, 18th Meeting of the Sixth Committee, October 24, 2011, Statement by Ms. Patricia O'Brien, Under-Secretary-General for Legal Affairs, http://untreaty.un.org/ola/media/info_from_lc/POB%20speech%20to%20the%20Sixth%20Committee%202011.pdf (accessed February 3, 2012).

32. U.N.'s General Conditions of Contract, Second Interim Revision, OLA Version, February 9, 2006, sec. 1, which states in part that a contractor "shall have the legal status of an independent contractor vis-à-vis the United Nations. The contractor's personnel and sub-contractors shall not be considered in any respect as being the employees or agents of the United Nations."

33 White, "Institutional Responsibility," 388.

34 *Behrami and Saramati v. France, Germany and Norway* (app. Nos. 71412/10 and 78166/01), para. 133.

35 Pierre Klein, "The Attribution of Acts to International Organizations," in *The Law of State Responsibility*, ed. James Crawford, Allain Pellet, and Simon Olleson (Oxford: Oxford University Press, 2010), 300–01.

36 Antonio Cassese, "The Nicaragua and Tadic Tests Revisited in the Light of the ICJ Judgment on Genocide," *European Journal of International Law* 18 (2007): 665–67. See also White, "Institutional Responsibility," 387–93.

37 Kjetil M. Larsen, "Attribution of Conduct in Peace Operations: The Ultimate Authority and Control Test," *European Journal of International Law* 19 (2008): 531; Marko Milanovic and Tatjana Papic, "As Bad as it Gets: The European Court of Human Rights' Behrami and Saramati Decision and General International Law," *International and Comparative Law Quarterly Review* 58 (2009): 267.

38 See generally the contribution of Andrew Alexandra, in this issue.

39 Neil Walker, "Late Sovereignty in the European Union," in *Sovereignty in Transition: Essays in European Law*, ed. Neil Walker (Oxford: Hart, 2003), 18, 17, 23.

40 Antony Anghie, *Imperialism, Sovereignty and the Making of International Law* (Oxford: Oxford University Press, 2004), 2.

41 Ibid., 6.

42 Gerry Simpson, *Great Powers and Outlaw States: Unequal Sovereigns in the International Legal Order* (Cambridge, UK: Cambridge University Press, 2004), 5.

43 See the contribution by Allison Stanger, in this issue.

44 Robert Nozick, *Anarchy, State and Utopia* (Oxford: Basil Blackwell, 1974), 113.

45 Allison Stanger, *One Nation Under Contract: The Outsourcing of American Power and the Future of Foreign Policy* (New Haven: Yale University Press, 2009).

46 Ibid., ix.

47 See Jan Klabbers, "Presumptive Personality: The European Union in International Law," in *International Law and Legal Aspects of the European Union*, ed. Martii Koskenniemi (The Hague: Kluwer, 1998), 243–49.

48 Commission on Human Rights, "Promotion and Protection of Human Rights: Interim Report of the Special Representative of the Secretary-General on the Issue of Human Rights and Transnational Corporations and Other Business Enterprises," U.N. Doc. E/CN.4/2006/97 (2006), para. 60.

49 Draft Convention, Arts. 40–42.

50 Anghie, *Imperialism*, 141.

51 Reflected in the decision of the Permanent Court of International Justice as late as 1927 in *The Case of the SS Lotus*, Permanent Court of International Justice Series A, No. 10 (1927), 18.

52 Ibid., 224.

53 http://www.g4s.com/en/Who%20we%20are/Where%20we%20operate (accessed February 3, 2012).

54 For a number of perspectives on this issue see *Non-State Actors and Human Rights*, ed. Philip Alson (Oxford: Oxford University Press, 2005), chaps. 5, 6, and 8. See also Sarah Joseph, "Taming the Leviathans: Multinational Enterprises and Human Rights," *Netherlands International Law Review* 46 (1999): 171.

55 See also the Organisation for Economic Co-operation and Development, "Guidelines for Multinational Enterprises" (rev. 2011; first produced in 1976). See also the International Labour Organization's "Tripartite Declaration of Principles Concerning Multinational Enterprises and Social Policy" (2006; first adopted in 1977).

56 U.N. Doc. A/HRC/17/31, March 21, 2011 (hereinafter Ruggie's "Framework").

57 U.N. Doc. A/HRC/RES/17/4, June 16, 2011.

58 Ruggie's "Framework," para. 6.

59 Ibid.

60 Sorcha MacLeod, "The Role of International Regulatory Initiatives on Business and Human Rights for Holding Private Military and Security Actors to Account," in *War by Contract*, ed. Francioni and Ronzitti, 350.

61 Ibid., 352.

62 See generally the contribution of Marcus Hedahl, in this issue.

63 Susan Marks and Fiorentina Azizi, "Responsibility for Violations of Human Rights Obligations: International Mechanism," in *International Responsibility*, ed. Crawford, Pellet, and Olleson, 729.

64 Susan Heathcote, "State Omissions and Due Diligence: Aspects of Fault, Damage and Contribution to Injury in the Law of State Responsibility," in *The ICJ and the Evolution of International Law: The Enduring Impact of the Corfu Channel Case*, ed. Karine Bannelier, Theodore Christakis, and Susan Heathcote (Abingdon, UK: Routledge, 2012), 308.

65 See Nigel D. White, "Regulatory Initiatives at the International Level," in *Multilevel Regulation of Private Military and Security Contractors*, ed. Christine Bakker and Mirko Sossai (Oxford: Hart, 2012), 11–30.

66 Ruggie's "Framework," commentary on Principle 1.

67 *Corfu Channel Case (Merits)*, International Court of Justice Reports 1949, 22.

68 Francesco Francioni, "The Role of the Home State in Ensuring Compliance with Human Rights by Private Military Contractors," in *War by Contract*, ed. Francioni and Ronzitti, 105–107. This is not without controversy—see the contribution of Benjamin Perrin, in this issue.

69 Ruggie's "Framework," commentary on Principle 2.

70 For a review and analysis see Christine Bakker, "Duties to Prevent, Investigate, and Redress Human Rights Violations by Private Military and Security Companies: The Role of the Host State," *War by Contract*, ed. Francioni and Ronzitti, 130.

71 *Velasquez Rodriguez,* Inter-American Court of Human Rights (Series C) No. 4 (1988), para. 172.

72 Ruggie's "Framework," commentary on Principle 7.

73 Ibid., commentary on Principle 5.

74 Ibid., Principles 5 and 6.

75 For a review and analysis, see Carsten Hoppe, "Positive Human Rights Obligations of the Hiring State in Connection with the Provision of Coercive Services by a Private Military or Security Company," in *War by Contract,* ed. Francioni and Ronzitti, 111.

76 *Reparation for Injuries Suffered in the Service of the United Nations,* International Court of Justice Reports 1949, 179.

77 The OIOS was established by GA Res. 48/218B, July 29, 1994, to assist the U.N. Secretary-General to fulfill his oversight responsibilities over staff and resources. The OIOS audits, evaluates, monitors, and inspects U.N. activities, including peacekeeping operations, and investigates reports of mismanagement and misconduct: www.un.org/depts/oios/pages/about_us/html (accessed February 3, 2012).

78 Ruggie's "Framework," Principle 11.

79 Ibid., Principle 12.

80 International Code of Conduct, paras. 2–3.

81 Ibid., para. 21.

82 This is reflected in Ruggie's "Framework," Principle 12.

83 International Code of Conduct, para. 14.

84 Montreux Document, Preface, paras. 2–4.

85 Ruggie's "Framework," Principle 17.

86 Ibid., Principles 17–21 plus commentary.

87 James Cockayne, "Regulating Private Military and Security Companies: The Content, Negotiations, Weaknesses and Promise of the Montreux Document," *Journal of Conflict and Security Law* 13 (2008): 427.

88 White, "Regulatory Initiatives."

89 Cockayne, "Regulating Private Military and Security Companies," 402.

90 Montreux Document, Part I.A, paras. 3–4 (contracting states), Part II.B, paras. 9–10 (host states), and Part II.C, paras. 14–15 (home states).

91 Ibid., Part II.A, paras. 5 and 14. But see U.S. practice in Doug Brooks and Hanna Streng's contribution, in this issue.

92 Montreux Document, Part II.B, paras. 26–40 (host states); Part II.C, paras. 54–73 (home states).

93 Ibid., Preface, para. 3.

94 Ibid., Part I.E, paras. 22–26.

95 International Code of Conduct, para. 21.

96 Ibid., paras. 2–3.

97 Ibid., paras. 35–42.

98 Ibid., para. 4.

99 Ibid., para. 7.

100 Ibid., paras. 45, 48, 50.

101 Ibid., para. 51.

102 Ibid., para. 55.

103 Ibid., para. 63.

104 Ibid., para. 6(d).

105 Ibid., paras. 66–68.

106 Ibid., paras. 9 and 11.

107 Draft Charter of the Oversight Mechanism for the International Code of Conduct for Private Security Providers, January 16, 2012, http://www.icoc-psp.org/uploads/Draft_Charter.pdf (accessed February 3, 2012) (hereinafter "Draft Charter").

108 Ibid., paras. III.B, IX.A.1, IX.D, IX.E.1, IXE.2.

109 See Alexander Bohm, Kerry Senior, and Adam White, "The UK: National Self-Regulation and International Norms," *Multilevel Regulation,* ed. Bakker and Sossai, 309–28.

110 Draft Convention, Preamble, para. 20.

111 Ibid., Art. 9.

112 Ibid., Arts. 7, 10. See also Art. 11.

113 Ibid., Art. 4(1)(2). See also Art. 5(3).

114 On jurisdiction, see ibid., Art. 21.

115 Ibid., Art. 5(2). See also Art. 7(1).

116 Ibid., Art. 7(2).

117 Ibid., Art. 19.

118 Ibid., Art. 12.

119 Ibid., Art. 13(1)(5)(6).

120 Ibid., Art. 14.

121 Ibid., Art. 11.

122 Ibid., Art. 15.

123 White, "Regulatory Initiatives."

124 Draft Convention, Art. 15(3).

125 Ibid., Art. 16.

126 Ibid., Art. 29.

127 Ibid., Arts. 31–32. The Committee is also requested to establish and maintain an international register of PMSCs, see Art. 30.

128 Ibid., Arts. 33 and 35.

129 White, "Regulatory Initiatives."

130 Draft Convention, Art. 34.

131 The current lack of domestic remedies is shown by the scarcity of domestic cases in which individuals have successfully sued PMSCs. In terms of litigation against PMSCs, there appears to be little more than a handful of U.S. cases—see the country-specific chapters in *Multilevel Regulation*, ed. Bakker and Sossai, 123–526.

132 Draft Convention, Art. 37.

133 White, "Regulatory Initiatives."

134 Ruggie's "Framework," Principle 25 and commentary.

135 Ibid., Principle 29 and commentary.

136 Draft Charter, X.A.

137 Ibid., X.B.4.5.

138 Draft Convention, Art. 28.

139 White, "Regulatory Initiatives."

140 Human Rights Council, Open-ended Intergovernmental Working Group to Consider the Possibility of Elaborating an International Regulatory Framework on the Regulation, Monitoring and Oversight of the Activities of Private Military and Security Companies, Summary of First Session, May 23–27, 2011. U.N. Doc. A/HRC/WG.10/1/CRP.2. The open-ended working group was established by Human Rights Council Resolution (A/HRC/RES/15/26, October 1, 2010), by 32 votes to 12 with 3 abstentions. Those voting against were Belgium, France, Hungary, Japan, Poland, Republic of Korea, Republic of Moldova, Slovakia, Spain, Ukraine, the United Kingdom, and the United States of America.

A U.N. Convention to Regulate PMSCs?

JOSÉ L. GÓMEZ DEL PRADO*

In the last 20 years the ruthless competition for natural resources, political instability, armed conflicts, and the terrorist attacks of 9/11 have paved the way for private military and security companies (PMSCs) to operate in areas which were until recently the preserve of the state. PMSCs, less regulated than the toy industry, commit grave human rights violations with impunity. The United Nations has elaborated an international binding instrument to regulate their activities but the opposition of the U.S., U.K., and other Western governments—and from PMSCs, which prefer self-regulation—have prevented any advancement.

The Context

The years that followed the decolonization period in the 1960s were marked by the activities of mercenaries. With the fall of the Berlin Wall, the collapse of the U.S.S.R., and the globalization of the world economy (a globalization which triggered a "ruthless competition for natural resources, political instability, armed conflicts and crisis situations"[1]), the last 20 years have been stamped by the activities of private military and security companies (PMSCs).

Military and security functions, considered inherently state functions, are being increasingly outsourced to the private sector.[2] The growth of this new industry, a direct consequence of merging public and private sectors (government and big business) with an unstoppable flow of money in a period of economic recession, has seen the increasing outsourcing of military functions to private contractors, with companies such as Blackwater (renamed Xe and Academi) and DynCorp doing the jobs of professional soldiers. In the field of

José L. Gómez del Prado is the former chairperson of the U.N. Working Group on the use of mercenaries.

intelligence, private contractors are hired to do the work of spies.[3]

This new industry is transnational in nature and has literally exploded with the privatization of war in the Afghan and Iraqi conflicts, where private contractor personnel have outnumbered those of the military.[4]

The reappearance of mercenaries in the 1960s, after their disappearance for almost a century, coincided with the decolonization process initiated by and conducted under the auspices of the United Nations. In 1977, with Protocol I Additional to the Geneva Conventions, the international community agreed on a definition of and a status for mercenaries operating in international armed conflicts. And in 1989, after many years of negotiations, the United Nations adopted the International Convention against the Recruitment, Use, Financing and Training of Mercenaries[5] which criminalized mercenary activities. The International Convention entered into force in 2001 when the mercenary phenomenon had been mostly replaced by the activities of PMSCs. By then, the convention was already considered obsolete.

However, the 2004 coup in Equatorial Guinea and the recent 2011 developments in Côte d'Ivoire and Libya remind us that mercenaries remain active in many parts of the world, particularly in Africa. The authorities of Côte d'Ivoire and Libya resorted to mercenaries to impede exercise of the right of the peoples to self-determination.[6] There have also been reports that former mercenaries have been contracted by PMSCs and deployed to Somalia.[7]

Only 32 states have ratified the International Convention against mercenaries. Even fewer countries (including Belgium, France, Italy, Namibia, and South Africa) have dealt with mercenary activities in their criminal or military codes using the definitions in Protocol I or the 1989 International Convention.

Since 1990, the world has witnessed a proliferation of private companies that profit from the military and security services they offer in armed and low-intensity conflicts and post-conflict situations, international relief, and contingency operations. Until recently, such services were considered to be the preserve of the state.

The United States, South Africa, the United Kingdom, Afghanistan, Iraq, and Sierra Leone, among others, have been confronted by human rights abuses committed by employees of PMSCs. The United States, the United Kingdom, and South Africa[8] are three of the major exporters of PMSC services to areas of conflict. Debates between their parliaments and government executives have revolved around how best to regulate these companies. Of the 464 PMSCs signatories to the International Code of Conduct being elaborated under the Swiss Initiative (as of September 10, 2012), 163 of the PMSCs are from United Kingdom, 54 from the United States, and 19 from South Africa.[9]

PMSCs also decide to place their headquarters in a given country because they calculate that they are not going to have regulatory difficulties with that particular government. Many PMSCs that have their headquarters in Washington or London are registered in tax havens such as the Bahamas or the Caymans.[10]

Similar to South Africa's legislation,[11] Afghanistan,[12] Iraq,[13] and Sierra Leone[14] have all established national regulatory frameworks. The Swiss government is studying possible frameworks of regulation at the national level in addition to the Montreux Document and the International Code of Conduct, and this work is being carried out in collaboration with the security industry and the U.S. and the U.K. governments.[15]

A third category of countries, including Colombia, Chile, Fiji, Nepal, Romania, and Uganda, has served as a pool from which former military and law enforcement personnel have been contracted as cheaper labor by PMSCs and their subsidiaries in order to increase their profits.

Although PMSC personnel carry out many of the activities that mercenaries have been conducting throughout history, they are not usually "mercenaries." Contrary to the "dogs of war" mercenaries of the past, PMSCs are legally registered business entities. The definition of mercenaries contained in international instruments does not generally apply to PMSC personnel.

The gross human rights violations in which PMSCs have been involved, and questions about their legitimacy and the type of activities they carry out, as well as the norms under which they should operate and how to monitor their activities, have galvanized the international community's attention.

Confronted with this new non-state actor, governments, the new security industry, and regional organizations,[16] as well as the United Nations and intergovernmental organizations, have reacted differently and adopted divergent approaches to dealing with this expanding phenomenon.

National Initiatives

Switzerland

The involvement of PMSCs in Iraq, following its occupation by American and Coalition Forces and the immunity status provided to foreign private contractors, led the Swiss government, as depository of the Geneva Conventions and headquarters of the International Committee of the Red Cross (ICRC), to react. In 2006, the Swiss government, together with the ICRC, launched the Swiss Initiative, which adopted the Montreux Document in 2008. The second phase of the Swiss Initiative consists of the elaboration of an international code of conduct for PMSCs, to be finalized in 2012.

Behind this move was also the embarrassment caused by the scandal of the 2004 coup in Equatorial Guinea. Several part-owners of Meteoric Tactical Systems—a company providing security to the Swiss Embassy in Baghdad—were involved in the coup during their holidays and were arrested in Zimbabwe.[17] In addition, the expansion of PMSCs in Switzerland forced the government to attempt harmonization of the legislation in the different Swiss cantons.[18] Legislation was drafted to be adopted in December 2007, but the Swiss government decided to provisionally renounce regulation of PMSCs in Switzerland that were active in zones of crisis or conflicts. In 2010, the Swiss government was again obliged to react following the scandal caused by the establishment in Basle of AEGIS Group Holdings SA, one of the major international PMSCs.[19] According to the Swiss Ministry of Justice, over 20 PMSCs established in different cantons were operating in conflict zones.[20] The Swiss government is now developing regulations to be adopted by its federal parliament.[21] A draft of the law was circulated in January 2012.[22] The legislation aims at preserving the domestic and external security of Switzerland and its neutrality as well as guaranteeing respect for international law. It foresees the legal prohibition of certain activities and the establishment of regulations. It will apply to persons and companies providing services abroad or in Switzerland.

As it stands, the draft law appears more like window dressing than a national mechanism aiming at effectively controlling and monitoring PMSC activities. The sanctions contained in its Article 17 are weak. Because it is not envisaged as a centralized body responsible for licensing, giving authorization to, and controlling private security companies, there will necessarily be delays and inefficiency in implementing the law.[23] Provisions regarding human rights protection could contain more specific standards, and gender issues particularly should be spelled out. The scope of application (Articles 2 and 4) contains activities that have been a matter of concern for the international community, including intelligence, espionage, and the detention[24] and interrogation of prisoners.

The law will also apply to firms established in Switzerland that have financial shares in companies operating abroad. It will prohibit direct participation in hostilities in an armed conflict, as well as activities in relation to either participation in hostilities or grave violations of human rights. In order to control their activities abroad, companies will have to declare themselves to the Swiss authorities. All activities contrary to the law will be forbidden. The law foresees administrative and penal sanctions and will also apply to federal authorities outsourcing functions of protection to an overseas private security company. Federal authorities will have to make sure that the company fulfills a number of prerequisite conditions and that its personnel have been adequately trained. The legislation determines under what conditions the use of force and weapons are authorized.

United Kingdom

On January 24, 2008, an Early Day Motion[25] was signed by 82 members of the U.K. Parliament, expressing the concern of the House of Commons about the "exponential growth of PMSCs since the invasion of Iraq."[26] Members of Parliament were "disturbed by the substantial rise of reported incidents of civilian killings and human rights abuses by PMSCs guards in Iraq who remain unregulated and unaccountable." The House of Commons noted that six years after the Green Paper that originated in a request from the Foreign Affairs Committee following the involvement of a British PMSC in Sierra Leone, there was still no United Kingdom legislation regulating PMSCs. The Members of Parliament believed that "self-regulation by the industry is not appropriate in this instance" and urged "the Government to bring forward legislative proposals for the control of the

PMSC sector as an urgent priority."[27] Civil society and concerned NGOs[28] had also identified and monitored a number of individuals and companies operating in this industry which had committed grave human rights violations.[29]

South Africa

Following the involvement of South African PMSCs in a number of armed conflicts in Africa, the government adopted the 1998 Regulation of Foreign Military Assistance Act (RFMAA). This prohibits mercenary activity and regulates the provision of "foreign military assistance" by South African citizens, companies, and permanent residents in South Africa. Under the RFMAA, "foreign military assistance" includes military assistance to a party to an armed conflict in the form of advice or training; personnel, financial, logistical, intelligence, and operational support; personnel recruitment; medical or paramedical services; and procurement of equipment. It also prohibits security services for the protection of individuals involved in armed conflict or their property; any action aimed at overthrowing a government or undermining the constitutional order, sovereignty, or territorial integrity of a state; and any other action that has the result of furthering the military interests of a party to the armed conflict. Any person or company who seeks to provide "foreign military assistance" must be specifically authorized to do so.

The RFMAA has had a very limited impact on South African mercenaries, PMSCs operating abroad, or South African nationals offering their services to foreign PMSCs. Between 2,000 and 4,000 South Africans were working in Iraq in 2010. Thirty-five South Africans employed by PMSCs were killed in Iraq between 2004 and 2010. Their bodies were repatriated to South Africa. Four others were abducted in 2006 and their status remains unknown. According to the Department of International Relations and Cooperation, the RFMAA has prompted a large part of the South African industry to relocate or go underground in order to escape regulation.[30] Following the 2004 Equatorial Guinea coup, in which several South African mercenaries were involved, new legislation was adopted in 2006, but it is not yet in force.

United States of America

The contracting out of a number of military and security activities to private companies in Iraq and Afghanistan has on numerous occasions been a source of embarrassment to the United States government. Employees of PMSCs have been accused, in high-profile incidents, of violating human rights, shooting civilians, using excessive force, being insensitive to local customs or beliefs, and treating local populations disrespectfully. Concerns over the lack of transparency, oversight, and accountability have also attracted media and public attention.[31]

In 2004, the killing of four Blackwater employees by Iraqi insurgents in Fallujah dramatically changed the course of the war. The U.S. Army unleashed Operation Phantom Fury and recaptured Fallujah in November 2004, leaving over 1350 insurgents dead, with some 95 U.S.

soldiers killed and 560 wounded.[32] According to several sources, in order to save money, Blackwater had failed to provide the appropriate safeguards for protecting a military convoy that needed to pass through an area controlled by insurgents.[33]

In 2006, a drunken Blackwater employee shot and killed a guard to the Iraqi Vice President. In 2007, the U.S. House of Representatives Committee on Oversight and Government Reform found that Blackwater had avoided paying Social Security, Medicare, and federal income and employment taxes.[34]

Also in 2007, the Special Inspector General for Iraq Reconstruction indicated that the U.S. State Department did not know specifically what it had received for most of the $1.2 billion in expenditures it had paid in its contract with DynCorp for the Iraqi Police Training Program. This was not the first time that DynCorp was suspected of illicit behavior. In the 1990s, during the Balkans operations, several DynCorp employees working in the U.N. Police task force were involved in a sex-trafficking scandal (including "owning" girls as young as 12 years old) and prostitution rackets. The supervisor of DynCorp in Bosnia videotaped himself raping two young women. None of these employees has been ever prosecuted.[35]

The Balkans allegations were brought to a Texas court in 2000 by an aircraft mechanic working for DynCorp who had ended up fired and was later forced into protective custody. On June 2, 2000, an investigation was launched in the DynCorp hangar at Comanche Base Camp, one of two U.S. bases in Bosnia and Herzegovina, and all DynCorp personnel were detained for questioning.[36] U.S. Army Criminal Investigation Division (CID) spent several weeks investigating and the results appear to support the allegations. DynCorp had fired five employees for similar illegal activities prior to the charges.[37] Many of the employees accused of sex trafficking were forced to resign under suspicion of illegal activity. DynCorp agreed to settle a suit brought by the former aircraft mechanic, Ben Johnston, two days before the case was set to go to trial in Texas. The amount of Johnston's settlement is confidential, but both Johnston and his attorney said they viewed the settlement as a victory—and as a vindication after two years of fighting the company.[38]

Kathryn Bolkovac, a U.N. International Police Force monitor, hired by DynCorp on another U.N.-related contract, also filed a lawsuit against DynCorp in Great Britain in 2001. She sued the company for unfair dismissal due to a protected disclosure (i.e., whistleblowing). She had reported that DynCorp police trainers in Bosnia were paying for prostitutes and participating in sex trafficking. On August 2, 2002 the court unanimously decided in her favor. At the time that she had reported that DynCorp officers were paying for prostitutes and participating in sex trafficking, DynCorp had a $15 million contract to hire and train police officers for duty in Bosnia and Herzegovina. None of the DynCorp employees were prosecuted, since they enjoyed immunity.[39] In 2010, Bolkovac's story was made into the film *The Whistleblower*.[40]

In 2009, photos were published showing employees of ArmorGroup North America—hired by the State Department to provide security at the U.S. Embassy in Kabul—engaging in lewd sexual hazing and harassment. Previous reports indicated a number of other allegations, including how the deficiencies of the company endangered the security of the embassy.[41]

A 2010 Senate Armed Services Committee investigation found that EOD Technology, another company contracted to protect the U.S. Kabul embassy, was suspected of hiring local warlords with possible Taliban ties. A report of the Subcommittee on National Security and Foreign Affairs of the U.S. Congress stated that the Department of Defense's contract had fueled a vast protection racket run by a shadowy network of warlords, strongmen, commanders, and corrupt Afghan officials. Not only did the system run afoul of the Department of Defense's own congressionally mandated rules and regulations, but it also appeared to risk undermining the U.S. strategy in Afghanistan.[42]

In April 2010, five former Blackwater employees were indicted for conspiring to violate federal firearm laws, for possession of unregistered fire arms, and for obstruction of justice. That same year, Xe Services LLC (formerly Blackwater) agreed to pay to the State Department a penalty of $42 million for 288 alleged violations of the Arms Export Control Act.[43]

Furthermore, there have been challenges to accountability asserted in a number of litigations against PMSCs in cases of torture and the abuse of detainees in the Abu Ghraib prison (involving employees of CACI and Titan), as well as in the 2007 shooting deaths of 17 Iraqi civilians by Blackwater employees in Nisoor square in Baghdad.[44]

In 2011, a congressional bill, the "Stop Outsourcing Security Act"—which was designed to phase out the use of private military contractors—was tabled again. Since 2007, the bill has been rejected four times.[45] Also rejected since 2003—despite having been reintroduced at four different sessions of Congress—is the "Transparency and Accountability in Security Contracting Act."[46] After a three-year investigation begun in 2008, a bipartisan congressional panel found that the U.S. had wasted or misspent $34 billion in the Iraq and Afghanistan wars.[47]

The U.S. Congress has regularly stated that it does not have complete access to information about all security contracts; the number of armed private security contractors working in Iraq, Afghanistan, and other combat zones; the number of contractors who have died; and any disciplinary actions taken against contract personnel or companies. The Special Inspector General for Iraq Reconstruction had not obtained information regarding the U.S. State Department's 2012 deployment in Iraq of some 5500 private security contractors.[48] In addition, there have been embarrassing reports to Congress indicating waste, fraud, and abuse running into the billions of dollars. A summary of the reports states: "for many years the government has abdicated its contracting responsibilities—too often using contractors as the default mechanism, driven by considerations other than whether they provide the best solution, and without consideration for the resources needed to manage them. That is how contractors have come to account for fully half the United States presence in contingency operations."[49]

The United Nations Draft Convention on PMSCs

Any national response to regulate PMSCs will have to take into consideration the transnational nature of the security industry. National legislative efforts, well intentioned as they may be, will never be successful without a coordinated response by the international community to the increasing role of the private sector in war and peace. To be effective, any regulatory framework will need to interlock legislation, regulation, and monitoring mechanisms at the national, regional, and international levels.[50]

Lack of transparency and accountability, human rights abuses, the outsourcing of inherently state functions to the private sector, the waste of resources, corruption, and rackets run by shadowy networks of warlords all pose real threats to the democratic ideals pursued by Western states as enshrined in the Magna Carta, the 1689 English Bill of Rights, the French and the U.S. constitutions,[51] as well as the U.N. Charter and its system of collective security based on sovereign states. As Martin van Creveld notes, the ascendancy of a kind of corporation that is not sovereign, and whose expansion with globalization is reaching all social dimensions, represents one of the greatest revolutions in modern times—and it is full of implications that we are only beginning to understand.[52]

The widespread contracting out of military and security operations—historically, inherently state functions—to the private sector has raised important issues and questions as to the extent that non-state actors can be held accountable for human rights violations. States have the responsibility to protect individuals against human rights violations committed by corporations such as private military and security companies. When such violations occur, victims have the right to an effective remedy and to appropriate reparation.

Two intrinsically contradictory strategies coexist at the threshold of the twenty-first century. On the one hand, in failing states such as Afghanistan and Iraq, U.N. peacekeeping and capacity-building missions backed by Western nations aim at building the state monopoly of legitimate force by capacitating a national army, police, and judiciary. On the other hand, these same Western states are increasingly outsourcing to the private sector large parts of their military and security forces and, therefore, undermining the state monopoly of force.[53]

The text of the Draft Convention developed for the United Nations by the Working Group on the use of mercenaries is based on the following paradigm:

The need of an international binding instrument as a means to invigorate cooperation among Member States in reaffirming that the sovereignty of States, the UN international collective security system and the strengthening of democracy lies on the responsibility of States to maintain the control of the legitimate use of force and States' obligations to investigate, prosecute, punish and ensure effective remedies to victims of human rights violations.

From May 23 to 27, 2011, the U.N. Open-ended Intergovernmental Working Group to consider the possibility of elaborating an international regulatory framework for PMSCs held its first session in Geneva. A few months previously, in September 2010, the U.N. Human Rights Council had decided to establish such a mechanism to consider the possibility of elaborating an international regulatory framework. The Human Rights Council had indicated that members of the intergovernmental working group should, inter alia, consider the option of developing a legally binding instrument on the regulation, monitoring, and oversight of the activities of PMSCs, including their accountability. Such an instrument would take into consideration the principles, main elements, and draft text as proposed by the Working Group on the use of mercenaries.[54]

Participants in the first and the second sessions of the Open-ended Intergovernmental Working Group, respectively held in May 2011 and August 2012, agreed that the activities of PMSCs should be properly regulated. There was, however, disagreement on the form that such regulation should take: whether an international convention was necessary or whether current international and national obligations combined with self-regulation were sufficient.

The debates during these sessions of the open-ended working group reflect the strongly divergent ideological and political positions of U.N. Member States regarding the activities of PMSCs, differences that will be difficult to resolve. However, the prospect of a human rights treaty focused on PMSCs remains and the participants have agreed to continue meeting and holding discussions.

Is the idea of an international binding instrument to regulate and monitor the activities of PMSC so far-fetched? Such a move has not only been proposed by a majority of Member States of the United Nations but also by members of the U.K. House of Commons[55] and by members of the Parliamentary Assembly of the Council of Europe.[56] They felt that a sensitive area involving the use of force and public security must not be left to corporations without strict delimitations of what are inherently state functions. They proposed establishing regulation and controls for those activities that may be carried out by the private sector.

Arguments in Favor of an International Binding Instrument

Taking into account the current legal vacuum covering the activities of PMSCs,[57] the dangerous activities they carry out, the types of environment in which they operate, and the impact of their activities on the enjoyment of human rights, states should register, license, regulate, and monitor their activities and ensure accountability through prosecution when necessary. Victims of human rights violations committed by PMSCs and their employees should be able to exercise their right to an effective remedy. As indicated earlier, the few national regulations so far adopted have serious limitations. Only an international legally binding instrument could ensure that states apply minimum standards to regulate PMSCs' activities.

The services provided by PMSCs cannot be considered as ordinary commercial commodities to be controlled through self-regulation initiatives. The functions filled by PMSCs are highly specific and dangerous and involve the trade-off of a wide variety of military and security services requiring the elaboration of international standards and monitoring mechanisms.

The fact that the definition of "mercenaries" under the two international conventions does not generally apply to the personnel of PMSCs[58] is also a strong argument for the adoption of a new instrument.

A majority of PMSCs has been created or is managed by former militaries or ex-policemen for whom this is big business:[59] they attract large numbers of military and police personnel looking for opportunities to make easy money. Unfortunately, they hollow out and weaken existing security institutions by draining resources and worsening public security.

The policy of outsourcing military and security functions from governments and intergovernmental organizations has not arisen as a result of spontaneous generation. A convergence of interests among key personalities in different national and international administrations with the security industry has been evident, including a revolving-door syndrome. The new security industry has placed key personalities within the administration and relevant institutions to secure its interests. The interest of governments in avoiding responsibility and monitoring by democratic institutions has also contributed to the development of such a policy.

Contrary to the arguments put forward by Doug Brooks and Hanna Streng,[60] there has been a regular and consistent lobbying from outside and from within the PMSC corporate community to obtain contracts from governments, intergovernmental organizations, and international organizations: the offer has stimulated the demand. A clear example has been the shift in the United Nations policy to outsource security since Gregory Starr, the person responsible for contracting Blackwater when he was at the U.S. State Department, was appointed U.N. Undersecretary General for Safety and Security.[61]

It has been argued that "*supply* in the market for force tends to self-perpetuate, as PMSCs turn out a new caste of security experts striving to fashion security understandings to defend and conquer market shares." On the other hand, "*demand* does not penalize firms that service 'illegitimate' clients in general. Consequently, the number of actors who can wield control over the use of force is limited mainly by their ability to pay."[62]

Arguments against a Binding International Instrument

Western states argue that what is really needed is better implementation of the existing international mechanisms, not new legislation, and contend that new self-regulatory mechanisms, such as the Montreux Document and the International Code of Conduct, have not yet been implemented.

Other reasons advanced are the lack of agreement among states on what are inherently state functions that cannot be contracted out to the private sector, as well as the conviction that the national licensing system envisaged by the Draft Convention would be too costly for governments. This argument is surprising, for licensing regimes already exist in most countries. Countries without a licensing regime for PMSCs, such as Canada, are the exception.[63]

The elaboration of a multilateral binding instrument needs the consensus of Member States. The proposed Draft Convention has the opposition of those governments in whose territories the majority of PMSCs is registered. They argue that a much broader consultation is needed in the development of a treaty. They also emphasize that the issue of regulating PMSCs intersects with several branches of international law, such as the law on the use of force, international humanitarian law, international criminal law, and the law on state responsibility, and it is not primarily a matter for the Human Rights Council.

The proposed U.N. Draft Convention, among other things, would:

- Reaffirm State Responsibility regarding the activities of PMSCs;
- Identify "inherently" state functions for which the state takes direct responsibility and that cannot be delegated or contracted out in order to ensure that states preserve their sovereignty and do not abdicate their responsibility toward their citizens and other states;
- Cover not only international armed conflicts but any other situation in which PMSCs operate;
- Extend responsibility to intergovernmental organizations, such as the U.N. or NATO;
- Require state parties to establish jurisdiction for the offenses addressed by the convention;
- Establish in each state a national regime of regulation and oversight over the activities in its territory of PMSCs and their personnel comprising (1) a register or governmental body, and (2) a national licensing system of import/export of military and security services;
- Create an International Committee on the Regulation, Oversight, and Monitoring of PMSCs;
- Establish (1) an Inquiry procedure, (2) an Inter-States Complaint mechanism, and (3) an Individual and Group petitions procedure;
- Envisage establishing an international fund to provide reparation to victims of offenses identified in the convention and/or assist in the victims' rehabilitation.

State Responsibility

PMSCs' security and military capabilities for hire have enabled states and non-state actors to overcome political limitations regarding the use of force. States have weak legal responsibility for the functions they outsource to PMSCs as well as for the behavior of their employees.[64] Current international law has several gaps concerning the accountability of PMSCs. Under international humanitarian law, PMSCs are not considered part of a state's armed forces or supporting militias. Moreover, states themselves rarely address PMSCs' violations.

As Nigel White notes, states and international organizations bear responsibility in international law when human rights are violated. However, there exists a gap regarding the responsibility of PMSCs to whom states and international organizations are increasingly outsourcing their security functions.[65]

In addition to defining the inherently state functions which PMSCs would not be allowed to fulfill, the proposed convention would reaffirm the responsibilities of states regarding the activities that PMSCs could perform in case states choose to contract out certain activities.[66] On the issue of transparency and accountability, the Draft Convention establishes strong provisions regarding these non-state actors who had formerly been protected by a cloak of immunity and subcontracting. States are required to adopt measures to investigate, prosecute, and punish abuses committed by PMSCs and to ensure effective remedies to

victims—therein ignoring preexisting immunity agreements.

In the Draft Convention, states are categorized into contracting states, states of operation, home states, and third states. Irrespective of this division, in accordance with Article 4 of the Draft Convention on General principles, "Each State party bears responsibility for military and security activities of PMSCs registered or operating in their jurisdiction, whether or not these entities are contracted by the state." However, the Draft Convention does not go into secondary levels of responsibility to address whether states should be responsible for the acts themselves, or for failing to apply the due diligence principle in cases of international human rights and humanitarian law violations. Last, but not least, the Draft Convention reflects the weaknesses of international law in not directly addressing PMSCs. Instead it imposes obligations on those states contracting with PMSCs or having them on their territories (either as home states or states of operation).

Inherently State Functions that Cannot Be Delegated

The Draft Convention is the first international instrument that attempts to draw a line between those activities that are state functions and cannot be delegated or contracted out to the private sector and those that may be outsourced but should, nonetheless, be regulated.

The main reason for identifying and prohibiting the delegating or outsourcing of such functions is to ensure that states preserve their

sovereignty in relation to other nations and provide equal security to their citizens. The monopoly on the use of force is closely linked to the emergence of the modern state and the strengthening of democracies in western European countries and other nations such as Canada, the U.S., Australia, Japan, India, and New Zealand.

The monopoly on the legitimate use of force is a central attribute of sovereignty. Nonetheless, a state may, in a manner consistent with human rights standards, delegate certain functions involving the use of force to private actors. This view is based on the understanding that sovereign states must maintain control of the legitimate use of force. This view, however, is not shared by all governments, particularly Western states that favor privatization at all costs.

It will be necessary for long negotiations to occur in order to reach a consensus on which activities constitute inherently state functions. For example, the Montreux Document permits private contractors to fulfill military and security services which include "prisoner detention and advice to or training of local forces and security personnel"[67] whereas the Draft Convention does not.

This is not the only gray area that must be diminished in terms of what PMSCs may and may not do. Among the functions that are consistent with the principle of the state monopoly on the legitimate use of force and the belief that a state cannot outsource or delegate this right to PMSCs under any circumstances, one also finds references to functions such as "direct participation in hostilities, waging war and/or combat operations." One must ask, under what circumstances would the activity of private contractors driving petrol or ammunitions to supply the military constitute "direct participation"?

Under international humanitarian law, "direct participation in the hostilities is not restricted to situations where individuals are involved in military deployment or are armed with a view to taking an active part in combat operations: direct partici-pation is not necessarily restricted to a minority" of PMSCs.[68] Although the Geneva Conventions and their Additional Protocols do not provide a definition of "direct participation in hostilities," the commentary on Additional Protocol I indicates that " 'direct' participation means acts of war which by their nature or purpose are likely to cause actual harm to the personnel and equipment of the enemy armed forces."[69]

The scope of other functions will also need to be discussed. For example, references to "intelligence, knowledge transfer with military, security and policing application." The actions of MPRI (Military Professional Resources Incorporated) resulted in the direct transfer of knowledge and military skills to the Croatian army in 1994–95. On that occasion, Croatia, after having separated from Yugoslavia, was militarily confronted by the Krajina Serbs, but the Croatian army was ill-equipped. The interest of the U.S. was to weaken the Serbs by bolstering the Croatian army. However, the U.N. Security Council embargo prohibited the direct assistance or sale of arms to one of the conflicting parties. In 1994 a Washington agreement permitted the State Department to issue a license by which the Croat government signed contracts with MPRI. The main aim of the contract was to make a professional Croatian army capable of launching a few months later the "Operation Storm," which defeated the Krajina Serb army. The MPRI operation not only included training but also tactics, unit strategy, and coordination (functions that would be forbiden under the Draft Convention).[70]

Regulation of the Use of Force and Firearms for those Activities that May Be Outsourced

The Draft Convention does not prohibit altogether the use of arms by PMSCs. It recognizes that employees may carry firearms in providing military and security services. It establishes measures to ensure that, in providing military and security services, employees of PMSCs shall, as far as possible, apply non-violent means before resorting to the use of force and firearms.

The Draft Convention stipulates that employees may use force or firearms[71] only under certain circumstances.[72] In all these circumstances, PMSCs shall identify themselves as such and give a clear warning of their intent to use firearms, if the situation permits. Whenever the use of force and firearms is unavoidable, PMSC personnel must exercise restraint, minimize damage and injury, and respect and preserve human life. They also must also ensure that assistance and medical aid are rendered to any injured or affected persons at the earliest possible moment, and that relatives or close friends of the injured or affected person are notified as soon as possible.

What is important to recognize is that there is a normative gap in international law. Despite indications of disapproval about some types of outsourcing, particularly with regard to direct participation in hostilities, international law does not prohibit the outsourcing of state functions to PMSCs or even the direct participation of contractors in hostilities.[73]

For this reason, in addition to identifying the inherently state functions, the Draft Convention could also have indicated a list of activities that should not be forbidden by an international legally binding instrument. Such activities could include protection services (humanitarian convoys, maritime convoys, close protection); guarding services (supply depots, embassies, refugee camps); and transport services (humanitarian aid, refugees). A list such as this would also assist in diminishing the gray areas of PMSC activities. However, the task might be accomplished through the jurisprudence of the proposed Oversight Committee.

In the case of convoys, an important distinction has to be made between humanitarian convoys and convoys that transport merchandise or goods for military purposes and can become targets in armed or low-intensity conflicts. In this context it is worth mentioning the suit against KBR and its former parent company, Halliburton, that was brought in U.S. courts by the families of victims. On April 9, 2004, Iraqi insurgents attacked a U.S. Army convoy and two drivers were killed.[74] The families accused the PMSC companies of fraud-in-recruiting for allegedly convincing drivers that they would be engaged only in rebuilding and not in combat activities. They also accused the companies of sending the drivers into a high-risk area, knowing they could be attacked and possibly killed.[75] A district court in Texas rejected KBR and Halliburton's request to dismiss the suit and allowed the case to proceed. But the 5th Circuit overturned the lower court's decision based on the fact the drivers were entitled to workers' compensation. The court said allowing the case to proceed would undercut the workers' compensation program, which is designed to provide "prompt relief for employees, and limited and predictable liability for employers," Judge Priscilla Owen wrote for the three-judge panel.[76]

The Draft Convention would not regulate the activities of "the vast majority of companies that operate in high risk environments even un-armed security companies"[77] in so far as the employees of those companies would not be performing intelligence work that would be considered under the convention as an inherently state function.

Support activities for protecting people, premises, or convoys conducted by PMSCs, such as the ones mentioned above, cannot be governed by softer law instruments alone but should be monitored by states party to the convention under the national regime of regulation and oversight.

In this regard it is interesting to note that in its interim report the U.S. Bipartisan Commission on Wartime Contracting in Iraq and Afghanistan came to several important conclusions regarding the contracting of security functions. It criticized the government for not having "clear standards and policy on inherently governmental functions" and called for the development of a single consistent definition to ensure that only officers or employees of the federal government or members of the armed forces perform inherently governmental and other critical functions.[78]

Criminal Responsibility

States parties are required to establish jurisdiction over acts that carry out inherently state functions or perform legitimately outsourced activities that violate the standards of international human rights law or, where applicable, international humanitarian law. Such violations can include the export/import of PMSC services without license or authorization; or unlawful use of force and firearms when the offense is committed within its territory, or on board a ship or aircraft registered under its laws; or when the offense is committed by its nationals; and when the victim is one of its nationals.

In conformity with the principle *aut dedere aut judicare*, state parties are

required to establish jurisdiction when the offender is present within its territory and the state does not extradite such a person to any other state party asserting jurisdiction over such a person. The Draft Convention also envisages individual criminal responsibility of the superiors of PMSC personnel.

Furthermore, it contains provisions to establish the liability of legal persons and entities for the offenses specified by the convention. The liability of legal persons may be criminal, civil, or administrative, or a combination of these, without prejudice to the criminal liability of the natural persons who have actually committed the offenses.

National Monitoring System

The Draft Convention provides for a monitoring system for PMSCs at the domestic and the international levels. An effective control and accountability of PMSCs is possible only if there is a robust system of national regulation and enforcement. States are, therefore, required

to establish a comprehensive domestic regime of regulation and oversight over the activities in [their] territory of PMSCs and their personnel including all foreign personnel, in order to prohibit and investigate illegal activities as defined by this Convention as well as by relevant national laws.[79]

In order to coordinate among the different law enforcement and other bodies at the domestic level as well as to cooperate and exchange information at the international level, in accordance with Article 16 of the Draft Convention, states are requested "to establish and maintain a general State Registry of PMSCs operating in their jurisdiction, including details of any subsidiaries or holding companies of each registered PMSC" and to "identify or establish a governmental body responsible for the registry of PMSCs and exercise oversight of their activities."[80]

States are requested to investigate reports of violations of international humanitarian law and human rights norms by PMSCs and ensure civil and criminal prosecution and punishment of offenders. Furthermore, they are requested to take appropriate action against companies that commit human rights violations or engage in any criminal activity, inter alia by revoking their licenses and reporting to the international committee established by the convention on the record of activities of these companies.

States will have to ensure that PMSCs and their personnel carry out their activities exclusively under their respective licenses and authorizations, and these must be registered in the general Registry of the State.[81] The criteria for granting licenses and authorizations will take into account any record of human rights violations committed by the companies, providing and/or ensuring training in international human rights and humanitarian law, and robust due diligence measures.

The Draft Convention also requires that PMSCs and their personnel import and export their services only under the appropriate licenses and authorizations, and that PMSC personnel are required to be professionally trained and vetted according to the applicable international standards—in particular regarding the use of specific equipment and firearms.

Such oversight activities cannot be left to self-regulation alone, as under the "mechanism" of the International Code of Conduct proposed by the security industry (a follow-up to the Montreux Document). The self-regulatory mechanism that the security industry is devising with the International Code of Conduct would eliminate a number of competitors among PMSCs. The security industry ultimately would be comprised of a core of multinational

PMSCs (those with sufficient resources) that would become a "de facto" oligopoly or monopoly without any control whatsoever by national authorities.

In addition, the majority of PMSCs excluded by this code of conduct would continue to operate by offering cheaper rates, without being controlled either by the industry (self-regulation) or by governments (national regulation under domestic legislation). What are needed are international standards and mechanisms of regulation integrated into domestic legislation and applied to all PMSCs. Or, as indicated by White, it is necessary to have a monitoring treaty mechanism to ensure that states and corporations fulfill their due diligence obligations.[82]

International Monitoring System

The Draft Convention envisages an international system of oversight and monitoring for the activities of PMSCs. For the purpose of reviewing the Draft Convention's application, a Committee on the Regulation, Oversight, and Monitoring of PMSCs is proposed, consisting of a given number of experts of high moral standing, impartiality, and recognized competence in the field covered by the convention. They are elected by Sstates Pparties from among their nationals, and such elected experts shall serve in their personal capacity, with consideration being given to equitable geographical distribution and to the principal legal systems.

After a given number of parties have signed up to the convention, the elected committee will establish its own procedural rules to provide—as is the case for other U.N. human rights organs—for interpretative comments on the provisions of the convention. The committee will be responsible for establishing and maintaining an International Register of PMSCs operating in the international market, based on information provided by states parties as well as the Periodic Reports mechanism. For the latter, state parties will have to submit to the committee periodic reports on the legislative, judicial, administrative, and other measures they have adopted to give effect to the convention. The committee, after having considered these reports, will make observations and recommendations to the states parties.

The committee will also be responsible for several optional procedures. Under an inquiry procedure, if the committee receives reliable information indicating "grave or systematic violations" of the convention, and after having sought observations from the state(s) in which the offenses occurred and from the companies involved, it may launch a confidential inquiry undertaken by one or more members of the committee. Such an inquiry could, with the agreement of the state(s) concerned, conduct a visit *in loco*. The findings are to be transmitted to the state(s) concerned and the proceedings will be confidential. However, the committee, after consultations with the state(s) concerned, may decide to include a summary account of the results of the proceedings in its annual report to the U.N. General Assembly.

Under the Inter-State Complaint Mechanism, if a state that is party to the convention (having made the appropriate declaration recognizing the competence of the committee to receive and examine interstate communications) considers that another state party is not giving effect to the provisions of the convention, it may bring the matter to the attention of the committee. The committee shall then transmit the complaint to the party concerned, requesting written explanations or statements clarifying the matter and the remedy, if any, that may have been instituted by that party. If a matter referred to the committee is not resolved to the satisfaction of the states parties concerned, the committee may, with the prior consent of those states parties, appoint an ad hoc Conciliation Commission comprising five persons—who may or may not be members of the committee—with a view to achieving an amicable solution on the basis of respect for the convention.

In addition, the convention contains an optional Individual and Group Petition Procedure under which the committee may receive and consider petitions from or on behalf of individuals claiming to be victims of a violation by a state party that has recognized the competence of the committee. Among the criteria for considering a petition by the committee is a requirement that all effective available domestic remedies must have been exhausted. This rule does not apply, however, where the application of the remedies is unreasonably prolonged. If it deems necessary, the committee can recommend that the state party take such interim measures as may be necessary to avoid possible irreparable damage to the victims of the alleged violation. When the procedure is finalized, the committee communicates its views to the state party and to the author of the petition. This type of procedure is the same as those of the other U.N. human rights treaty organs.

Compensation to Victims: The Right to an Effective Remedy

The Draft Convention recognizes the need for victims of human rights violations committed by PMSCs to have access to justice. It contains a provision requiring states to consider establishing an international fund to be administered by the U.N. Secretary General to provide reparation to victims and/or assist in their rehabilitation. This, however, may not be considered sufficiently strong to reflect the growing need for stronger procedures at the international level. Considering the ineffectiveness of a large number of domestic legal systems, victims of human rights abuses committed by PMSCs should have direct access to justice. This could involve the creation of an ombudsman mechanism to guarantee access to justice to the victims, using models such as the Kosovo Ombudsman and the office of the ombudsperson created by the Security Council for individuals targeted by sanctions.[83]

Concluding Remarks

The state monopoly on the legitimate use of force, a central attribute of sovereignty on which the U.N. system of collective security is based, is a fairly recent political concept and one that is closely linked to the emergence of the modern state and the development of democratic institutions in Western Europe.

Although certain functions involving the use of force may be delegated to private actors, PMSCs' activities raise questions having different implications in countries with a firm monopoly on the use of force and in countries that have not reached that stage and lack such a monopoly. In the latter countries, such as Afghanistan and most African countries, or in countries where a monopoly has been destroyed, such as Iraq, the use of private force can be extremely problematic for building state democratic institutions.

At present, there is no comprehensive regulatory framework for the activities of PMSCs. States, nonetheless, bear the responsibility for holding private military and security companies accountable for human rights violations and are therefore required to develop national rules to regulate PMSCs. These rules must ensure that PMSCs are held criminally responsible for the conduct of their employees and that compensation mechanisms are established for victims of human rights violations.

Any national response to regulate PMSCs will have to take into consideration the transnational nature of the security industry. National legislative efforts, well intentioned though they may be, will never be successful without a coordinated response by the international community to the increasing role of the private sector in war and peace. In order for any regulatory framework to be effective it is vital to interlock legislation, regulation, and monitoring mechanisms at the national, regional, and international levels.

The research carried out by the U.N. Working Group on the use of mercenaries underscores that a national/international system based on self-regulation is insufficient. Democracies are being hollowed out by the development of a multinational security industry that merges the public and the private sectors, government, and big business. If we do not want to see the market of the security industry imposing its own rules on democracy,[84] it becomes imperative to establish international and national frameworks that are regulated and monitored by states.

Given the lack of agreement on a number of issues and the strong opposition of influential Western governments to a binding international instrument in the form proposed by the U.N. Working Group on the use of mercenaries, there is a need for the Open-ended Intergovernmental Working Group to identify and synchronize the complementarities that do exist between the Draft Convention, on one side, and the Swiss Initiative comprising the Montreux Document and the International Code of Conduct, on the other.[85]

The sessions of the Open-ended Intergovernmental Working Group provide member states that are in favor of an international binding regulatory framework with the opportunity to convince those Western states that favor a self-regulatory framework that

certain functions such as combat, arrest, detention, interrogation, and intelligence gathering, are acts of states no matter who performs them. They therefore give rise to state responsibility. Under this approach the outsourcing of state functions is permitted but the outsourcing of state responsibility is not.[86]

The Swiss draft law points out, albeit insufficiently, how complementarities that already exist between a binding instrument such as the international Draft Convention and a self-regulatory code of conduct could be integrated into a national regulatory framework.

This approach may also enable the integration into an international binding regulatory framework of the international code of conduct for PMSCs, developed under the Swiss Initiative, as well as any other regulations developed by the security industry. It would also be necessary to translate a number of the "Good Practices" included in the Montreux Document into binding international legal obligations.

Because there exists a protection gap—due to the fact that the contents of international human rights obligations of states are not always specifically determined in international law, with a consequent lack of effective remedies for human rights violations—the proposed convention would fill such a gap. States should not be relieved from their obligations and responsibilities under international law by the mediation procedure proposed under the "mechanism" foreseen in the international code of conduct. It is the responsibility of sovereign states to ensure that effective access to justice and appropriate remedies are available to victims of human rights violations committed by PMSC personnel.[87]

Notes

1 M. Kurtz, "The Social Foundations of Institutional Order: Reconsidering War and the Resource Curse in Third World State Building," *Politics and Society* 37, no. 4 (2009): 479.

2 Tanya Cook, "Dogs of War or Tomorrow's Peacekeepers? The Role of Mercenaries in the Future Management of Conflict," *Culture Mandala: The Bulletin of the Centre for East-West Cultural and Economic Studies* 5, no. 1 (2002): Article 1, available at http://epublications.bond.edu.au/cm/vol5/iss1/1

3 Paul Harris, "How Private Firms have Cashed in on the Climate of Fear since

9/11," *Guardian*, September 5, 2011: "Generals, government officials and intelligence chiefs flock to private industry and embark on new careers selling services back to government."

4 Scott Horton, "One Nation under Contract: Six Questions for Allison Stanger," *Harper's Magazine*, April 22, 2011.

5 International Convention Against the Recruitment, Use, Financing and Training of Mercenaries, December 4, 1989, 2163 UNTS 75.

6 United Nations Human Rights Council, Report, A/HRC/17/48 (2011); and United

Nations Human Rights Council, Report, A/HRC/17/49 (2011).

7 Jeffrey Gettleman, Mark Mazetti, and Eric Schmitt, "U.S. Relies on Contractors in Somalia Conflict," *New York Times*, August 10, 2011. See also Jeremy Scahill, "The CIA's Secret Sites in Somalia," *Nation*, July 12, 2011; and United Nations Human Rights Council, Report, A/HRC/18/32/Add.3, para. 34 (2011).

8 International Code of Conduct for Private Security Service Providers (ICoC), www.icoc-psp.org (accessed December 1, 2011).

9 In 2006, in order to address the demand for a clarification of legal obligations under international humanitarian law and international human rights law, as regards PMSCs, the government of Switzerland and the International Committee of the Red Cross launched what has been known as the Swiss Initiative, an international process of consultations with main stakeholders: governments, the new industry of PMSCs, and civil society. The Swiss Initiative has been strongly supported by the governments of the U.S. and the U.K., where most of the industry (70%) and the lobbies of the new security industry are located: the International Peace Operations Association (IPOA renamed ISOA) and the British Association of Private Security Companies (BAPSC). On September 17, 2008, the process led to the adoption of the Montreux Document on Pertinent International Legal Obligations and Good Practices for States Related to Operations of Private Military and Security Companies during Armed Conflict (the Montreux Document on Private Military and Security Companies, Switzerland, Federal Department of Foreign Affairs, http://www.eda.admin.ch/psc). In June 2009 following the adoption of the Montreux Document, under the Swiss Initiative, a parallel project was launched. It has led to an International Code of Conduct for Private Security Service Providers, which was partially approved in 2010. Supporting this project are industry associations, in particular ISOA and BAPSC, corporations and individual business leaders, the Swiss, the U.K. and the U.S. governments. In contrast with the Montreux Document under the Swiss Initiative, the International Committee of the Red Cross has only been participating as an observer to the International Code of Conduct project. José L. Gómez del Prado, "A United Nations Instrument to Regulate and Monitor Private Military and Security Contractors," *Notre Dame Journal of International, Comparative, and Human Rights Law* 1, no. 1 (2011): 28–37.

10 P. W. Singer, *Corporate Warriors* (Ithaca: Cornell University Press, 2004), chap. 5.

11 United Nations Human Rights Council, Report, A/HRC/18/32/Add. 3: 8–17.

12 United Nations Human Rights Council, Report, A/HRC/15/25/Add. 2: 7–13.

13 United Nations Human Rights Council, Report, A/HRC/18/32/Add. 4: 8–13.

14 *National Security and Central Intelligence Act*, section on the "Control and issuing of licenses to private security companies," *Sierra Leone Gazette* 132, no. 42 (July 4, 2002): Supplement.

15 Rapport de l'Office fédérale de la justice concernant une éventuelle règlementation sur les entreprises de sécurité privées opérant depuis la Suisse dans des zones de crise ou de conflit, December 30, 2010 (on file with the author).

16 Parliamentary Assembly of the Council of Europe, Report of the Political Affairs Committee, *Private Military and Security Firms and the Erosion of the State Monopoly on the Use of Force*, Parl. Eur. Doc. 11787 (December 22, 2008); and Opinion of the Committee on Legal Affairs and Human Rights, *Private Military and Security Firms and the Erosion of the State Monopoly on the Use of Force*, sec. 1, Parl. Eur. Doc. 11801 (January 27, 2009). Also the Project PRIV-WAR, financed by the European Commission, to explore ways in which the European Union could regulate or facilitate the regulation of PMSC with a view to assuring compliance with human rights law and international humanitarian law: PRIV-WAR, http://priv-war.eu (accessed August 14, 2011).

17 Adam Roberts, *The Wonga Coup: Guns, Thugs and a Ruthless Determination to Create Mayhem in an Oil-rich Corner of Africa* (New York: PublicAffairs, 2006), 144.

18 Conseil fédéral Suisse, http://www.ejpd.admin.ch/content/ejpd/fr/home/dokumentation/mi/2005/2005-12-050

(accessed February 10, 2012). In addition, the government wished to make a significant contribution to the codification and clarification of international humanitarian norms. See also "Nouveaux mercenaires en Suisse," *Le Temps* [Times], January 31, 2006, and "Les sociétés de sécurité et leurs mercenaires dans la ligne de mire de la Suisse et du CICR," *Le Temps* [Times], October 20, 2006, regarding the establishment of PMSCs in Switzerland that offer their services in zones of armed conflict.

19 "Un vide juridique profite aux armées privées [Private Armies Take Advantage of Legal Loophole]," Reuters, August 10, 2010, and "Les armées privées s'installent en Suisse en toute légalité [Private Armies Established Legally in Switzerland]," ATS, August 10, 2010.

20 Confédération Suisse, Département Fédéral de Justice et Police, "Rapport de l'Office fédéral de la justice concernant une éventuelle réglementation sur les entreprises de sécurité privées opérant depuis la Suisse dans des zones de crise ou de conflit [Swiss Confederation, Federal Department of Justice and Police, "Report of the Federal Bureau of Justice on a Possible Regulation of Private Security Companies Operating from Switzerland in Zones of Crisis or Conflict"]," December 30, 2010.

21 Confédération Suisse, Département Fédéral de Justice et Police, "Soumettre les entreprises de sécurité à l'obligation d'informer et à l'interdiction d'exercer certaines activités [Swiss Confederation, Federal Department of Justice and Police, "Obligation for Security Companies to Inform and the Prohibition to Fulfill Given Activities"]," available at http://www.ejpd.admin.ch/content/ejpd/fr/home/dokumentation/mi/2011/2011-02-160... 20/04/2011 (accessed February 10, 2012).

22. Confédération Suisse, Département Fédéral de Justice et Police, "Loi fédérale sur les prestations de sécurité privées fournies à l'étranger [Swiss Confederation, Federal Department of Justice and Police, "Federal Law on Private Security Operations Abroad"]," available at http://www.ejpd.admin.ch/content/ejpd/fr/home/themen/sicherheit/ref_gesetzgebung/ref_sicherheitsfirmen.html (accessed August 27, 2012).

23 Ibid., Arts. 14, 24, and 31.

24 Regarding the privatization of prisons, Eyal Zamir and Barak Medina write: "the Israeli Supreme Court recently decided to strike down legislation to establish a privately operated prison." Zamir and Medina, *Law, Economics, and Morality* (New York: Oxford University Press, 2010). Reference originally appeared in the abstract of "Constitutional Limits to Privatization: The Israeli Supreme Court Decision to Invalidate Prison Privatization," Barak Medina, Hebrew University of Jerusalem, Faculty of Law (August 30, 2010). See also Avirama Golan, "Beinisch Drops a Bombshell," *Haaretz*, November 20, 2009.

25 Early Day Motion 785, "Private Military and Security Companies," January 24, 2008, Primary Sponsor: David Anderson. Available at http://www.parliament.uk/edm/2007-08/785 or http://edmi.parliament.uk (accessed February 23, 2012).

26 Ibid.

27 Ibid.

28 Damian Lilly, "Regulating Private Military Companies: The Need for a Multidimensional Approach," *International Alert* (June 24, 2002), 2.

29 War on Want, "Private Armies," *Up Front* (February 2008).

30 United Nations Human Rights Council, A/HRC/18/32/Add.2.

31 Moshe Schartz, "The Department of Defense's Use of Private Security in Iraq and Afghanistan: Background, Analysis, and Options for Congress," U.S. Congressional Research Series, June 22, 2010.

32 J. Scahill, "A Very Private War," *Guardian*, August 1, 2007.

33 Louis Hamsen, "Families Sue Blackwater Over Deaths in Fallujah," *Virginia Pilot*, January 6, 2005, available at www.corpwatch.org; J. Scahill, "Blood is Thicker than Blackwater," *Nation*, May 1, 2006.

34 U.S. Congress, "Stop Outsourcing Security Act," HR 2665, 112th Congress, July 27, 2011.

35 Singer, *Corporate Warriors*, 222.

36 Human Rights Watch, *Hopes Betrayed: Trafficking of Women and Girls to Post-conflict*

Bosnia and Herzegovina for Forced Prostitution 14, No. 9 (D), November 26, 2002, 63–64.

37 Kelly Patricia O'Meara, "CorpWatch, January 14, 2002; Kelly Patricia O'Meara, "DynCorp Disgrace," *Insight Magazine*, August 19, 2003, available at http://www.prisonplanet.com/dyncorp_disgrace.html (accessed February 23, 2012).

38 O'Meara, "DynCorp Disgrace."

39 CorpWatch, "CSC/DynCorp," http://www.corpwatch.org/article.php?list=type&type=18 (accessed February 23, 2012).

40 "Accusation Against the Transnational DynCorp," Permanent Peoples' Tribunal Session on Colombia, Hearing on Biodiversity, Humanitarian Zone (Cacarica, February 24–27, 2007). Prepared by the José Alvear Restrepo Lawyers' Collective, *Corporación Colectivo de Abogados "José Alvear Restrepo,"* available at http://www.prensarural.org/spip/spip.php?article673 (accessed January 18, 2012)

41 Ibid.

42 *Warlord, Inc.: Extortion and Corruption Along the U.S. Supply Chain in Afghanistan,* Report of the Majority Staff, Subcommittee on National Security and Foreign Affairs, Committee on Oversight and Government Reform, U.S. House of Representatives, June 2010.

43 U.S. Congress, "Stop Outsourcing Security Act," HR 2665.

44 United Nations Human Rights Council, A/HRC/15/25/Add.3.

45 U.S. Congress, "Stop Outsourcing Security Act," HR 2665.

46 U.S. Congress, "Transparency and Accountability in Security Contracting Act of 2009," HR 2177, 111th Congress, April 29, 2009, available at http://www.govtrack.us/congress/bill.xpd?bill=h111-2177 (accessed January 20, 2012).

47 Nathan Hodge, "Report Finds Vast Waste in U.S. War Contracts," *Wall Street Journal*, July 23, 2011.

48. Stuart Ackerman, "U.S. Blocks Oversight of Its Mercenary Army in Iraq," Wired.com, July 22, 2011, available at http://www.wired.com/dangerroom/2011/07/iraq-merc-army/ (accessed January 20, 2012).

49 U.S. Bipartisan Congressional Commission on Wartime Contracting in Iraq and Afghanistan, Second Interim Report to Congress, "At What Risk," February 24, 2011, available at www.wartimecontracting.gov (accessed January 20, 2012).

50 Raenette Taljaard, "Implementing South Africa's Regulation of Foreign Military Assistance Act," in *Private Actors and Security Governance*, ed. A. Bryden and M. Caparini (Zurich: Verlag Munster, 2006), chap. 9.

51 Helena Torroja, "Hacia el reconocimiento internacional del Principio del monopolio del poder de coerción del Estado: fundamentos jurídicos y delimitación," U.N. Expert Seminar on the State Monopoly on the Legitimate Use of Force, New York, July 6–7, 2011.

52 Martin van Creveld, "The State: Its Rise and Decline," *Mises Daily*, October 16, 2000, available at http://mises.org/daily/527 (accessed February 23, 2012).

53 Herbert Wulf, "The Privatization of Violence: A Challenge to State Building and the Monopoly of Force," *Brown Journal of World Affairs* 18, no. 1 (2011): 137–49.

54 United Nations Resolution, A/RES/15/26; and United National Human Rights Council, A/HRC/15/25.

55 Ninth Report of the Foreign Affairs Committee, U.K. House of Commons (2001–02), *Private Military Companies*, HC 922, para. 25.

56 See note 15 above.

57 United Nations Human Rights Council, A/HRC/18/32; and United Nations Document, A/65/325 (2010).

58 See Protocol I Additional to the Geneva Conventions of August 12, 1949, and Relating to the Protection of Victims of International Armed Conflict, Art. 47(2), June 8, 1977, 1125 UNTS. 3. See also International Convention against the Recruitment, Use, Financing and Training of Mercenaries, Art. 1, December 4, 1989, 2163 UNTS. 75.

59. See the collection of articles under "National Security" at the Center for Public Integrity website, such as M. Asif Ismail, "Investing in War: The Carlyle Group Profits from Government and Conflict;" Dan Guttman, "The Shadow Pentagon;" and Larry

Makinson, "Who Benefits from the Politics and Economics of National Security," available at www.publicintegrity.org. See also Amy Farnsworth, "Romney Names Terrorism Policy Advisors," Boston.com (September 13, 2007), http://www.boston.com/news/politics/politicalintelligence/2007/09/romney_names_te.html (accessed February 23, 2012).

60 Doug Brooks and Hanna Streng, "The Stability Operations Industry: The Shared Responsibility of Compliance and Ethics," in this issue.

61 Alejandro Teitelbaum, Comentarios al Informe del Secretario General de la ONU: Las empresas y los derechos humanos, *Argenpress* [Comments to the UN Secretary General's Report on Business Companies and Human Rights], August 22, 2012: 8–11; Lou Pingeot, "Dangerous Partnership: Private Military and Security Companies and the UN," Global Policy Forum and Rosa Luxemburg Foundation (New York, June 2012), 23–29.

62 Anna Leander, "The Market for Force: The Consequences of Privatizing Security," *Journal of International Relations and Development* 11, no. 1 (2008): 75–77 (emphasis added).

63 O. Quirico, "National Regulatory Models for PMSCs and Implications for Future International Regulation," EUI MWP Working Paper 2009/25, cited in Carsten Hoppe and Ottavio Quirico, "Codes of Conduct for Private Military and Security Companies: The State of Self-Regulation in the Industry," in *War by Contract: Human Rights, Humanitarian Law, and Private Contractors,* ed. F. Francioni and N. Ronzitti (New York: Oxford University Press, 2011), chap. 18.

64 E. L. Gaston, "Mercenarism 2.0? The Rise of the Modern Private Security Industry and Its Implications for International Humanitarian Law Enforcement," *Harvard International Law Journal* 49, no. 1 (Winter 2008): 222.

65 Nigel White, "Due Diligence Obligations of Conduct: Developing a Responsibility Regime for PMSCs," in this issue, see the Responsibility Matrix section.

66 U.N. Human Rights Committee, *Cabal and Pasini v. Australia,* Communication no. 1020/2001, para. 7.2, United Nations Document CCPR/C/78/D/1020/2001 (2003).

67 Montreux Document, Preface, para. 9, a.

68 Alexandre Faite, "Involvement of Private Contractors in Armed Conflict: Implications Under International Humanitarian Law," International Committee of the Red Cross 7 (2004), available at http://www.icrc.org/eng/assets/files/other/pmc-article-a-faite.pdf (accessed February 23, 2012).

69 International Committee of the Red Cross, Commentary on the Additional Protocols of 8 June 1977 to the Geneva Conventions of 12 August 1949 619 (1987). See also Nils Melzer, "Interpretive Guidance on the Notion of Direct Participation in Hostilities under International Humanitarian Law," *International Review of the Red Cross* 872 (2008): 991, 1020 n. 114, available at http://www.icrc.org/eng/assets/files/other/irrc-872-reports-documents.pdf (accessed February 23, 2012).

70 Singer, *Corporate Warriors,* 124–30.

71 United Nations Human Rights Council, Report, A/HRC/15/24, Annex, Art. 18.

72 Ibid.

73 The Swiss legislation that is being developed would specifically prohibit direct PMSC participation in hostilities.

74 Terry Baynes, "U.S. Court Rejects Iraq Convoy Drivers' Suit Against KBR," CNCBC, January 12, 2012.

75 Ibid.

76 Accident and Work Injury Law Group, http://accidentandworkinjurylawgroup.com/2012/01/14/court-rejects-iraq-convoy-drivers-suit-against-kbr/ (accessed September 10, 2012).

77 Brooks and Streng, "Stability Operations Industry," in this issue.

78 U.S. Commission on Wartime Contracting in Iraq and Afghanistan, *At What Cost? Contingency Contracting in Iraq and Afghanistan,* Interim Report (June 2009).

79 United Nations Human Rights Council, A/HRC/15/25, 2 July 2010, Annex, Art. 13.

80 Ibid, Art. 16.

81 U.K. Government Green Paper, "Private Military Companies: Options for Regulation," HC 577 (London, February 2002), para. 73.

82 White, "Due Diligence Obligations of Conduct," see the Conclusion.

83 Nigel White, "The Privatization of Military and Security Functions and Human Rights: Comments on the U.N. Working Group's Draft Convention," *Human Rights Law Review* 11 (2011): 149.

84 Sharon Weinberg, "Windfalls of War: Pentagon's No-bid Contracts Triple in 10 Years," *i.watch news*, August 29, 2011. See also Commission on Wartime Contracting in Iraq and Afghanistan, Final Report to Congress, *Transforming Wartime Contracting, Controlling Costs Reducing Risks* (August 31, 2011); and Sarah Stillman, "The Invisible Army," *New Yorker*, June 6, 2011.

85 I cannot but underscore the ethical implications of the U.N. mandate and refer to the point raised by John Kleinig during our workshop as to whether contractors are ethical or whether they do "unacceptable damage to the dignity of" the human being.

86 White, "Due Diligence Obligations of Conduct," see the Conclusion.

87 The principle of effective remedy or effective reparation is enshrined in all modern international human rights treaties. International law requires states to provide an effective remedy of a right guaranteed by international law.

Transparency as a Core Public Value and Mechanism of Compliance

ALLISON STANGER*

Private security contractors are just the tip of an outsourcing iceberg. Across the three Ds of defense, diplomacy, and development, American foreign policy has been privatized. The Obama administration inherited a government that had been hollowed out to an unprecedented extent, and in many realms it had and has no choice but to depend on contractors to conduct what used to be state business. This essay examines the reasons for and unintended negative consequences of this outsourcing of American power. It argues that turning the clock back and returning everything to in-house assignments is both undesirable and impossible. Instead, government must pursue contracting in ways that do not undermine the public interest. It can do this by identifying the things that should never be outsourced and ensuring that the letter and spirit of the Federal Funding Transparency and Accountability Act is upheld. Greater transparency in contractor–government relations will foster private security contractor compliance with ethical norms while bolstering our capacity for self-government. Transparency is thus both an end in itself and a means to sustainable democratic deliberation. While tension can exist between national security and open government, that tension is often overestimated.

Allison Stanger is Russell Leng Professor of International Politics and Economics and Chair of the Political Science Department at Middlebury College, VT. Her most recent book, One Nation Under Contract: The Outsourcing of American Power and the Future of Foreign Policy, *was published by Yale University Press (2009/2011). She has three times testified before Congress on contracting issues.*

The origins of the privatized military industry have been effectively explored elsewhere,[1] but the privatization turn has not been confined to private security contractors and the Department of Defense (DOD) alone. Under Democrats and Republicans alike, the State Department and the United States Agency for International Development (USAID) have also embraced contracting out to the private sector what was once the work of government. These government entities do this whenever possible, both as a perceived cost-savings measure and as a mechanism for getting things done more efficiently. When the international agenda grew more ambitious after 9/11, the Bush administration took the unprecedented step of privatizing oversight of its contractors, with disastrous consequences. America became what I have called one nation under contract.[2]

Extreme privatization has had unfortunate and unintended consequences for public values essential for self-government. Because the circumstances in which Washington finds itself are in part of its own making, the situation is not irreversible, even though the status quo has an inexorable force of its own. But the wrong strategic choices are likely to follow if globalization's central role in empowering private actors—both malevolent and benevolent—is not properly acknowledged. The gains in agility, efficiency, and innovative problem-solving that appropriate outsourcing can facilitate are not insignificant, but they have come with an ethical cost. The solution is not to turn the clock back and bring everything back in-house, because the requisite expertise in government

no longer exists and cannot be re-created in the digital age. Instead, we must pursue appropriate contracting in ways that do not undermine the public interest and we must initiate a public discussion on those things that should never be outsourced. Greater transparency in contracting practices is a necessary precondition for securing both of these ends.

The remarks that follow are divided into five principal sections. The first traces the emergence of the contractor industrial complex and the unintended consequences of that development. The second explores the impact of privatization on core public values. The third argues that armed security contractors have performed inherently governmental functions in Iraq and Afghanistan and sketches the moral implications of our current practices. The fourth section demonstrates the critical importance of transparency, both as an end in itself and as a means to more sustainable democratic processes. The network of private actors that advances American interests overseas cannot be held to norms and standards, regardless of the origins of the rules, if its practices are hidden from public view.

1. From Military Industrial Complex to Contractor Industrial Complex

The shadow government can trace its founding moment to the Eisenhower administration, when fiscal concerns led the president to instruct government agencies to purchase as much as possible from private sources. Eisenhower issued an executive order prohibiting the federal government from engaging

in "any commercial activity to provide a service or product for its own use if such product or service can be procured from private enterprise through ordinary business channels."[3] This order became the point of departure for Office of Management and Budget (OMB) Circular Number A-76, whose basic aim was to put activities currently performed by government out for public-private competition. Functions identified as "inherently governmental" were not to be candidates for outsourcing.

Eisenhower's concerns were a rational response to a changed postwar institutional environment. The National Security Act of 1947 had created a brand new national security architecture that included the new Department of Defense and made wartime-sized federal budgets a peacetime norm, increasing both the size of government and the scope for outsourcing. Prior to World War II, the United States had neither a permanently entrenched armaments industry nor a peacetime defense establishment. That changed with the National Security Act of 1947. Despite the dramatic demobilization of American forces, after World War II the federal budget would never return to pre-war levels. The government's projected total outlays for 1947 were roughly four times what they had been in 1940, and they escalated exponentially from there. Even with the reductions in military spending after the Cold War's end, America's 1995 military budget approximately equaled the 1980 military budget in real terms.[4]

Eisenhower was well aware of the dangerous path that the United States was on during the Cold War. His prescient farewell address argued that the current "conjunction of an immense military establishment and a large arms industry" combined to have grave implications. "In the councils of government," Eisenhower warned, "We must guard against the acquisition of unwarranted influence, whether sought or unsought, by the military-industrial complex." The military-industrial complex presents a vast opportunity for "the disastrous rise of misplaced power," and is something about which Americans must be ever vigilant:

We must never let the weight of this combination endanger our liberties or democratic processes. We should take nothing for granted. Only an alert and knowledgeable citizenry can compel the proper meshing of huge industrial and military machinery of defense with our peaceful methods and goals, so that security and liberty may prosper together.[5]

Despite Eisenhower's grave warning, the trends that alarmed him continued unabated and have combined to transform Eisenhower's military-industrial complex into something else entirely. For Eisenhower, the military-industrial complex was a result of annual spending on the military exceeding the total net income of U.S. corporations. It was the product of an economy overly focused, proportionately, on security concerns at the expense of private sector activity. Even at today's record highs, however, defense spending is now dwarfed by the net income of U.S. corporations. In 2002, for example, the U.S. budgeted $344.9 billion for defense and the military, and the net income of all U.S. corporations that year came to $1.08 trillion.[6] Thus, while defense spending in the Eisenhower years exceeded corporate income, today corporate income exceeds military spending almost threefold. Globalization has empowered the private sector and transformed the calculus of government power in wholly unprecedented ways, remaking Eisenhower's military-industrial complex into a private sector juggernaut: the contractor-industrial complex.

	Contracts in 2000	Contracts in 2010	Change in Contracts	Grants in 2000	Grants in 2010	Change in Grants
Defense	$133.2 billion	$367.1 billion	176%	$2.3 billion	$4.5 billion	96%
USAID	$478.6 million	$6.7 billion	1300%	0	$8.9 billion	N/A
State	$1.3 billion	$8.1 billion	523%	$102.5 million	$1.4 billion	1266%

The basic pattern is striking. In 2000, the Department of Defense spent $133.2 billion on contracts. By 2010, that figure had grown to $367.1 billion, an almost three-fold increase. In 2000, the State Department spent $1.3 billion on contracts and $102.5 million on grants. By 2010, grant spending had grown to $1.4 billion and contract spending had grown to $8.1 billion. In 2000, USAID spent $0 on grants[7] and $478.6 million on contracts. By 2010, those figures had climbed to $8.9 billion and $6.7 billion, respectively.[8] Foreign affairs outsourcing had become the new normal.

With two wars simultaneously raging in Iraq and Afghanistan, allocations for private security contractors comprised a large proportion of the 1300% and 523% increase in contracts at the State Department and USAID.[9] As Washington draws down uniformed personnel in Iraq, the State Department and USAID of necessity must try to plug the resultant security gap. Since neither has the requisite personnel in house, they have no choice but to contract out for the security they need. One result is that more civil-ian contractors lost their lives in Afghanistan in 2011 than soldiers. If L-3 Communications—a government services company—were a country, it would have the third highest number of fatalities in Iraq and Afghanistan after the United States and Britain.[10] As Steve Schooner has put it, we have even outsourced "the ultimate sacrifice."[11] Although the general public is not yet fully aware, Iraq and Afghanistan were America's first contractor wars. Contractors usually outnumbered uniformed personnel on the ground in both theaters, and security contractors have featured prominently in U.S. operations, especially in situations in which the U.S. military has withdrawn its forces but the State Department has stayed behind.

Although wartime contracting and successive supplemental appropriations have fueled these dramatic developments, it is important to note that this is not a partisan issue. Whenever possible, Democrats and Republicans alike have embraced outsourcing the work of government to the private sector, both as a perceived cost-savings measure and as a mechanism for getting things done more efficiently. But the Bush administration's wildly ambitious overseas agenda and its belief that government itself is the problem combined to fuel what I have called laissez-faire outsourcing. Laissez-faire outsourcing meant that government footed the bill and largely got out of the way, trusting the private sector to oversee itself. The laissez-faire outsourcing—or to use Defense Secretary Gates's language, the "willy-nilly" contracting—that accompanied the wars in both Iraq and Afghanistan often meant that oversight and management were outsourced as well as implementation, with predictable consequences. With private security contractors standing in as proxies for American military might, this would turn out to be a toxic brew.

That pattern has largely continued unabated under the Obama administration, as the 2011 final report of the Commission on Wartime Contracting revealed. It found that at least $31 billion and as much as $100 billion had been lost to contract waste and fraud in Iraq and Afghanistan. The commission concluded that this gross mismanagement of public resources had three primary causes. First, agencies over-relied on contractors for contingency operations. Second, "inherently governmental" rules did not guide the deployment of contractors in war zones. Finally, across the board, agencies have not treated contracting as a strategic issue. The commission concluded that the nation's security demands sweeping reform of our wartime contracting practices.[12]

Laissez-faire outsourcing and its disastrous consequences were prominent in the most controversial inci-

dents in Iraq and Afghanistan. At Abu Ghraib prison that year, 27 of the 37 interrogators were employees of the private military company CACI International, and 22 of the linguists who assisted them were employed by California-based Titan International.[13] None of the contractors to date has been prosecuted. Until President Obama's new CIA director banned it, the CIA's secret interrogation program made extensive use of contractors, in roles that included the waterboarding (simulated drowning) of terrorist suspects—contractors designed the very program itself. Stuart Bowen, Jr, Inspector General for Iraq Reconstruction, told Congress in March 2009 that the U.S. government had appropriated 25 times more for Iraq reconstruction than had been originally anticipated, resulting in "pervasive waste and inefficiency."[14] There were over 300 reported cases of contracting mistakes or abuses in Iraq from 2003 through 2007. There has not been a single instance of anyone being fired or denied promotion in connection with those cases.[15] In a stunning confession, the Pentagon itself acknowledged that $8.2 billion of taxpayer money flowed through contracts into Iraq, some in stacks or pallets of cash, without appropriate recordkeeping or oversight. For example, $68.2 million went to the UK, $45.3 million to Poland, and $21.3 million to Korea, yet Pentagon auditors were unable to determine why the payments were made.[16]

Above and beyond squandering taxpayer money, laissez-faire subcontracting has also undermined larger U.S. strategic ends. For example, a House Committee Majority Report in June 2010 found that DOD oversight of the multi-billion-dollar Host Nation Trucking contract in Afghanistan was virtually non-existent. DOD essentially designed a contract that put responsibility for the security of U.S. supply lines in the hands of wholly unaccountable Afghan subcontractors:

This arrangement has fueled a vast protection racket run by a shadowy network of warlords, strongmen, commanders, corrupt Afghan officials, and perhaps others. Not only does the system run afoul of the Department's own rules and regulations mandated by Congress, it also appears to risk undermining the U.S. strategy for achieving its goals in Afghanistan.[17]

In other words, U.S. taxpayer money has been flowing through subcontracts in Iraq into the pockets of the Taliban. Funding the enemy as one fights them is not typically viewed as prudent strategy.

Although it may feel good to blame "business" for the rampant waste, fraud, and abuse, the truth is vastly more complicated. Business offers what the government requests. Scapegoating contractors means that government is not forced to reflect on whether it has requested the right things.

In short, laissez-faire contracting has undermined American power. Contracting itself was not the root cause; rather, the problem lay with Washington's supersized aspirations. In his first inaugural address, Ronald Reagan said, "Government is not the solution to our problem; government is the problem."[18] Reagan was right to champion the private sector as a source of energy, efficiency, and innovation, but in citing government as the problem, he was very wrong. Business can be hired to solve problems, but there are some problems that only government can solve since business absent good government will always sacrifice sustainability to short-term gain. In war zones such as Iraq and Afghanistan, that dynamic has been on full display.

2. Privatization and Public Values

The opaque nature of foreign affairs outsourcing has had an unfortunate impact on the healthy functioning of self-government. Such outsourcing slowly eats away at public values.

In *Outsourcing War and Peace*, Laura Dickinson argues that our public values have been compromised and diminished by the rampant outsourcing of government services to private companies. She identifies the core public values as human dignity, public participation, and transparency. Dickinson's book surveys four distinct mechanisms of constraint, each of which may be deployed as a means of shaping the behavior of foreign affairs contractors so that they are more likely to respect these core public values. The four accountability mechanisms considered are (1) pursuing litigation under international and domestic law, as well as changing existing domestic statutes; (2) writing better contracts and improving the entire oversight regime; (3) fostering public participation; and (4) remaking organizational structure and culture through programs such as placing JAG lawyers on the battlefield.[19]

Using Dickinson's categories, transparency both improves the entire oversight regime (mechanism 2) and fosters public participation (mechanism 3). In this sense, transparency is actually much more than a civic virtue. I shall argue below that transparency is our most important core public value, since it is also an underappreciated mechanism of compliance that increases the prospects for strengthening all other means of constraint on self-interested behavior. Perhaps most importantly, transparency is a necessary condition for vital democracy, because transparency is what makes public participation possible: no transparency, no self-government.

In this issue, Brooks and Streng draw our attention to Dickinson's second mechanism. They make a strong point when they demonstrate the myriad ways that the underspecified content of contracts can produce outcomes that look like corruption or abuse but are actually within the letter of the law. Writing better contracts, ones that more clearly specify the results the government seeks, would ameliorate the appearance of strictly self-interested behavior. The point is an important one. We cannot blame contractors for undesirable results when the desired results were poorly delineated. And if government does not insist on applying the full weight of its ethics rules to contractors, then we should not be surprised to find behavior that most would agree deviates from the ethical.

Dickinson believes we can best protect public values by embedding them in the privatization framework, rather than turning the clock back on outsourcing.[20] She acknowledges that there are potential difficulties with all four mechanisms and that one big objection would be that they are all inherently unrealistic, "because one of the main reasons governments privatize is precisely to avoid the kinds of constraints I seek to impose."[21] Determining motives is a tricky business and ultimately an unnecessary exercise because they do not determine outcomes. Governments can privatize with the best of intentions and still wind up inadvertently undermining public values. Add in ubiquitous time constraints and the shortage of government personnel that extensive privatization has facilitated, and one can get suboptimal outcomes without any deliberate attempts to manipulate the public. Market imperatives can trump civic ones in ways that combine to undermine our capacity for self-government. This is the heart of the enforcement problem. Privatization produces a fragmentation of authority that can weaken the will to enforce the spirit of the law.

Dickinson rightly argues that the outsourcing horse is out of the barn, so the clock cannot be turned back, yet the prospects for upholding public values through the market solutions proposed by Dickinson seem problematic. The waste, fraud, and abuse associated with wartime contracting all have been fueled by the very profit motive that makes capitalism's wheels turn. When public values collide with market imperatives in a privatized world, the demands of the market typically triumph—and the logic for this outcome seems iron clad. Put another way, it may be easy to coax public servants to adopt a market outlook and think more like businessmen to uphold common values. But getting businessmen to think like public servants? That conflicts with the private sector's raison d'être, which is to ensure the profitability of any given enterprise on a day-to-day basis. There are competing values at work, and when the profit motive leads in one direction and the common good in another, why should we expect private sector employees to act against their own self-interest?

One potential way of squaring this circle is to deploy Tocqueville's famous doctrine of self-interest well understood. Tocqueville considered this doctrine the unifying creed in America, where virtue is pursued not for its own sake but because it is in the long-run self-interest of the virtuous. In *Democracy in America*, Tocqueville writes: "The Doctrine of self-interest well understood does not inspire great sacrifices, but every day it prompts some small ones . . . if it does not lead the will directly to virtue, it establishes habits which unconsciously turn it that way."[22] Tocqueville saw in this distinctly American approach to virtue something new and powerful. He drew a direct connection between the wholly self-interested drive to make money and its potential to spawn virtuous circles of action. When virtue pays, individuals and organizations alike will be inclined to be virtuous.

We can understand the corporate social responsibility movement as the globalization of Tocqueville's doctrine of self-interest well understood. Corporate social responsibility is addressed to two audiences: consumers and company employees. With respect to the former, since revenues fall after a product has been identified with corporate ruthlessness, it should not surprise us to see businesses striving to be seen as socially responsible. With respect to the latter, corporations also strive for social responsibility so as to hire the best employees in a competitive labor market. People want to work for a company that stands for something beyond mere profit. By this logic, it pays to be virtuous, and we should strive for policies that promote this market for virtue.

Although this reasoning can hold successfully in peacetime, it is another matter in wartime environments. When the nation is at war and national security is seen to be at stake, the inexcusable is often overlooked, making the market for virtue hard to locate, let alone promote. By definition, wartime is a state of emergency, during which ordinary procedures are suspended. Tocqueville's doctrine of self-interest well understood functions differently when lives are on the line. When one can do good and do well, that is ideal, but public values are likely to be the first casualty when they confront the insatiable demands of war.

3. Inherently Governmental Functions and Armed Security Contractors

Drawing a clear line of demarcation around inherently governmental functions is one way to ensure that public values are protected in challenging environments. Contractors doing laundry and preparing food are unlikely to be performing inherently governmental functions.

But what about those carrying weapons and performing activities indistinguishable from those of uniformed personnel? Are armed security contractors currently performing inherently governmental functions in Iraq and Afghanistan?

Armed security contractors can be divided into two main categories: static security (guarding a particular location, such as an embassy or camp) and moving security (guarding personnel or convoys as they pursue work in different locations). Contractors providing static security do not venture out on missions. Those providing moving security are the ones who often perform jobs indistinguishable from those of uniformed personnel and are most likely to wind up using their weapons. The use of contractors to guard U.S. embassies is a practice that began in the 1980s and it has been a long-standing source of employment for local nationals. Contracting for moving security is largely a post-Cold War development, and our missions in Iraq and Afghanistan today are wholly dependent on it.

Although there is a general consensus that there are activities so intrinsic to the nature of government that they should not be contracted out, there is little agreement on what those activities are. Both the Office of Management and Budget and Congress have repeatedly focused attention on the topic of inherently governmental functions, but to date have largely refrained from providing specific guidelines as to what particular activities must never be outsourced.

Restricting the focus to those contractors able to deploy lethal force makes it easier to render a judgment. A leading advocate of minimal government, Milton Friedman, maintained: "The basic functions of government are to defend the nation against foreign enemies, to prevent coercion of some individuals by others within the country, to provide a means of deciding on our rules, and to adjudicate disputes."[23] Using Friedman's minimalist definition, the use of contractors in the realms of security and justice demand strict scrutiny, since defending the nation and preventing coercion are "basic functions of government." Yet even under this leanest of definitions, moving security contractors are performing inherently governmental functions, since they are actively involved in defending the nation against foreign enemies.

Section 5 of the Federal Activities Inventory Reform Act defines an inherently governmental function in potentially broader terms as "a function that is so intimately related to the public interest as to require performance by Federal Government employees." The Office of Federal Procurement Policy issued further guidance on this definition in September 2011. Its final policy letter added to the illustrative list of inherently governmental functions "all combat" and "security operations in certain situations connected with combat or potential combat."[24] It follows that many armed contractors in Iraq and Afghanistan have been performing inherently governmental functions. The final report of the Commission on Wartime Contracting in Iraq and Afghanistan carefully navigated this issue by endorsing the application of "inherently governmental" rules to the use of contractors in war zones. Taking up arms to defend the interests of the United States, whether remotely pulling triggers on drone flights or guarding government personnel as they travel in war zones, would seem to constitute active involvement in defending the nation against foreign enemies. Such actions would clear Milton Friedman's minimalist inherently governmental threshold and arguably constitute "security operations in certain situations connected with combat or potential combat" as well. In short, if anything at all is inherently governmental, armed security contractors deployed in war zones would seem to be it.

As John Kleinig pointed out in our October 2011 workshop, the debate over inherently governmental functions has moral significance.[25] Inherently governmental functions are those things that only government can do well. By implication, this means there are some things that should never be for sale. The "inherently governmental" debate thus ultimately points to the moral limits of markets—the line that outsourcing and commodification must not cross if justice is to be upheld. When we violate those limits and privatize what is actually inherently governmental, we both diminish ourselves and harm American constitutional democracy.

According to Michael Sandel, there are two arguments that can be voiced about the moral limits of markets. The first is an argument from coercion. The injustice arises when people buy and sell things because they are in dire financial circumstances and really have no choice. A peasant may agree to sell his kidney to feed his starving family, but he is not really doing so voluntarily. He cannot be said to have granted consent if necessity dictates his alleged "choice." The second is an argument from corruption. A society that allows desperate individuals to sell vital body parts is degraded by the practice. The activity is wrong, not because the peasant has no real choice in the matter but because selling body parts compromises human dignity, both the peasant's and our own. If there are some things that money cannot or should not be allowed to buy, we harm ourselves when we commodify them, whether we freely choose to do so or not.[26]

The argument from coercion certainly does not apply to security contractors. Choosing a job that pays more than the same work in a government uniform is not the same as being forced to do something to put food on the family table. The argument from corruption, however, potentially resonates. A former member of the military earning two to three times the pay that a current soldier receives for performing comparable tasks arguably undermines the honor and dignity of military service. In addition, if the contractor is not a U.S. citizen but instead a third party or foreign national, he is taking up arms for a country not his own. The official sanctioning of mercenary-like behavior undermines the public value of patriotism and civic duty. There seems to be a good deal at stake, ethically and practically speaking, in our current practice of extensively relying on security contractors to plug the gap between the all-volunteer force and the demand for military expertise in service of the United States.

Since their duties most closely mirror those of uniformed personnel, moving security contractors inhabit the most morally troubling realm.

The American addiction to them thus may come at a higher cost than the simple price tag for their services alone.

4. The Importance of Transparency for Accountability and Self-Government

As we have seen, greater transparency in our contracting practices is a step in the right direction for both strategic and moral reasons. Until very recently, data on the broadening scope of government-wide procurement were unavailable to the general public. That changed in 2003 with the launch of the General Services Administration's Federal Procurement Data System (FPDS), which made data on contract spending (both for-profit and not-for-profit) available to registered users. Since FPDS issues annual reports and makes them publicly available on its website, its launch marked the start of a new era of relative transparency.

In 2006, the Federal Funding Accountability and Transparency Act (FFATA) took things a step further when it instructed the Office of Management and Budget to create and maintain a searchable database that covers all federal spending in a user-friendly way. To public acclaim, USAspending.gov came online one month ahead of schedule, in December 2007. For the first time, the public could see in detail how the federal government spends taxpayer money. The website crossed all sorts of divides. Not only did Barack Obama, then just the junior senator from Illinois, and Sen. Tom Coburn, the Republican from Oklahoma, co-sponsor the legislation, but OMB partnered with OMB Watch—a non-profit organization founded to keep OMB honest—to devise the new website's software.

The new website dramatically expanded the scope and quality of information available to the public on contracting and subcontracting. It allowed me, a Vermont-based professor, to get a good understanding of basic issues without a security clearance. The legislation mandated that OMB's database be expanded by January 2009 to include information on subcontracts and subgrants. USAspending.gov relies on FPDS contracting numbers, but it corrects for inaccuracies that it detects in its by-agency figures before presenting them to the public.[27]

FFATA was long overdue. Despite the tremendous amounts of money involved, government needed a push to launch a concerted effort to track those flows accurately. Putting together a government-wide system for tracking contracts and subcontracts was spurred by FFATA and remains a work in progress.

Some time in early 2010, USAspending.gov's platform and interface were totally redesigned. The makeover was supposed to endow USAspending.gov "with greater capacity for fulfilling FFATA requirements."[28] However, the site's FAQs did not include any references to this revamping or the reasons for it. Unless a person, like me, had done extensive work with the previous website, the user would indeed have no idea that anything at all had changed.

So what had changed? The site's new incarnation temporarily eliminated the subcontracts and subgrants pages. In its earlier form, the old subcontracts page had reported that the site was "under development," and it provided a clear placeholder for important forthcoming information. The new and improved Obama administration site not only did away with the subcontracts page, it also eliminated an earlier FAQ section that had told the user that FFATA mandated that information on subcontracts be provided to the public by 1 January 2009. In short, the Bush OMB site made it clear that important data were missing and soon to be forthcoming; the Obama administration's renovation at first removed explicit references to aspects of FFATA that had yet to be fulfilled.

Some time after I testified before the Senate Budget Committee in July 2010 and noted these puzzling changes, both items were restored to the USAspending.gov site. But while the subcontracts and subgrants categories have been reinstated, with data flowing in, full compliance remains a distant goal and the available data remains wildly erratic and incomplete.

Given recent revelations that U.S. taxpayer money has been flowing through subcontracts into the pockets of the Taliban,[29] the primitive state of the subcontracts database is troubling. Without transparency in subcontracts, we have effectively been pouring taxpayer money into a black hole in Afghanistan, with no real means of knowing how well that money is likely to be spent or even who is receiving it.[30] It is precisely the opposite of what we need at a

time when our fiscal imprudence has become a national security issue. Secrecy prevails because the general public tolerates it; the American people do not protest because we have a long-standing tradition of tolerating constraints on liberty in exchange for the promise of greater security.

Although the First Amendment upholds freedom of the press and freedom of speech, the Supreme Court has also acknowledged that there are limits to free expression when security is at stake. As Justice Holmes famously argued in *Schenck v. The United States* (1919), a man does not have the right to falsely shout "Fire!" in a crowded theater. Yet the secrecy imperative for national security reasons can make it very difficult for the public to know whether what is being shouted is true or false. The claim that Saddam Hussein had weapons of mass destruction, which was used to justify the invasion of Iraq, turned out to be false. The Bush administration never provided firm evidence to support this claim, allegedly for fear of compromising intelligence sources, but in reality, we now know, it was because it did not have the firm proof in hand.

Why do elites always err on the side of secrecy? Fortunes and empires are built by exploiting information disparities. Above and beyond national security claims of its importance, secrecy remains a vital component of any functioning capitalist system. Since profit is derived from knowing just a bit more than your competitors, every profit margin that ever lived has its origins in some modicum of secrecy. The idea of proprietary information in business exists to protect against piracy. Yet just as the secrecy imperative can be exploited as a power resource in the national security realm, so too can it be manipulated by financial elites in ways that undermine democracy. Financial fraud flourishes in the shadows, as do profit margins. Demands for transparency are sand in the gears of any moneymaking enterprise. It is certainly the case that secrecy is sometimes necessary to defend the United States and to protect legitimate financial accomplishments. But it is also the case that there are enormous incentives for the powerful to insist on excessive secrecy.

Secrecy, therefore, has been and always will be a power resource. Those in positions of power will always have a vested short-term interest in asserting its necessity. But in the long run, excessive secrecy can be damaging to both security itself and democratic values. As the late Senator Patrick Moynihan put it in his book *Secrecy*, "At times, in the name of national security, secrecy has put that very security in harm's way."[31] As he concludes, "secrecy is for losers."[32]

Lest I be misunderstood, I am well aware that the demands of national security must sometimes trump the public's right to know. When our enemy was the Soviet Union, there were many instances where this imperative rightfully prevailed. But the Cold War is long over, and our enemy today is not another state but a network of order-subverting terrorists who threaten our most cherished values. Fighting that new threat demands unprecedented cooperation, collaboration, and information sharing between the public-private sectors, between federal, state, and local government, and with our NATO allies. Transparency serves each of those ends rather than undermining them. Thus, when our na-

tional security interests are properly understood, transparency does not threaten the national interest but instead upholds it. In the simplest of terms, transparency is the widespread availability of information; it fosters the cooperation and teamwork on which our homeland security depends. I stand ready to be persuaded otherwise, but I have found most concerns about the costs of transparency to be misplaced, excessively focused on the short term at the expense of the sustainable.

So why has the quest for transparency in government spending proven so difficult to date? That transparency undermines a significant power resource of elites is one part of the story, but it is not all of it. The simple truth is that bolstering transparency is a challenging proposition for public servants. The explosion of government outsourcing was not originally accompanied by the development of appropriate accounting systems for monitoring these flows. Getting the work done took precedence over ensuring that the right systems were in place to ensure that the work would be done well. Responding to the requirements of FFATA, for example, often meant being asked for data that one had not made a habit of collecting. Upholding transparency requires significant expenditures of time—if the leadership does not make it clear that its employees will fulfill the spirit of the law or suffer consequences, the most common outcome will always be perpetuation of the status quo. Data quality was and is a persistent concern because the government's accounting systems have not yet fully adapted to the new normal, where the majority of the government's work is in private hands.

Conclusion

When so much of the work of government is in private hands, standard approaches to transparency will no longer suffice. As we have seen, transparency is often the first casualty when the work of government is outsourced, even though transparency is both a core public value and the lifeblood of self-government. In terms of transparency and accountability, Congress could be enormously helpful in providing incentives to get us where we need to go sooner rather than later. They simply need to make it clear that they want the existing law upheld. When in doubt, Congress should err on the side of transparency and full disclosure. This may mean redefining our understanding of business proprietary when the business in question is actually the work of government.

The American people always need to be able to see where and how their tax dollars are spent—right through to the sub-award level. To ensure that this is possible, the spirit and letter of FFATA must be fulfilled, regardless of whether Democrats or Republicans are at the helm. Companies as well as governments can operate with the purest of intentions, but if their most important transactions are opaque to the public, they will lose trust and effectiveness. FFATA recognizes the importance of transparency for healthy democracy. Much good could come from Congress and the American people simply insisting that the existing laws be upheld.

Notes

1 For example, see Peter W. Singer, *Corporate Warriors: The Rise of the Privatized Military Industry* (Ithaca, NY: Cornell University Press, 2003); Deborah Avant, *The Market for Force: The Consequences of Privatizing Security* (New York: Cambridge University Press, 2005).

2 Allison Stanger, *One Nation under Contract: The Outsourcing of American Power and the Future of Foreign Policy* (New Haven: Yale University Press, 2009).

3 Donald Kettl, *Sharing Power: Public Governance and Private Markets* (Washington, DC: Brookings Institution, 1993), 41.

4. Kenneth Waltz, "Globalization and American Power," *National Interest* (Spring 2000).

5 Dwight D. Eisenhower, Farewell Address to the Nation, January 17, 1961.

6 Figures are from the White House Office of Management and Budget, "Budget of the United States Government (Historical Tables)" (Washington, DC: U.S. Government Printing Office, 2008); and the Internal Revenue Service, "SOI Tax Stats—Integrated Business Data" (Washington, DC: United States Department of Treasury). Unfortunately, 2002 is the latest year for which data are available. It would obviously be interesting to see how the statistic has changed with wartime spending in full gear.

7 USAID's problematic past accounting practices are currently on full public display at USAspending.gov. No data on grants are provided for FY2000–06. FY2010 figures were retrieved from USAspending.gov on September 27, 2011.

8 Data quality appears extremely variable, but for general trends, it can suffice. I use 2010 numbers for the comparison, since the aggregate numbers for 2011 were still a moving target.

9 The available data do not allow one to break out exact expenditures, primarily because subcontracting chains are still shrouded in secrecy.

10 Rod Nordland, "Risks of Afghan War Shift from Soldiers to Contractors," *New York Times*, February 11, 2012, available at http://www.nytimes.com/2012/02/12/world/asia/afghan-war-risks-are-shifting-to-contractors.html?_r=1

11 L. Schooner and Collin D. Schwann, "Dead Contractors: The Un-Examined Effect of Surrogates on the Public's Casualty Sensitivity," *Journal of National Security Law and Policy* (forthcoming). See http://papers.ssrn.com/sol3/papers.cfm?abstract_id=1826242, p. 6.

12 Commission on Wartime Contracting in Iraq and Afghanistan, Final Report to Congress, *Transforming Wartime Contracting, Controlling Costs Reducing Risks* (August 31, 2011).

13 Deborah Avant, "The Privatization of Security and Change in the Control of the Use of Force," *International Studies Perspectives* 5 (2004); Lynda Hurst, "The Privatization of Abu Ghraib," *Toronto Star*, May 16, 2004.

14 http://www.sigir.mil/files/testimony/SIGIR_Testimony_09-002T.pdf#view=fit

15 Walter Pincus, "U.S. Cannot Manage Contractors In Wars, Officials Testify on Hill," *Washington Post*, January 5, 2008.

16 James Glanz, "Iraq Spending Ignored Rules, Pentagon Says," *New York Times*, May 23, 2008.

17 John F. Tierney, Chair (U.S. House of Representatives, Committee on Oversight and Government Reform, Subcommittee on National Security and Foreign Affairs), *Warlord, Inc.: Extortion and Corruption Along the U.S. Supply Chain in Afghanistan* (June 2010), 1, available at http://oversight.house.gov/images/stories/subcommittees/NS_Subcommittee/6.22.10_HNT_HEARING/Warlord_Inc_compress.pdf

18. http://www.reagan.utexas.edu/archives/speeches/1981/12081a.htm

19 Laura A. Dickinson, *Outsourcing War and Peace: Preserving Public Values in a World of Privatized Foreign Affairs* (New Haven: Yale University Press, 2011), 13.

20 Ibid., 15–17.

21 Ibid., 20.

22 Alexis de Tocqueville, *Democracy in America*, trans. Harvey C. Mansfield and Delba Winthrop (Chicago: University of Chicago Press, 2000), 500–03.

23 Milton Friedman, *Why Government is the Problem* (Palo Alto, CA: Hoover Institution Press, 1993), 6.

24 White House Office of Management and Budget, Office of Federal Procurement Policy, "Publication of the Office of Federal Procurement Policy (OFPP) Policy Letter 11–01, Performance of Inherently Governmental and Critical Functions," *Federal Register* 76, no. 176 (September 12, 2011).

25 John Kleinig, Remarks at "Outsourcing Security: Private Military and Security Companies (PMSCs) and the Quest for Accountability," John Jay College of Criminal Justice, October 8, 2011.

26 Michael J. Sandel, "What Money Can't Buy: The Moral Limits of Markets," Tanner Lectures on Human Values (Oxford University, May 11–12, 1998), 94–95.

27 Allison Stanger, "Your Tax Dollars at Work: If You Can Find Them," *Washington Post*, May 18, 2008.

28 White House Office of Management and Budget, "Open Government Plan" (April 7, 2010), 10–11, available at http://www.whitehouse.gov/sites/default/files/microsites/100407-omb-opengov-plan.pdf

29 Tierney, "Warlord, Inc."

30 Allison Stanger, "Addicted to Contractors," *Foreign Policy* (December 1, 2009), available at http://www.foreignpolicy.com/articles/2009/12/01/addicted_to_contractors

31 Daniel Patrick Moynihan, *Secrecy: The American Experience* (New Haven: Yale University Press, 1998), 60.

32 Ibid., 227.

The Stability Operations Industry: The Shared Responsibility of Compliance and Ethics

DOUG BROOKS* AND HANNA STRENG

Companies in the stability operations industry have been subjected to painstaking scrutiny while critics have ignored the value they bring to contingency operations and government clients. Moreover, the scope of the industry is often overlooked by critics who paint a picture of uncontrollable companies making ridiculous profits. In response, this article offers some insight on stability operations, contracting processes, pitfalls, and opportunities. The article then discusses some of the criticisms that surround the industry. These criticisms are often due to sensationalized reporting, and a significant problem is that reports on criminal activity such as fraud and abuse are exaggerated. In contrast, the far larger problem of waste due to poor client planning and oversight is glossed over. Finally, the article discusses industry self-policing efforts that have emerged to support the use of professional and compliant businesses in stability operations. Ultimately it is governmental regulatory enforcement and quality contracting practices that will do the most to marginalize unethical companies, reward better firms, and improve partnerships and success rates in stability operations globally.

Doug Brooks is President of ISOA, the International Stability Operations Association. He is a specialist on private sector capabilities and African security issues and has written extensively on the regulation and constructive utilization of the private sector for international peacekeeping and humanitarian missions. He has testified before the US Congress, South African Parliament and to UN functions, and as an advocate for the industry he makes frequent appearances on news programs and in documentaries.

Hanna Streng is a Security & New Business Analyst for a London-based insurance broker specialized in insurance for security companies. She co-wrote this article during her position as Senior Programs Associate for ISOA. She obtained an MA in Conflict, Security and Development from King's College London's War Studies Department in 2010, and a BA from University College Utrecht in the Netherlands. She has lived and worked in the Netherlands, Switzerland, the USA and the UK.

Despite an increasing acceptance of the advantages of private services in contingency operations by governments and other large clients, sensationalistic and anecdotally based media reports regularly evoke emotion and dismay toward the use of contractors in contingency operations. Even well-respected media outlets continue to slip into derogatory and colloquial terms when discussing the industry.[1] Though opinions are often influenced by a sensationalistic media, one-sided perspectives inhibit an informed understanding of the industry's origin and influences, and deny a full appreciation of its importance in contingency operations, in disaster relief, and in the high-risk environments in which these companies operate.

More to the point, allegations against contractors are generalized as "waste, fraud, and abuse" of government funds and thus taxpayer money. Accountability and oversight are certainly problematic in contingency environments; however, ire should be tempered since evidence clearly demonstrates that the biggest causes of waste are poor planning and inadequate coordination between government clients. As one wag put it, "if you order an ugly fountain for your front yard, don't be outraged when a contractor builds an ugly fountain in your front yard." In other words, analysts should differentiate poor planning, coordination, and design from fraud and abuse because the latter involve deceit and criminal activity. By focusing on the "fraud and abuse" instead of waste, misinformation and sensationalization, such emphasis has an adverse effect on policy formulation, and policy cures tend to focus on the smallest parts of the larger problem.

Overview

The United States and many other countries rely on the private sector to provide services that supplement and support, not replace, their military capabilities. The industry exists to satisfy these demands. It is not engaged to make strategic decisions; it is brought in to support those decisions. Ultimately, so long as states are not willing or able to comprehensively commit their own existing resources to enact critical policies domestically and internationally, the industry will continue to respond to market demands. The 2011 Commission on Wartime Contracting report highlighted the importance of the industry to U.S. stability operations:

Contractors represent more than half of the U.S. presence in the contingency operations in Iraq and Afghanistan, at times employing more than a quarter-million people. They have performed vital tasks in support of U.S. defense, diplomatic, and development objectives.[2]

In terms of the international scene, Alex Bellamy and Paul Williams, in the second edition of their seminal work, *Understanding Peacekeeping*, consider the topic important enough to include a special new chapter on privatization, and state: "private contractors have played important roles in the conduct of peace operations and have done so for a considerable period."[3] Thus, policy analysts are wise to focus more on maximizing the utilization as well as the ethics and value of the industry, rather than seeking artificial limits and increasing costs that must come from already limited budgets. The success of international policies related to stabilization and humanitarian intervention now and in the future will rely on the prudent and effective use of these organizations, not on overzealous restriction and certainly not on their elimination.

Partnership, not confrontation, is the key to success in stability operations. Although the stability operations industry itself must also be responsible in setting and enforcing basic principles through codes of conduct and the development of standards, ultimately contractual compliance is essentially and most effectively the responsibility of the client. Ensuring legal enforcement requires an active role for governments (sometimes clients and governments are one and the same). It is the original contract design and structure that ensures that projects enable and comply with comprehensive relief, reconstruction, and development plans. Coordination with interagency partners, other international actors, and host nation governments is also vital to minimizing the enormous problem of waste. Ultimately, effective stability operations require partnership and communication among all actors in stability operations: governmental, nongovernmental, international, and industry. The chaotic nature of contingency operations means that there must be a working partnership if vital international operations are to succeed.

This essay will describe the industry, clarify terminology, and address some of the criticisms that surround the industry. It examines successful self-policing efforts in the industry and the increase in international efforts among both governments and companies to set international standards through the Montreux Document and the International Code of Conduct for private security providers (ICoC).

Terminology

It is helpful to differentiate between types of contingency operations and organizations rather than lumping the wide variety of services into a single category. The fashionable term "private military and security companies" (PMSCs) is inherently faulty and deceptive, as only a small percentage of the industry—in both numbers and contract value—is devoted to armed security, and the term does not fully reflect the diverse roles of the industry beyond that function. Generally less than 20%—and more commonly only 5–10%—of the industry performs security tasks. The use of the term "military" is also inaccurate, as the companies are civilian and it is misleading to imply they have the legal rights and responsibilities of soldiers under international law, as discussed below. The majority of companies provide the more ordinary services that are essential to contingency operations, but the companies provide them more cost-effectively or on a short-term emergency basis. Various analysts have described the industry in different ways and there are no agreed upon categorizations, but generally we can distinguish among four types of companies:

(1) Logistics and Support organizations, that essentially provide services that might be mundane in other environments, including aviation, logistics, and construction;

(2) Private Security companies (PSC) that protect 'nouns'- people, places and things including site and convoy protection, body guard services and diplomatic protection, threat assessments, and advice;

(3) Security Sector Reform and Development organizations that help with the long-term solutions for state-building, including legal and law enforcement training, reforming educational systems, military and peacekeeper training, development projects, capacity building, governmental mentoring, and other similar services; and

(4) Industry Support companies, which include legal services, accounting, public relations, recruitment and vetting of personnel, and insurance firms.

Thus the larger industry is more encompassing than is usually assumed and the "PMSC" terminology does not begin to cover the range of services that the industry provides. In fact, the term "Stability Operations Industry" is more apt. This phrase reflects the fact that companies do not only provide security in war zones, but also provide services that range from training to construction, demining to information technology, and ground transportation to risk management. They operate in areas disrupted by war, natural disasters, or humanitarian emergencies and in service to NGOs, the private sector, international organizations, and governments.

The terminology used to characterize the industry has an effect on attitudes toward contractors, as well as on their own self-perception. Differentiating between the tasks and role of the military and industry is important as it connects with the fact that the rights and responsibilities of the private sector differ fundamentally from the role that the military has, even though they frequently operate in the same high-risk environments. For those contractors doing security, labeling them "military" inaccurately implies that they have the same role as militaries. For example, military forces in the field are guided by secret Rules of Engagement (ROE), which provide the legal guidelines for the military to engage proactively with lethal force and indicate when it is appropriate to advance their mission. Security contractors are guided by the public Rules for the Use of Force (RUF), usually included as part of any contract for security companies. These rules allow for very limited and reactive use of force. The RUF for contractors in Iraq in 2004 and Afghanistan in 2011 allowed the use of force in the following situations:

(1) in self-defense;
(2) in defense of persons as specified in the contract;

(3) to prevent life-threatening offenses against civilians; and

(4) in defense of Coalition-approved property specified in the contract.[4]

Moreover, military personnel fall under military law—the Uniform Code of Military Justice (UCMJ) in the case of the U.S. military. Contractors are covered by civilian law, in most cases local law or some national laws that have international reach, such as the Military Extraterritorial Jurisdiction Act. In most operations local hires make up the bulk of personnel and they are always under local laws. Hence, there are inherent differences in the role and guidelines for contractors and military personnel.

Who are contractors?

Although media attention has been primarily on western contractors who operate in high-risk environments, Westerners form only a small minority of the contractors on the ground. They are relatively expensive due to higher wage structures, travel, housing, and security costs, and these factors make them uncompetitive if alternatives are available. In many cases the only reason Westerners are utilized is because some clients, for security reasons, specifically require them in the contracts.

In fact, the majority of contractors are local hires and Third Country Nationals (TCNs). Local hires are the best and cheapest option and hiring locals provides valuable jobs and capacity-building skills, supports the local economy, and engenders ownership in the success of the stability operation. They obviously speak the local languages and understand the society better than any foreign national, and this is particularly advantageous. TCNs are employees from countries unrelated to the area of operation and they usually come from countries where economic opportunities do not compare with the relatively lucrative employment available for short-term contracts in contingency operations. Whereas local nationals generally earn market wages, TCNs generally earn several times as much as they could make in their home countries. It should always be kept in mind that local wages impact the larger mission, and if they rise too high, members of other professions, such as doctors and lawyers, may leave their jobs for better pay as cooks and mechanics. Nevertheless, the skills and cost-effectiveness that TCNs and LNs bring to the missions add enormously to the potential success of any operation.

Importing labor and specialized skills is a necessary and common practice in stability operations and it has vast benefits both for the policy and the employees. However, the potential for labor trafficking abuse is very real. Working for the international community can be dangerous in stability operations and it is important to note that employees must be allowed the opportunity to make a rational choice to work in such high-risk environments. They often do so in order to better provide for their families. Hiring locals and TCNs usually requires the use of labor agents, and it is critical that companies ensure these labor agents are legitimate and compliant to international laws and regulations. Prime contractors have a responsibility in such circumstances, and the ones that have been regularly operating in contingency operations will have elaborate structures and networks in place to minimize the labor trafficking issue. The biggest problems tend to come from local firms or companies from countries where they are unfamiliar with the detailed regulations of Western governments (such as the extensive U.S. Federal Acquisition Regulations). In fact, the proper vetting of labor agents and personnel is in a company's own best interest to maintain a good reputation and thus remain profitable.[5]

Legally, contractors are bound by domestic and international legal frameworks, depending on the area and kind of operation. Most importantly, primary jurisdiction is, if available, always the legal system of the country of operations. For local nationals, this is always the case, despite the fact that legal systems in countries of operation may be in a shambles or even non-existent. For international contractors, however, if there are non-existent or ineffective local legal avenues, there are other provisions. As mentioned, the U.S. Military Extraterritorial Jurisdiction Act (MEJA) provides jurisdiction to prosecute criminal acts that would be felonies if they happened on United States territory. MEJA applies to all nationals working on U.S. contracts except for local nationals, and non-U.S. nationals can and have been brought to the United States for prosecution—though their home states must provide permission for the prosecution to go forward. Of course, these laws are on top of the many other laws and legal requirements that apply to a company's operation in any foreign country.

It is worth noting that contractual stipulations are generally easier to modify than laws. Companies are bound by their contracts and these can be used to bring flexibility in addressing emerging concerns, something that is important in fluid, high-risk environments. When governments are the clients, they have been able to use the contracts to change the rules relatively quickly to ensure problems unique to an operation are addressed in all future contracts. For example, the Rules for the Use of Force were inserted into PSC contracts, and modifications to vehicles and additional training and reporting requirements have been added over time.[6] These contractual terms can be an incredibly useful tool in maximizing the flexibility that the industry brings to international operations.

Criticisms

Stability operations are inherently high profile and even the most minor incidents and problems frequently make headlines. For a number of reasons, there is almost always a side to the story that is rarely publicized, or only much later. Furthermore, as one would expect of an industry that operates in highly dangerous and unstable areas, there are numerous unusual and complex problems unique to these environments. In many cases, contractors are not allowed to speak to the media due to their governmental contractual obligations. In other cases, contractors prefer to take blame rather than shame their current—and possibly future—clients. Worse, many journalists, academics, and self-proclaimed experts have sensationalized and exaggerated anecdotal incidents, sometimes deliberately, creating a situation where policies are being developed based on overbroad assumptions. Primary research is all too rare, and too often the most motivated correspondents are in fact those with specific agendas already in mind.

The controversy and intrigue surrounding contracting helps to sell books and articles but often ignores the essential role, valuable services, and critical contributions that contractors provide to stability operations. Successful logistics or professional and effective security operations are not considered newsworthy. At the same time, critics rarely offer an alternative to the private sector while mythologizing a past when contractors allegedly did not exist, and this has hampered objective and constructive viewpoints. The very policy of outsourcing, for example, is often blamed on contractors without examining the demand factor that created the market for contingency contractors in the first place. Contingency contractors can exist only because of an international demand for their services, and those who drive the industry are former government and military personnel who know well

how to fill the real capacity limitations faced by international policymakers. The industry did not create the need for government outsourcing, but they are there to fill the vital demands.

In that sense, there seems to be a disconnect between the perception of what services governments should be providing and what they can actually provide quickly, effectively, and cheaply. Private firms offer enormously cost-effective options. A Congressional Research Service's (CRS) report on contractors in Department of Defense operations acknowledges that "hiring contractors only as needed can be cheaper in the long run than maintaining a permanent in-house capability."[7] Consider the huge costs in personnel pensions that the military has to pay long after a conflict ends, while any such costs are included up front in private contracts. The Government Accountability Office came to a similar conclusion for the U.S. State Department.[8] Finally, it has to be asked whether the government should set aside the vast resources necessary for a permanent, in-house contingency operations capability that gets used sporadically over the years, or simply exploit the off-the-shelf, as-needed capabilities the industry already offers. Considering that few governments believe contingency operations are a "normal" role for their military forces (least of all the United States), funding, equipping, and maintaining a "contingency capability" is extremely unlikely, thus leaving the off-the-shelf private sector options as the only real solution.

The Stability Operations Industry does not make decisions; it is made up of companies that respond to client demands and to policymaker requirements. On occasion, the industry is accused of benefitting from conflicts and devastation, implying they actively advocate for policies and operations causing chaos. The industry certainly lobbies to influence and improve rules and regulations that directly impact industry operations. To date, however, there has been no documented evidence of lobbying policymakers to stimulate new conflicts. Indeed, it would be remarkable were such a small industry to have that kind of influence in a democratic society.

There are many reasons why private companies are better suited to perform certain tasks than governments, international organizations, or NGOs. Due to their competitive nature, private companies are more cost-efficient, flexible, and innovative, especially compared to governments, which are notoriously the opposite. As academic Thomas Bruneau highlights, "In fact, the whole premise for replacing government employees with private contractors rests on the assumption that competition for making a profit in an open marketplace guarantees the best quality product or service for the least cost."[9] Contracts can be terminated if a company does not perform, services can be bought on a temporary as-needed basis, and competition in the industry drives down the price of services and creates innovation.[10] These beneficial traits require competition, but competition can be reduced by regulations (necessarily), risk, and thin profit margins common to the industry. Wise clients and governments seek to ensure healthy

numbers of competitors from around the world to maximize value.

There is no empirical evidence that contractors, even security contractors, lead to an increase in casualties or are less ethical than military counterparts. Indeed, the few systematic studies demonstrate the opposite.[11] What is true is that contingency contractors are more likely to get negative press for their missteps than regular militaries or peacekeepers. For example, in 2005 during the peacekeeping operation in Haiti, Brazilian MINUSTAH soldiers fired 20,000 rounds of ammunition into a crowded slum during a raid on the gang leader Emmanuel Wilme. Scores of women and children were killed or wounded.[12] Outside of Haiti few are aware of the incident, yet comparatively small PSC incidents in the far more volatile Iraq operations were regular features on the front pages of most international media. Deadly incidents happen in contingency operations, but the goal must be to minimize such deadly occurrences via professionalism and training. Clients can help by writing quality standards and training standards into PSC contracts and actually enforcing those requirements. On the other hand, for many international stability operations there is often no choice about which military units are proffered and the quality varies greatly, thus increasing the risk to civilians.

Claims that the use of PSCs in security operations has developed into the "privatization" or "outsourcing" of policy or strategy have emerged during the last two decades and the United States appears more reliant on contractors than ever.[13]

However, it is not policies that are being privatized; it is their execution. Private sector actors are contracted to carry out policy or to provide the necessary logistical support for government actors to pursue strategic decisions. In reality, the U.S. government in particular demands that contractors follow elaborate and detailed contractual guidelines—this leaves less room for flexible solutions as challenges arise. Moreover, because the activities of security companies oftentimes are either "tacitly or explicitly sanctioned by governments, accountability lies with the government and can be linked to the accountability of the state."[14]

In 2008 the Montreux Document addressed this issue, and in fact it may be more difficult for a government to claim "plausible deniability" due to the enormously detailed contracts and various reporting requirements of modern contingency contracting. Contractual fraud and abuse have often been cited as the main problems with contracting practice.[15] Cases of fraud and abuse have obviously occurred and have been frequently highlighted by both the Government Accountability Office (GAO) and the Commission on Wartime Contracting in Iraq and Afghanistan (CWC), among others, yet both organizations reveal that *waste* is a far more important and prominent issue than fraud and abuse. Waste is not an issue over which the private sector has much control, and examples of enormous projects that are redundant or irrelevant, or, once they have been finished, never get adopted by the host nation governments for which they are built, characterize the issue of waste.[16] In most cases, the problem of waste cannot be blamed on the contractors who are hired to carry out these tasks. According to a GAO report, waste costs accumulate from "poor planning, bad designs, poorly written government contracts, poor government management, and other similarly draining errors."[17] Clark Irwin of the Commission on Wartime Contracting emphasized that point when he commented, "Waste is a bigger issue than fraud or abuse ... bad planning, bad coordination— those are probably the biggest problems."[18] Nevertheless, addressing fraud and abuse is important, especially since they can undermine the legitimacy of a mission. From an industry perspective, when governments are able to address fraud and abuse effectively and to punish the guilty firms, it rewards the better companies. Given this result, industry has consistently supported strong oversight and enforcement.

There are also better ways to address the waste issue. Absentee client oversight is one of the main reasons for waste. Especially in the early days of the Afghanistan and Iraq conflicts, U.S. government contract oversight staff were being rotated in and out of war zones far too quickly, sometimes after less than four months in the field. Inadequate oversight and the absence of a contract officer, or a well-trained and effective contract officer representative (COR)—the official charged with observing contract progress and quality—were the norm. Worse, poor oversight limits the flexibility to modify contracts to address changing mission requirements, and limits the ability of the government to refocus personnel and material according to evolving mission needs, something that is essential in effective contingency operations. Changing conditions, crises, and setbacks cannot be responded to immediately and effectively because CORs on the ground, often junior military officers hastily trained for the oversight tasks, do not have the authority to authorize necessary contractual changes when the situation on the ground is different from expected. Hence, proper contract management is essential to ensuring operational success, operational compliance, and thus effective policy implementation. Despite this necessity, the government significantly decreased the number of contract officers in the years prior to the Iraq invasion in 2003.[19]

Compliance

To maximize advantages when using private sector companies takes management capacity, and this capacity has been lacking in the past. The Gansler Report explains:

[T]imely and efficient contracting for materiel, supplies and services in support of expeditionary operations, and the subsequent management of those contracts, are and will be a key component of our achieving success in future military operations. Contracting is the nexus between our warfighters' requirements and the contractors that fulfill those requirements— whether for food service, interpreters, communications operations, equipment repair, new or modified equipment, or other supplies and services indispensable to warfighting operations. In support of critical military operations, contractor personnel must provide timely services and equipment to the warfighter; and the Army contracting community must acquire those services and equipment effectively, efficiently, and legally.[20]

Although the U.S. government's procurement and contract management procedures are among the most rigorous and comprehensive around the world, the sheer scale of current operations has overwhelmed the contract oversight force and meant that monitoring and enforcement have been spotty. An inadequate contract monitoring capability limits the ability of the government to assess fluid situations and modify contracts to match situational needs, creating needless waste and too often increasing the risk for contractors. Governments can build improved quality, flexibility, efficiency, and ethics of services into contracts, but ultimately an adequate contract oversight capability is necessary to ensure companies adhere to their contractual obligations, and to weed out the bad companies while rewarding the good ones.

The opportunity for innovation is increasingly constrained by contracting practice and laws added in attempts to reduce costs. Government contracts are designed to address a specific policy, but they often contractually enumerate the specific way of achieving the policy. This seems understandable: clients are afraid poorly enacted contracts could negatively influence the wider policy. However, it leaves little room for innovation and limits the potential benefits that the private sector can offer. This contracting practice is derived from the standard procurement method in U.S. contingency contracting, which is branded "lowest price, technically acceptable" (LPTA) contracting. LPTA contracting denotes the practice that as long as competing bidders meet the minimum provisions of the policy and the mission, the contract is by law awarded to the absolute lowest bidder. Logically speaking, this policy tries to guarantee that the government does not overpay for services and equipment. However, the policy necessarily disregards the quality of the delivered services and makes high-end companies cut value elements from their proposals in order to be competitive for a bid. This leads to cutbacks on the provision of quality services that result in operational problems on the ground. This is particularly true when cuts are made in vetting and training, for such cuts will undermine political stakes, will imperil the policy the government set out, and will even jeopardize lives, given the high-risk environments in which these operations take place.

There are alternatives to LPTA contracting. "Best value" bids depend on the discretion of the procurement official to award the proposal that will best serve the broader goals of the mission. Best value allows companies to offer better quality and innovation, as well as value enhancements. As companies still compete with one another, this does not necessarily drive up the price. Cost will always be a factor, of course, but best value encourages quality as well as price. The tradeoff is that best value requires more time and personnel to make a selection, and often in contingency operations the contracting community is already overtaxed because of other operational requirements.

The Commission on Wartime Contracting (CWC) itself specifically recommended that the LPTA should no longer be the norm for private security services in one of their earliest reports. As all contractors compete to be the cheapest, rather than the best, it should be the goal of governments to broaden the CWC recommendation to include all services provided in contingency operations.[21] The argument of LPTA advocates stems from the idea of decreasing overall government spending. This argument is generally not conducive to the broader debate about how best to improve the quality of contingency contracting.[22] It does not recognize that in the long term the government's investment in quality might have a far more beneficial return, especially in foreign operations where international policies and humanitarian needs would put a premium on rapid and effective policy implementation. Clients should pay close attention to the performance quality of companies in this process.[23]

On the side of the contracting companies, it is logical that good companies benefit from good oversight and therefore will willingly and frequently submit to remarkably invasive oversight procedures. In fact, companies in the industry undergo regular audits from all clients, but especially when working for the U.S. government. These normally come from their contract officers, but also from independent organizations such as the Defense Contract Management Agency (DCMA), which is the Department of Defense's component to ensure quality and punctuality of services and supplies that meet cost requirements, and the Defense Contract Audit Agency (DCAA), which is the arm of Department of Defense that audits contracts of defense contractors. Other audits are conducted by the Inspector Generals of the organizations they work with (Department of Defense, Department of State, U.S. AID, Corps of Engineers, etc.) and, since 2003, the audits and inspections have markedly increased with the creation of the Commission on Wartime Contracting, the Special Inspector Generals for Iraq and Afghanistan Reconstruction (SIGIR and SIGAR respectively), and additional reports from the Government Accountability Office, Congressional Research Service (CRS), and numerous congressional investigations. In fact, numerous repetitive audits and inspections are recognized as part of the job and the cost of doing business with the U.S. government. Enforcement of contractual requirements and quality standards means that good companies regularly remove incapable subcontractors that do not meet the standards and policies required by the client, the contract, and the company. Clients can and do penalize prime contractors that are not appropriately managing their subcontractors.[24] Thus, effec-

tive oversight and accountability are beneficial to good companies and boost standards in the entire industry.

In short, with LPTA determinations the client can expect to get what it pays for: a company meeting the minimum requirement and the possibility that better companies will lower their own standards to a universal bottom-level of competency in order to win contracts. With best value determinations, in contrast, the client should expect and demand a higher quality. As we have explained, it is not always an easy task to increase oversight in high-risk environments and stability operations. Oversight bodies do not always have the necessary capacity. For example, "the number of DCMA personnel assigned to review purchasing systems decreased from 102 personnel in 1994 to 70 in 2002, to 14 in 2009."[25] Moreover, the different oversight bodies send contradictory or divergent messages to contractors, as indicated by a study by the CWC.[26] Thus, if government agencies do not speak with one voice and the right direction is undetermined, doing the right thing is nigh impossible.

Industry Efforts to Improve Quality

As mentioned above, better companies benefit from better oversight and regulations. Therefore, companies over the last 10 years have increasingly been supportive of self-policing in the industry. The International Stability Operations Association (ISOA)[27] is an international trade association for companies that work

in contingency operations. Over 50 companies have joined ISOA and subscribe to the ISOA Code of Conduct.[28] The ISOA Code of Conduct was first drafted in 2001 and it is a living document originally created by NGOs, human rights organizations, and academics. It has been updated every few years to address concerns raised both within the industry and by academics, NGOs, governments, and other interested parties. The accountability mechanism allows that any individual or organization can file a complaint against an ISOA Member Company based on the Code of Conduct, and the case will be heard by the ISOA Standards Committee (essentially a jury of industry peers). The interest and support that the private sector has shown for this demonstrates the awareness among companies that ethics and standards are beneficial to the industry and have a real market value. As a trade association, ISOA's mission is to improve standards in the industry. It is therefore not the goal to remove member companies that have been accused of breaching the ISOA Code of Conduct, but to ensure that wayward companies return to compliance. ISOA has been clear that its Code of Conduct and its Standards Committee are not a substitute for police or government law courts. A private entity should not have such legal powers. Nevertheless, such efforts are effective and do serve to improve the industry's quality.

Associations that bring together a variety of constituents—competing companies, big companies with small businesses, U.S. and non-U.S. based companies—to share ideas, interests, and standards are indicative of an industry that understands the importance of self-regulation. Although cynics have been critical, the industry and its NGO and academic partners recognize that self-regulation, though necessarily working within limits, does have meaningful results. Codes of conduct should not be used to hide abuses—they should be there to set and maintain standards for the entire industry.[29] The ISOA Code of Conduct does not necessarily have to be the primary reason that an organization joins ISOA; but by having to comply with the Code of Conduct, the standards of the larger industry will be raised as a result. The ISOA Code of Conduct promotes the standards of member companies and promotes the profile of those companies by doing so. It is then up to governments and other clients to support those standards and hire those companies that are deemed ethical.

Despite the fact that self-regulation cannot substitute for government legislation and judicial prosecutions, it shows that ethical companies can and do make an effort to improve standards in an industry, particularly when their specialty is providing critical services to zones with limited legal structures. ISOA, like other industry associations, has strongly supported and advocated on behalf of the industry for improved accountability for those accused of crimes and breaches of international laws in stability operations, especially those related to conflict and post-conflict environments. For example, ISOA has twice supported the expansion of the U.S. Military Extraterritorial Jurisdiction Act (MEJA)[30]—the key tool for prosecuting contractors that has been used in numerous cases since 2001—as well as the creation of the Civilian Extraterritorial Jurisdiction Act (CEJA) which will, when passed, address some loopholes in MEJA.[31]

The industry has advocated for increased accountability and supported international initiatives as well, including the Montreux Document and the International Code of

Conduct for Private Security Providers (ICoC). The Swiss government and the International Committee of the Red Cross initiated the Montreux process to clarify how international laws should be applied to international personnel working in contingency operations.[32] Over 30 governments, including some of the recipient countries such as Afghanistan, Angola, and Iraq, as well as contracting clients such as the United States, the United Kingdom, and South Africa, have joined in supporting the Montreux Document. The developments of Montreux have led to an initiative primarily for PSCs: the International Code of Conduct for Private Security Providers.[33] The U.S. and U.K. governments have both stated that they will contract only to companies who have signed the ICoC and have agreed to the compliance process, the design of which is still in progress as of this writing. It is hoped that in the future other clients, such as international organizations and NGOs, will join in as well. It is the responsibility of governments to be vigilant about this, to increase the efficiency of this effort, and to put a premium on quality.[34] Once the ICoC process is fully implemented, it should do much to increase overall quality, ethics, and standards in the industry, as contracting practices will encourage companies to abide by the rules of the ICoC. It should also enhance the confidence of potential clients in the industry, and should broaden the market as well. Ultimately, this process is expected to reach far beyond PSCs to cover the entire industry.

Conclusion

The stability operations industry is necessary and valuable, and as planning, oversight, accountability, and partnerships are improved, it can be more so in the future. The Commission in Wartime Contracting co-chair, Michael Thibault, recently said at a news conference:

During our extensive travel in-theatre, we heard emphatic appreciation constantly at all levels with the quality and effectiveness of contractor support for the U.S. military effort. Our focus on problems derives from our concern that the cost of contractor support has been unnecessarily high, and that government has not effectively managed contracts to promote competition, reward good performance, and impose accountability for poor performance and misconduct by both government and contractor personnel.[35]

During the same conference, the other co-chair of the CWC, Christopher Shays, mentioned that senior "U.S. defense officials have testified that the U.S. cannot go to war without large scale contracting support."[36] Although often in denial about it, the United States has always been involved in stability operations and will continue to be involved in such operations—thus demand for the use of contractors will persist. To make these successful, more attention has to be paid to the role of U.S. contracting, procurement, and contract management.

Indeed, for any government, the lessons of Afghanistan and Iraq are that in-house recruiting and retaining the expertise, as well as maintaining skills and equipment necessary to be able to undertake contingency operations, is far too costly. However, a relatively small investment in an expandable professional contract management capacity to effectively oversee and manage stability operations makes sense. That kind of trained and knowledgeable capacity could foster the mutually beneficial partner relationship between governments and contractors, thus focusing missions on successful policies rather than on the destructive internal wranglings and disputes that characterize too many contemporary contingency operations.

We should not lose sight of the fact that clients are most responsible for determining the level of professionalism and quality that they desire of their contractors. Their willingness to ignore and downplay standards has been the bane of the industry. Good rules and regulations, combined with effective enforcement, reward the better companies that are willing and able to address those issues. Poor procurement policies, such as lowest price contracts, and poor management practices, including poor or non-existent oversight, undermine both quality firms and the incentive for the private sector to provide professionalism and ethics in their operations. Worse, by misunderstanding the nature of the largest problems in reconstruction, development, and security in contingency operations and by obsessing on "fraud and abuse" when the far larger issue is waste—due to poor planning and coordination—governments fixate on less significant problems while not addressing the larger problem that challenges success. No serious analysts contest the importance of the private sector supporting international policies. If policies such as those involving Afghanistan and Iraq, and humanitarian missions such as famine relief in Somalia, are vital and important, then improving the way we hire and manage stability operations companies is critical.

Notes

1 The *New York Times* is unique in that it continues to use the derogatory "mercenary" label for contingency contractors, a practice long discarded by other professional media sources and serious academics. For example, see Mark Mazzetti and Emily B. Hager, "Blackwater Founder Forms Secret Army for Arab State," *New York Times*, May 15, 2011. Deborah Avant argues, "The term 'mercenary' describes a wide variety of military activities, many of which bear little resemblance to those of today's private security companies." Avant, "Think Again: Mercenaries," *Foreign Policy* 143 (July 1, 2004): 20. See also Volker Franke, "Service Versus Profit," *Journal of International Peace Operations* 7, no. 21 (July 2011):

28–29, available at http://web.peaceops.com/; and Volker Franke and Marc von Boemcken, "Guns for Hire: Motivations and Attitudes of Private Security Contractors," *Armed Forces and Society* (forthcoming).

2 Commission on Wartime Contracting in Iraq and Afghanistan, Final Report to Congress, *Transforming Wartime Contracting, Controlling Costs Reducing Risks* (August 31, 2011), 2.

3 Alex J. Bellamy and Paul Williams, *Understanding Peacekeeping*, 2nd ed. (Cambridge, UK: Polity Press, 2010), 322.

4 From the Coalition Provisional Authority, Memorandum No. 17, June 26, 2004;

and CENTCOM RUF, September 6, 2011. The guideline also requires contractors to "report incident immediately and break contact," a little-known requirement that has led many journalists to report that PSCs 'flee' after incidents.

5. Conclusions from the International Peace Operations Association conference, "Combating Trafficking in Persons: FAR Compliance Training for Government Contractors," Washington, DC (July 17, 2007).

6 Dan Kuwali, "Legal Perspective: Do Private Military Companies Have a Legitimate Place in Peacekeeping?" in *From Market for Force to Market for Peace: Private Military and Security Companies in Peacekeeping Operations*, ed. Sabelo Gumedze (Institute for Security Studies, Monograph No. 183), 97, available at http://kms1.isn. ethz.ch/serviceengine/Files/ISN/135461/ ipublicationdocument_singledocument/6f3 3d2ce-4111-43ec-aab3-b2de05f6828e/en/Mo no183.pdf

7 Moshe Schwartz, "Department of Defense Contractors in Iraq and Afghanistan: Background Analysis," Congressional Research Service (August 13, 2009), available at http://fpc.state.gov/documents/organi zation/128824.pdf

8 Government Accountability Office, "Warfighter Support: A Cost Comparison of Using State Department Employees versus Contractors for Security Services in Iraq," GAO-10-266R (Washington, DC, March 4, 2010), available at http://www. gao.gov/assets/100/96571.pdf

9 Thomas C. Bruneau, *Patriots for Profit: Contractors and the Military in U.S. National Security* (Stanford: Stanford University Press, 2011), 110.

10 Commission on Wartime Contracting in Iraq and Afghanistan, *At What Cost? Contingency Contracting in Iraq and Afghanistan*, Interim Report (June 2009); Commission on Wartime Contracting in Iraq and Afghanistan, *Transforming Wartime Contacting*.

11 Mariya Keller "Private Military Companies and Civilian Casualties: The Iraq Story" (master's thesis, Uppsala University, 2011); see also Sarah Martin "Boys Must Be Boys? Ending Sexual Exploitation and Abuse in UN Peacekeeping Missions," Refugees International, October 2005.

12 Colum Lynch, "UN Peacekeeping More Assertive, Creating Risk for Civilians," *Washington Post*, August 15, 2005.

13 Examples include Allison Stanger, *One Nation Under Contract: The Outsourcing of American Power and the Future of Foreign Policy* (New Haven: Yale University Press, 2009); and Laura A. Dickinson, *Outsourcing War and Peace: Preserving Public Values in a World of Privatized Foreign Affairs* (New Haven: Yale University Press, 2011).

14 Kuwali, "Legal Perspective: Do Private Military Companies Have a Legitimate Place in Peacekeeping?" 104.

15 Taxpayers for Common Sense is an example. See Laura Peterson, "Troop Surge Dollars Must be Watched," Taxpayers for Common Sense (December 3, 2009), available at http://taxpayer.net/projects.php? action = view&category = &type = Project& proj_id = 2982

16 For a summary of some of the most infamous examples of waste, fraud, and abuse, see Bruce Burton and Lauren McLean, "The Black and White of Fraud, Waste, and Abuse," *Defense AT&L*, 38, no. 2 (2009): 36–41, available at http://www. dau.mil/pubscats/PubsCats/atl/damtoc/ burt_ma09.pdf

17 Richard Lardner, "U.S. Oversight of War-zone Contractors Labeled Weak," *Washington Post*, February 22, 2011, available at http://www.washingtonpost.com/ wp-dyn/content/article/2011/02/22/AR20 11022205739.html

18 Scott Canon, "Black & Veatch's Fog-of-War Contract in Afghanistan," *Kansas City Star*, February 19, 2011.

19 Steve Schooner, "Iraq Contracting: Predictable Lessons Learned," Statement, United States Senate Democratic Policy Committee, Washington, DC, September 10, 2004.

20 Gansler Commission Report, *Urgent Reform Required: Army Expeditionary Contracting*, U.S. Commission on Army Acquisition and Program Management in Expeditionary Operations (October 31, 2007), 3, available at http://www.army.

mil/docs/Gansler_Commission_Report_Final_071031.pdf

21 Commission on Wartime Contracting in Iraq and Afghanistan, *Special Report on Embassy Security Contracts: Lowest-priced Security Not Good Enough for War-zone Embassies*, CWC Special Report 2, October 1, 2009, available at http://www.wartime-contracting.gov/docs/CWC_SR2-2009-10-01.pdf

22 Danielle Brian, "CWC Findings on Embassy Guards Fiasco Amount to 'Blame Shifting,'" Project on Government Oversight, October 6, 2009, available at http://pogoblog.typepad.com/pogo/2009/10/cwc-findings-on-embassy-guards-fiasco-amount-to-blame-shifting.html

23 Kuwali, "Legal Perspective: Do Private Military Companies Have a Legitimate Place in Peacekeeping?" 106–07.

24 Currently, information on penalized contractors and subcontractors can be found on the "Excluded Parties List System," available at https://www.epls.gov. However, this was being replaced at the end of July 2012 by the "System for Award Management" (SAM). See https://www.sam.gov. EPLS also includes a list of past penalties and suspensions, and uses a detailed code system to explain reasons for listings.

25 Commission on Wartime Contracting in Iraq and Afghanistan, *Special Report On Contractor Business Systems: Defense Agencies Must Improve Their Oversight of Contractor Business Systems to Reduce Waste, Fraud, and Abuse*, CWC Special Report 1, September 21, 2009, n. 14: "Information provided to the Commission by DCMA on August 4, 2009." Report available at http://www.wartimecontracting.gov/docs/CWC_SR1_business-systems_2009-09-21.pdf

26 Commission on Wartime Contracting, *Special Report on Contractor Business Systems*, April 2009; http://www.wartimecontracting.gov/docs/CWC_SR1_business-systems_2009-09-21.pdf

27 Formerly known as the International Peace Operations Association (IPOA).

28 The latest version is available on the ISOA web page, www.stability-operations.org

29 Daphné Richemond-Barak, "Regulating War: A Taxonomy in Global Administrative Law," *European Journal of International Law* 22 (2011): 1027.

30. For a good article on the origins of MEJA, see Major Joseph R. Perlak, "The Military Extraterritorial Jurisdiction Act Of 2000: Implications for Contractor Personnel," *Military Law Review* 169 (2001): 91–140.

31 Information on CEJA is located on the Human Rights First website, "Senate Judiciary Committee Passes Bill on U.S. Civilian Contractor Accountability Abroad," June 23, 2011, available at http://www.human-rightsfirst.org/2011/06/23/senate-judiciary-committee-passes-bill-on-u-s-civilian-contractor-accountability-abroad/

32 Montreux Document, Federal Department of Foreign Affairs, Switzerland, available at http://www.eda.admin.ch/psc. See also Nigel White's discussion of the Montreux Document, in this issue.

33 ICoC information can be found online at http://www.icoc-psp.org/

34 Advisory Council on International Affairs, "Employing Private Military Companies – A Question of Responsibility," No. 59 (The Hague: December, 2010), available at http://www.aiv-advies.nl/ContentSuite/upload/aiv/doc/webversie_AIV_59 eng(1).pdf

35 The entire news conference can be seen at http://www.c-span.org/Events/Wartime-Contract-Commission-Finds-quot At-Least-31-Billionquot-Lost-to-Waste-amp-Fraud/10737423790/

36 Ibid.

Index

abuses 77–8, 97, 126–31, 156: Abu Ghraib 57, 61, 66, 98, 131, 154; accountability 2, 12, 50; Basra Fallujah incident 31, 66–7, 129–30; labor trafficking 169–70; Nisoor Square Massacre 12, 32, 50, 57, 63, 65–7, 131; remedies 142, 144; sex trafficking 130; stability operations industry 166, 169–70, 172–3, 177, 179

Academi (formerly Blackwater) 57, 125

accountability 1–4, 38–52, 129, 131, 155: 'accountability for', meaning of 57; being accountable and being held accountable, relationship between 44–5; change, proposals for 45–52; citizen armies 25; collective accountability 47, 49; Contracting phase 14, 58–9, 60, 63–4, 67–8, 70–1; contractual accountability 40–6, 49, 58, 64; corporate social responsibility 9, 11, 42–3, 106; crime rates of PMSCs and US Army, comparison between 45; criminal responsibility 14, 39, 43–7, 50, 57, 59, 65–6, 80–2, 90, 97–8; current system 38–52; divergent interests, problem of 39–42, 50; due diligence 11, 63–4, 67; employees 39, 42–3, 46–7; ethics 14, 34, 38–9, 41–2, 45, 47–8, 51; held accountable, being 44–5; human rights 8–9, 13, 60–3, 65, 67–8, 70, 84; In-the-Field phase 14, 58, 59, 60–2, 64, 67–71; individual criminal responsibility 39, 43, 46–7, 50, 97–8; international humanitarian law 8, 12, 13, 60, 63–5, 67–9; international law 10–11, 14, 56–71, 77, 80–1, 82, 84, 90–1; legal accountability 9–11; one-shop accountability 42–3; oversight 12, 14, 38–41, 46–52, 59–60, 67; peer accountability 9, 11; personal accountability 39, 42–3, 46–7, 74; Post-Conduct phase 14, 57, 58, 59–60, 63–5, 67–8, 70–1; public reputational accountability 9; recent developments 66–70; relational concept, as 8, 42; responsibility regime, development of 15, 97–9, 104, 106, 109, 114–16, 119; soft law 9, 11, 16; stability operations industry 15,

166, 173, 176–8; standards 8, 11, 45, 58, 92; state responsibility 11, 14, 16, 57, 60, 64–71, 82; three-phase construct 56–71; transparency 11–13, 15, 160–3; UN Draft Convention 67, 68–71, 97–9, 114–16, 132–6, 140, 143; universal accountability 44

AEGIS 39–40, 127–8

Aerospace Corporation 51

Afghanistan 1–2, 126: accountability 45, 51; capacity-building missions 132; Commission on Wartime Contracting 40–1, 139, 154, 158–9, 166, 173, 175–6, 178; contractor industrial complex, emergence of 153; cost efficiencies 178–9; distinction, principle of 31–2; governmental functions, exercise of 151, 158; human rights 67, 87; laissez-faire outsourcing 154–5; military provider firms 30; Rules for Use of Force 168; Special Inspector General for Afghanistan 176; state and citizen, relationship between 27–8, 29; Taliban 131, 155, 161; use of force, state monopoly of 143; waste and fraud 40, 154–5, 161, 173

Africa: African Crisis Response Initiative 8; African Commission on Human and Peoples' Rights 84; Elimination of Mercenarism in Africa Convention 10; mercenaries 6–7, 10 see also particular countries

Agency for International Development (USAID) 150–1

Alston, Philip 85

American Convention of Human Rights (ACHR) 84

Anghie, Antony 103, 105

Angola 8

Arendt, Hannah 98

Argentina and Brazil, 1830 war between 6

ArmorGroup 130–1

attribution 80–1, 89, 98–102

audits and inspections 40, 50, 52, 175–6

Azizi, Fiorentina 106

For Product Safety Concerns and Information please contact our EU
representative GPSR@taylorandfrancis.com Taylor & Francis Verlag GmbH,
Kaufingerstraße 24, 80331 München, Germany

Printed and bound by CPI Group (UK) Ltd, Croydon, CR0 4YY
08/05/2025
01864518-0002